What I Wish I Had Told My Children

What I Wish I Had Told My Children

Michel Bastarache and Antoine Trépanier

Translated by Julie da Silva

University of Ottawa Press 2023

 Les **Presses** de l'Université d'Ottawa
University of Ottawa **Press**

The University of Ottawa Press (UOP) is proud to be the oldest of the francophone university presses in Canada and the oldest bilingual university publisher in North America. Since 1936, UOP has been enriching intellectual and cultural discourse by producing peer-reviewed and award-winning books in the humanities and social sciences, in French and in English.

Library and Archives Canada Cataloguing in Publication
Title: What I wish I had told my children / Michel Bastarache and Antoine Trépanier.
Names: Bastarache, Michel, author. | Trépanier, Antoine, author.
Description: Includes bibliographical references.
Identifiers: Canadiana (print) 20220472580 | Canadiana (ebook) 20220472629 | ISBN 9780776640143 (hardcover) | ISBN 9780776639598 (softcover) | ISBN 9780776640129 (PDF) | ISBN 9780776640136 (EPUB)
Subjects: LCSH: Bastarache, Michel. | LCSH: Canada. Supreme Court—Biography. | LCSH: Judges—Canada— Biography. | LCSH: Acadians—Canada—Biography. | LCGFT: Autobiographies.
Classification: LCC KE8248.B37 A3 2023 | DDC 347/.014092—dc23

Legal Deposit: Second Quarter 2023
Library and Archives Canada

© University of Ottawa Press 2023
All right reserved.

Production Team
Copy-editing   Tanina Drvar
Proofreading   Robbie McCaw and Crystal Chan
Typesetting   Édiscript enr.
Cover Design   Lefrançois Agence B2B

Cover Image
Michel Bastarache at the Supreme Court of Canada, collection from Michel Bastarache.

We acknowledge the financial support of the Canada Council for the Arts for the translation of this book.

The University of Ottawa Press gratefully acknowledges the support extended to its publishing list by the Government of Canada, the Canada Council for the Arts, the Ontario Arts Council, the Social Sciences and Humanities Research Council and the Canadian Federation for the Humanities and Social Sciences through the Awards to Scholarly Publications Program, and by the University of Ottawa.

Table of Contents

Foreword		ix
Acknowledgements		xi
Preface		1
Chapter 1	"Speak White"	3
Chapter 2	The Path	13
Chapter 3	Stand Up	23
Chapter 4	Activist	33
Chapter 5	Dead Ducks	43
Chapter 6	What of Acadia?	57
Chapter 7	Duality, Eh!	63
Chapter 8	The Task Force That Would Change Everything	75
Chapter 9	The Dream	87
Chapter 10	The Battle of Alberta	101
Chapter 11	Salesman, Teacher, Bureaucrat, Lawyer	117
Chapter 12	Assumption	129
Chapter 13	Politics	139
Chapter 14	The New Justice	155
Chapter 15	Globetrotter	173
Chapter 16	A Historic Case	183
Chapter 17	Not in my My Back Yard	197
Chapter 18	The Battle Rages On	207
Chapter 19	Farewell to the Court	221
Chapter 20	One Hellish Commission	235
Chapter 21	One Last Fascinating Chapter	251
Conclusion		265

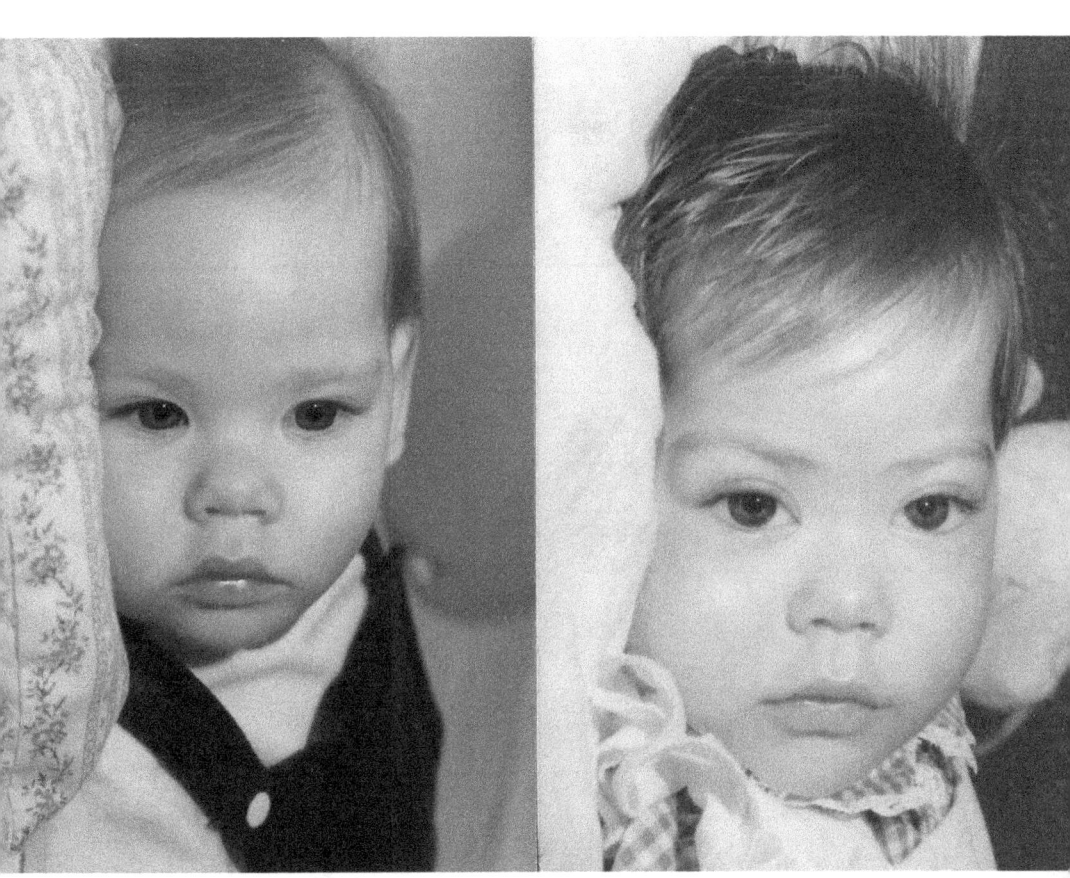

My two children, Jean-François and Émilie.
Source: Collection of Michel Bastarache.

Foreword

FORMER SUPREME COURT OF CANADA JUSTICE MICHEL BASTARACHE, a man of few words, got straight to the point: he was calling to ask if I would write the foreword to his autobiography. I have been a writer for a long time, but I have only ever written one foreword. It was for Michel Cormier's biography of Louis Robichaud. I should probably have given it some thought before embarking on this particular adventure—I am a fiction writer, after all—but I did not hesitate. To me, my extraordinary compatriot's life was like that of a character skirting the bounds of imagination and reality. The manuscript of *Ce que je voudrais dire à mes enfants* arrived the very next day.

Immersing myself in the life story written by a father to his two children, both of whom died young of an extremely rare disease that denied them the opportunity to grow up, I realized I myself was wandering back in time to the days before my own arrival in this world, in an uncertain place and time. What might the future hold for a *La Sagouine* or a *Pélagie* with no certainty their people would survive, their memory endure or their words, vestiges of old, old French, persist? I was suddenly struck by the utter randomness, or perhaps the alignment, that resulted in the birth, around the same time and within a few miles of my village, of Louis Robichaud and Jeanne de Valois in Saint-Antoine, of Michel Cormier in Cocagne, and of the Bastarache children in a suburb of my hometown of Bouctouche, whose true name is Great Little Harbour. Could it be the hand of Destiny tapping softly at our doors?

Let us accept this invitation to share in the intimate thoughts of one of our most eminent jurists, a man who made his way to the Supreme Court of Canada yet presents his autobiography like a bedtime story to his children. I truly believe that this account of one man's life, informed as much by the heart as by the head, is an indispensable treasure for all those contemplating their own existence because it casts light not only on the shadowlands of our past and the ambiguities of our present, but also, and most importantly, on the unforeseeable hopes of our future.

Born in Québec City to a Québécoise mother and an Acadian father of Basque descent, an extremely talented physician, young Michel searched for his path in Acadia at the dawn of a new era in a land attempting to define itself. Better hustle; you only have one life to live.

So he rolled up his sleeves, dabbled in economics and sociology, then threw himself into the study of law, the real kind, the pursuit of justice. The young lawyer began to emerge. He navigated the currents of history, writing his thesis on the law of the sea. The law of the sea led to the law of the land, and from there to the law of culture, of language. In his autobiography, he himself acknowledges that he was well ahead of his time, as he was in taking up the thorny issue of official languages in cases that went all the way to the Supreme Court. Arguing one case after another for Francophones in Alberta, in Manitoba, and, of course, in the Maritimes, he doggedly led the charge, perhaps seeking to deepen and strengthen his own roots.

Jeanne de Valois fought to save French language and culture in Acadia by promoting higher education for women. Premier Louis Robichaud awakened the Acadian people's political power and pride. Clément Cormier, founder of the Université de Moncton, along with countless others, engaged in a battle for their survival. Following in their footsteps, a young lawyer pledged to give his lost children a people. That is what drove Michel Bastarache to launch innumerable battles for the betterment of both Quebec and the Canadian Francophonie.

I now understand the true meaning of the title he gave his autobiography. As a father to children who died too young, he dedicated his own life to giving them an identity, a homeland, and a people against all odds. In the process, he dreamed a bigger dream, the dream we all share, of living in a right and just world, a world that embraces every hue, tint, tone, and shade.

Did the tragic loss of Michel Bastarache's son, Jean-François, followed by that of his daughter, Émilie, help bring about an opportunity for as-yet-unborn children to one day be part of a gloriously reborn Acadia?

This book, Michel Bastarache's life story, gives us reason to hope so.

ANTONINE MAILLET

Acknowledgements

I HAVE OFTEN BEEN ASKED TO WRITE MY MEMOIRS, but, for one thing, I do not really like talking about myself. For another, I did not really feel I had documented my work or my participation in important events well enough to produce an interesting read. I had recorded ideas and anecdotes in a personal journal, but other than that, I was not sure I had enough material to tell my life story accurately and completely.

In the fall of 2016, the University of Ottawa Press suggested I work with journalist Antoine Trépanier to publish my biography. Antoine and I spent about thirty hours together going over the salient events of my career and personal life. We spent more than two years on the manuscript, working closely every step of the way to produce the book you are now holding.

I want to thank everyone who agreed to help and took the time to talk about some of the significant events in my life. Their comments added a more personal dimension to historical facts and enriched the narrative immeasurably. I also wanted to give certain individuals an opportunity to respond to some of the anecdotes I felt were interesting. I am grateful to them for answering questions that were sometimes quite sensitive, thereby enabling readers to hear both sides of the story.

Our sources included numerous newspaper and magazine articles. To create the style and flow I was looking for, I opted not to add the footnotes and bibliography one would typically find in a biography. I was committed to the concept of telling my story as a letter to my children, and I appreciate Marc-François Bernier and the Press being so flexible in that regard.

I also want to thank Library and Archives Canada, Bibliothèque et Archives nationales du Québec, the Legislative Library of New Brunswick, the Provincial Archives of New Brunswick, the Supreme Court of Canada, the Supreme Court of Prince Edward Island, the Court of Queen's Bench of Alberta, the University of Ottawa, the Université de Moncton, the Université de Montréal, the Université de Sherbrooke, Université Laval, the University of Alberta, the Université de Nice, the Université de Moncton's Centre d'études acadiennes Anselme-Chiasson, the Association des juristes d'expression française du Nouveau-Brunswick, the Société de l'Acadie du Nouveau-Brunswick, and the Société nationale de l'Acadie, whose services and resources contributed directly and indirectly to the completion of this project.

I also want to thank my family and friends who supported me throughout this process.

And, of course, Yolande. Thank you for everything. Absolutely everything.

Preface

AYLMER, 1984. I can hear my feet swishing through the snow. Startled, I realize I have been watching them. Unconsciously, I stare at my toes as they lift with each step, imagining how they press against the top of my boot. I focus on the sound and movement of my feet. My mind is so blank that I suddenly lose my balance and almost fall over. I get a grip on myself and lift my eyes to the nearby street and houses. All at once, I remember why I am walking. I need exercise. I need to organize my thoughts, weigh them, classify them, clarify them. I feel as though all my free time is spent processing.

We had left New Brunswick to settle in the national capital. That year, I had resigned as director general for the promotion of official languages at the Secretary of State for Canada and joined the University of Ottawa as a professor and associate dean while taking on cases from one end of the country to the other. I was working non-stop. Meanwhile, at home, my children were suffering from an incurable neurological disease that left them completely disabled and eventually caused their early deaths. Jean-François died in 1985 and Émilie in 1996, about a year before my Supreme Court appointment. Life at home was never easy, and my wife, Yolande, went to great lengths as she fought, often alone, to keep my precious children alive. To keep us alive.

This particular winter evening, I am weighed down by my responsibilities, by my work, by my never-ending battle to give francophone minorities the right to the same quality of life as our anglophone friends and, most of all, my struggle to find the time to save my children from imminent death. I am not walking to escape my children and Yolande; I am walking to clear away the cobwebs and find fresh perspective. I think of my father, my hero, who is dying. As I walk, I follow that train of thought. I think back a few months to the summer of 1983, the whole family was gathered at my parents' cottage. An idyllic spot in the tiny town of Shediac Bridge, some thirty kilometres from Moncton, New Brunswick, and not far from Shediac, where tourists stop to have their picture taken with a giant lobster statue. Strong winds. Turbulent seas. A perfect place to relax.

Every evening, my father gets up to go smoke. He smokes like a chimney, chain-smokes three or four packs a day. But this warm July morning, I hear noises that worry me more than usual. I do not know why. When I walk into the living room, my father is there, standing in front of a little mirror on the wall. His neck is grotesquely swollen. There is no mistaking it.

"See my neck? That's lung cancer," he says as he examines his reflection. I cannot believe my eyes. I am skeptical. I tell him he cannot just go diagnosing himself with cancer in the middle of the night. It is ridiculous. But he was right. The cancer had progressed and would take his life. My father was right again. He died a few months after that winter evening walk.

I owe my father everything. He encouraged me to pursue law and was always there for my family and me. His passing left a huge void, as did my mother's thirty years later, but nothing scarred me as much as the death of my two children. I had the career I had, but nothing can fill that emptiness.

I never got to teach my children to walk or ride a bike. I never got to help them with their homework. I never saw them graduate. They were not there the first time I took my seat as a justice of the Supreme Court of Canada. I wish I could have told them about our lives, about our hopes and dreams, but their illness made that impossible. Or was it my lack of courage? I fled reality by burying myself in my work, and I had no stories left to tell.

Now I would like to tell my children a little about my life. I am not trying to justify my choices or explain myself. I am not asking anyone to understand. All I want to do is tell a little story. I wish the story had played out differently. This is a letter to my two dead children. Émile and Jean-François, this is my story.

1

"Speak White"

YOUR GRANDFATHER'S NAME WAS ALFRED, Alfred Bastarache, and he was born to Michel Bastarache and Claire Allain on January 11, 1921. Known to many as "Fred" for short, my father was one of six children, one of whom died young. He was born into a very poor family in a poverty-stricken part of New Brunswick. In his hometown, Bouctouche, jobs and education were scarce. Even now, Kent County is one of the province's poorest regions, and its unemployment rate is extremely high.

Back then, kids could not go to school in French past primary school, and, of course, your grandfather, my father, spoke only French. The only way he could keep studying in French was at private school, and the only French private schools then were *séminaires* and *collèges* run by the Church. People quickly realized that your grandfather was a clever and exceptionally bright boy. He was so smart that he got one of the scholarships that the Archbishop of Moncton gave to a handful of students to attend the Petit Séminaire de Rimouski.

Just between you and me, the only issue was that his schooling prepared him for a career in either medicine or... the priesthood. At a time when religion dominated francophone society, my father was not the most devout Catholic. He was a bit of a black sheep in that respect. He completed his studies in Rimouski with great distinction and earned his way into Université Laval's Faculty of Medicine, which was quite an honour. That was where things really clicked for him. He was treading the halls of an institution that, over the years, had been home to some of the greatest political figures in Canada and Quebec. My father was interested in medicine, but, above all, he was curious about everything. His interests spanned the spectrum from the hard sciences to the soft. Hanging out with young people who were studying social sciences with the "father of the Quiet Revolution," Father Georges-Henri Lévesque, a Dominican priest who founded Université Laval's School of Social Sciences, meant just as much to him as medicine. Father Lévesque had a huge influence on many students who would later leave their mark on Quebec and Acadian society.

My father never actually knew Father Lévesque, but he embraced the man's liberal social justice ideology and, in a way, brought it back to New Brunswick. And that was not the only thing he came home with. In Québec City, he met a woman from Chicoutimi, a *Québécoise pure laine*, a descendant of the first French settlers, whose family moved to the area when she was a child. Her name was Madeleine Claveau.

Born on February 27, 1918, to Jean-Arthur Claveau and Yvonne Rouleau, Madeleine was quite a character. An iron fist in a glove of steel. A take-charge woman who was studying to be a nurse. It is hard to say how she came by that personality. Did it have something to do with being one of fourteen children? I do not know. What I do know is that, although your grandfather turned many heads in Québec City, it was Madeleine Claveau from Chicoutimi who settled down with flamboyant Fred. She was three years older than your grandfather. A nurse and a doctor.

Fred Bastarache and Madeleine Claveau married on July 13, 1946, at the Église Saint-Dominique on the Grande-Allée in Québec City, and that is the city I was born in, a year later, on June 10, 1947. I am Québécois, but only by birth.

✦✦✦

> Children, we Acadians tend to take an interest in our family history. We want to understand where we came from.

Children, we Acadians tend to take an interest in our family history. We want to understand where we came from. One day, some friends gave me a copy of my father's family tree, and that is when I found out that my ancestors emigrated from Bayonne in 1640. I was astounded to discover that they were described as *flibustiers*. Flibu-what? Essentially, they were government-sponsored pirates called "Besteretchea" before their name was Frenchified. Apparently, they did not change much when they settled in the village of Paradis in southwestern Nova Scotia, not far from the Université Saint-Anne. I mention this because I read in a magnificent book called *A Great and Noble Scheme* that my many-times-great-grandfather and his brother were deported to North Carolina, where they were jailed because they had sunk English ships with Beausoleil Broussard. Few other deportees suffered that fate. I also learned that they escaped and made their way on foot to New Brunswick. During their journey, they were taken captive by the Iroquois, but were released with the help of a priest. They went through Memramcook before settling in Bouctouche. One of the two brothers then carried on northward, eventually founding the town of Tracadie. At the time, they went by the name Basque.

Children, I am going to go off on a genealogical tangent here to tell you about my first trip to Louisiana. I was invited to give a speech at Codofil, the Council for the Development of French in Louisiana. I got to their offices early and casually approached the entrance. I did not see anyone there, so I decided to wander around until the meeting started. Suddenly, an elderly man came out and beckoned me over.

"Come on in, Mr. Mouton," he said to me in French.

"I'm afraid you're mistaken, sir," I replied. "My name is Michel Bastarache, and I'm an Acadian from New Brunswick."

"Young man, I know a Mouton when I see one. Come on in."

I followed him, reiterating that he was mistaken about my identity. He invited me to take a seat and turned away to look for something. He pulled out a large book and opened it to a page with a photo of a Mr. Mouton. I believe he said the man had founded Vermillonville or Lafayette. I could not believe my eyes! The man was a dead ringer for me. I could have been looking at a picture of myself in period costume. My companion told me that, during the deportation, three Bastarache sisters were sent to Louisiana and married three Mouton brothers. The family resemblance was clear.

According to Bastarache family lore, many of those who bore the Basque surname were fishermen—whalers and cod fishers who came to work the Atlantic in places like Labrador around the fourteenth century. There were very few families of Basque origin in New Brunswick then. There were some in Port Royal along with some Besteretcheas. It was a small family that had no connection to the much more numerous LeBlancs, Cormiers, and Robichauds.

★★★

My first sojourn in Quebec lasted just a few months. Although I was born in Quebec and spent some of my life there, I am not Québécois. Acadia was so ingrained in my father's body and soul that he convinced my mother to go live in New Brunswick with him. And that is how a francophone woman who did not speak a single, solitary word of English ended up in the greater Moncton area.

You see, my father belonged to a generation of young men who left to study outside New Brunswick but felt a moral obligation to return home. It was their mission, in a way, a calling, kind of like a priest's calling. They believed they had been fortunate and had a duty to give back. He was much more Francophone when he returned to his home province than when he left it. From then on, and for the rest of his life, he was involved in a number of major initiatives to improve the lives of New Brunswick's Francophones and Acadians, especially in the province's southeast.

He wanted to contribute. He wanted to foster a sense of pride in the community and among individual Acadians. He wanted to nurture their independence. It was quite revolutionary. The 1940s and 1950s in New Brunswick were a dark time. There was virtually no social safety net, and people were struggling to survive. Things were especially bad in rural regions like the southeast, and they were even worse for Francophones.

Do not get me wrong, Jean-François and Émilie! I am not complaining. I did not have an unhappy childhood. We were considered a middle-class family. We lived in downtown Moncton, we owned a cottage by the sea, and my father was a doctor. Even so, your grandparents experienced the *grande noirceur*, as it was called in Quebec, in their own way. He was a doctor, she was a nurse, and together they went from house to house around Kent County, in Saint-Antoine, Bouctouche, and Sainte-Marie, to care for the sick and help women give birth. Payment was often in the form of a chicken, a pig, some vegetables, or a simple "thank you."

My parents may have been middle class, but they were kind and generous people. Helping others was in their DNA, and family was very important to them too. Under no circumstances were we allowed to miss a meal, especially on weekends. That was mainly because of my mother, but my father was fully on board. On a typical Sunday, we would go visit relatives. My parents would call out, "Let's go make the rounds!" All four children were welcome to go along, and together we called on extended family. My father was hyperactive and could not keep still, so we would stop in, catch up on everyone's news, and then move on.

We all valued our close family ties, and my father also forged a network of strong friendships. He loved to talk and tell us all kinds of stories. He had a keen sense of humour. A few weeks before his death, he asked my brother Marc to show him the cemetery where he would be buried. Marc was uncomfortable. My father said to him, "Death isn't the hard part; the hard part is resurrection." The hospital stories were definitely his best ones. I understood early on that my father became attached to people he did not even know. Many of them were terminal, at death's door. My father did not know them, but he connected with them. He wanted to provide them with the best possible quality of life.

***

Martin, Louis, Joe, and the others walked into the house. They took off their hats, greeted us, and sat at the table. They were all there in our Dominion Street kitchen in Moncton. They lit their cigarettes, and a thick cloud of smoke drifted gracefully up to the ceiling lights. There were usually three, four, or five men at the table, sometimes more. They drank and smoked. Little kitchen klatches. I did not usually know why they were getting together, but eventually I realized that they talked about anything and everything. Education, money, health. Politics came up a lot, of course. My father loved politics, but he was not partisan by nature. Affairs of state, all these new ideas for practical, effective ways to improve people's lives. Theirs was a nitty-gritty, grassroots kind of politics. Liberal Party honchos rarely saw him at political gatherings, but when my cousin, Bertin LeBlanc, who lived with me after his father died, was elected to the Legislative Assembly of New Brunswick as the member for Kent South in 1978, my parents celebrated openly.

Although Fred was not an influential Liberal Party player, he did carry some weight because his opinion mattered to important people. In the 1950s, people were willing to try anything to get rid of Hugh John Flemming's Conservatives. My father's friend Louis was practising law in Richibucto, in north Kent County. He was a little younger than my father, but the two got along swimmingly. Their affection for each other went beyond their shared passion for civic engagement. Theirs was a deep friendship. I still remember waking up in the Shediac Bridge cottage to the sound of Louis coming in and sitting down with my parents. Louis and my father would get drunk together—unless Louis was already so drunk when he showed up that my mother went about trying to sober him up. Their friendship was so great that, when my father died, Louis sent my mother a long, handwritten letter, a letter so heartfelt and poignant that my family will never forget it.

Louis got into politics quite young. He was twenty-seven in 1952 when he became the member for Kent in the Legislative Assembly. He was re-elected in 1956 and then became the leader of the Liberal Party. In 1960, Louis-Joseph Robichaud became the premier of New Brunswick. He—we—had arrived. Our friend, P'tit Louis, was the first Acadian ever to be elected as premier of our beautiful province.

***

The New Brunswick I grew up in was changing fast. This was during the years leading up to Quebec's Quiet Revolution. I do not remember much about my childhood. My life was pretty uneventful. The 1940s and 1950s were not great years in New Brunswick. Despite our considerable numbers, Francophones like us were treated like good-for-nothings. Truth be told, we were an underclass. Loyalists—Anglophones who were proud of their British roots and fierce defenders of the monarchy—stuck together, hardly sparing a thought for the "Frenchies." *L'Acadie, l'Acadie?!?*, a film by Michel Brault and Pierre Perrault, captures the mood of the day, especially in the scene where hundreds of Loyalists gather in community halls and church basements. Not only were Francophones not invited, they were not allowed. The men and women start their meetings with a rendition of "God Save the Queen," then some of them take turns stepping up to the microphone to speak. For the most part, they do not have very nice things to say about Francophones. These people do not see the presence of two languages as a cultural treasure; they see it as an affront to British and Canadian identity. Let us just say that an Acadian family like ours, some of whose ancestors were deported from the region in 1755, did not share that sentiment. It was not the eighteenth century anymore, but it sure felt like it. When we discussed issues with the Anglos, they tried to shut down the conversation by saying that they, the English, won the war against the French. The war had ended over three hundred years before, but that mentality persisted. In 1982, during the work of the Poirier-Bastarache task force on the equality of official languages in New Brunswick, I asked sociologist René-Jean Raveau to study people's attitudes towards the French language. His findings are no less chilling now than they were then. He reported that, in the early 1980s, about forty percent of Anglophones believed bilingualism to be unacceptable because the English won the Battle of the Plains of Abraham. That is crucial information for anyone attempting to understand people and come up with a way to change their attitudes.

When I was young, it was much more complicated because most of the provisions of the *New Brunswick Official Languages Act* would not come into force until six years after it was passed, in 1969. The Act had legal significance at the time, but, for all intents and purposes, a law cannot eliminate racist attitudes. Let us not mince words, children, it was most certainly racism.

★★★

As a child, I often ran errands with my mother and my brother Marc. We would leave the house and go downtown to buy groceries, clothes, and whatnot. That seems pretty basic, but it could turn out to be quite challenging. You see, my mother spoke hardly any English, and she did not tend to see herself as inferior to anyone. She never let anyone humiliate her.

We lived in Moncton, one of the biggest cities in the Maritimes, and we were lucky enough to have an Eaton's. It was right downtown, where Highfield Square was later built and then demolished in the 2000s to make way for the new multi-purpose arena. Eaton's was the department store then, and it carried just about everything. On this particular occasion, we were browsing the aisles, and an employee addressed my mother in English. Oops. My mother immediately replied in French. The man did not speak French and had no intention of finding an immediate solution to this communication quandary. Like many of his colleagues at the store and other Anglophones in town, the employee thought it was okay to be rude and to imply that my mother had some kind of disease. As if being Francophone were a disease. She did not back down. Unflappable, she shot back, "I insist that you find me a bilingual salesperson and that patrons be treated politely." Your grandmother was not one to take discrimination lying down.

That kind of thing has happened dozens of times throughout my life. Some days, on my way to school, students from the nearby English school threw rocks at my francophone friends and me. "Speak White!" and "Speak the Queen's language!" they taunted. Now, when a worker addresses me in English, the first thing I do is make sure they do not speak French. Just in case. It is never okay to let things slide. It is never okay to say nothing for fear of disturbing the established order. Complacency is death.

> Like many of his colleagues at the store and other Anglophones in town, the employee thought it was okay to be rude and to imply that my mother had some kind of disease. As if being Francophone were a disease.

★★★

We were not dead. We were alive and well. Our father was extremely involved, and our mother was demanding, endowed with a sense of activism that commanded attention. We lived in a nice house in Moncton. I was the eldest of four children, and I was just four years older than my youngest brother, Jean. I was always closest to the second oldest, Marc, but we three boys and my sister, Monique, have always enjoyed a cordial relationship.

My brother Marc was always the black sheep of the family, in a way. My mother often scolded him for his disruptive behaviour. I am sure he got that from my father, whom everyone thought of as an engaging host, a first-class speaker, and quite a clown when kids were around. As for me, even as a child, I preferred tidiness and timeliness. I liked knowing what to expect. I wanted to make sure I did what I was supposed to do properly and on time. I always had a strong sense of duty. It is hard to explain. It is part of my value system, an attitude, a character trait. According to my brothers and sister, I get it from my mother. My relationship with my mother was unique. I did not exactly make choices to please my parents, but I felt enslaved by my outlook on life. Life was too serious for fun. It is true, my mother was like that too. She was good, warm, brave, and methodical. She behaved as though she had a job description, a predetermined role and a duty to fulfill. I have to admit I liked it.

Children, your mother would tell you that my mother was a big influence in my life. I am not sure she is right about that, but she says that, subconsciously, I have always wanted to please my mother and live up to her standards. She says that is why I have always had such an exaggerated drive to do the right thing, always keep a promise, and never be late. Apparently, I get all that from my mother. To measure up to Madeleine Claveau was to be the best. She was extremely competitive her whole life. In her view, if I was not top of my class, I was being lazy. I kept telling her that there were other smart people out there, but when I said things like that, she would reply, "No, you're as smart as anyone else, and if you're not top of your class, you must not be working as hard as the others." I think my coming in second would have made any parent happy, except my mother. Second was not good enough. She was not as demanding with Marc though, whose unruly behaviour she found exasperating. I think Monique and Jean were spared as well.

That lasted my whole life. My mother never really made much of my accomplishments. Deep down, that bothered me. I never understood why. When I became president of Assumption Life, a big life insurance company in Moncton, she did not seem all that impressed. She thought it was just a job and that I was doing my best. Come to think of it, my father never said much either. I do not think he ever congratulated me on succeeding at anything. I cannot recall him ever praising me, ever. One day, my father's close friend, Dr. Léon Richard, told me that my dad was always saying how proud he was of me. I was astounded. I wonder why he never told me so himself.

When I was appointed to the Supreme Court of Canada, Roland Maurice, another friend of my father's whom I never saw, called me up to congratulate me. The only thing he said to me was, "It's so sad that your father isn't here to see it." And then he said the same thing: "Your father was always talking about you."

★★★

When I was a kid, sitting in class and looking at the other students, I felt like a stranger. That was how I felt in Moncton, in Montréal, where we lived while my father was studying pathology, and in Shediac. It is not that I was not interested in others; I just felt out of place. I think that sense of isolation came from a feeling of being unable to communicate with other people in any meaningful way. For example, when everyone laughed at a student or a teacher for some silly reason, I could not join in. On the contrary, I did not find these things funny at all, and I wondered why everyone was trying so hard to laugh. I did not suffer, but I felt uncomfortable. Things did not improve as I got older, unfortunately. As a child, I always felt more comfortable in class than anywhere else, simply because that was where I could express myself, speak most freely, and be spontaneous. I was very keen on debate, and I appreciated thoughtful dialogue that had a point. I was not bullied or rejected, but I felt disconnected, and that was frustrating. It felt like something was missing. I felt like an observer of my own actions.

But why? It is strange, I know. I did not want people to think of me as cold and indifferent, because I was not. At least, that was not how I saw myself. Even now, some people see me as austere and impatient. I get that; I understand it. It takes a very good argument to make me change my mind. Sometimes I can be downright unforgiving, especially with journalists who do not know how to speak on TV. I listen to them and get all worked up because of their inability to speak French properly. Back then, I was often impatient, harshly correcting people and then immediately feeling bad for hurting their feelings.

Was I as good at taking criticism as I was at dishing it out? Of course not. I did not take well to anyone correcting me, mainly because I noticed my own mistakes quickly and easily. Even when I was very young, I did not need anyone to point them out. In conversation, others found me antagonistic, though I did not usually realize I was coming across that way. It is just that I was direct; I did not seek consensus. I was like my Québécoise mother in that regard. For example, I had no time for folklore or, generally speaking, amateur performances. I would say so candidly even though local culture depended on it. This trait made it hard for me to fit in with groups of students or young people.

It goes without saying that I resisted confiding in anyone on a personal level. On those rare occasions when I spoke freely, I shared too much and always ended up feeling vulnerable and uncomfortable. I had no filter, and I was too trusting. That was naive of me because I did not take into account the impact of my words and many people's tendency to gossip, often distorting what I said. Every time I revealed too much, I regretted it, wondering if what I saw as an indiscretion would come back to bite me. As a young person, I worried that I might never have real friends because I could not really open up to people. I did not have the social acumen to figure out if other people confided in their friends and if doing so was essential to friendship.

Eventually, I came to understand and accept that people were different because of their individual circumstances, background, culture, and strengths. We have to respect individuals for who they are, but that is a daily practice that is not always perfect. I feel deep compassion for those whose lives are difficult, but I also have little patience for anyone who does not try to improve their life. Nowadays, I am often seen as severe, but I would argue that I am just a person with high standards. Friends who know me best can tell you that I am always willing to help build up a secretary's confidence, offer advice to a student, or orient a young lawyer struggling with a case and needing a few doors opened.

Émilie and Jean-François, it is very hard to live with the idea that people do not really understand who you are, but you cannot spend your life explaining yourself. You have to act! Ever since childhood, I have been nothing if not a person of action. That trait would bring me both success and distress.

The Path

I WAS NEVER ONE TO PICK A FIGHT, though my brother Marc would tell you that, when we were kids, he could count on me to leap to his defence. I was in pretty good shape back then, and I played lots of sports. I was not much of a troublemaker, but in my late teens, I still do not really know why, I would sometimes lash out when provoked. A few times, I thought I might have seriously injured someone.

The first incident happened on a train on our way to Bathurst. Two or three young guys were walking down the aisle, making a racket. They seemed drunk. When they got to where I was sitting, the first guy stopped and stared at me. He did not say anything. Then, out of nowhere, he threw a cup of coffee in my face and howled with laughter. I leaped up and punched him right in the nose. He was out like a light. The train slowed and then stopped. He was still lying there on the ground. Passengers stepped right over him to get off the train. I turned to his companions and told them to pick him up and deal with him. Then I got off the train.

The second incident was eerily like the first. It was convocation day at the Université de Moncton. That afternoon, I stopped in at a little shop, and as I was leaving, I saw that a car had parked behind mine, blocking me in. I went back into the shop to look for the driver. Nobody stepped up, so I went back out, but I felt like I was being followed. I turned around and saw a big guy. He beckoned me over. I approached to talk to him. Out of nowhere, he hit me in the face. I lost my balance for a second, recovered a little, then attacked, walloping him in the jaw. The impact was clearly audible, and I saw his jaw slide to the right. He was out like a light. His friends came over but could not revive him. A small crowd gathered. I was starting to worry, and I told the young guy in front of me that he had thirty seconds to get his car out of the way. Nervously, he moved the car, and I took off. Let us just say my graduation photo was not pretty. I was not a fighter, but if someone hit me, I hit back. Surprisingly, my mother was proud of her son. Never let anyone push you around, my dears.

★★★

When I was a child, we could do just six years of public school in French. After that, we had to switch to English school or go to private school. There were three options for boys in and around Moncton: the Collège Saint-Joseph in Memramcook, the Collège de l'Assomption in downtown Moncton, and the Séminaire Notre-Dame-du-Perpétuel-Secours in Humphrey, a suburb of Moncton. My parents opted for the Séminaire, a school run by the Quebec-based Redemptorists, where I could study the classics curriculum that was traditional in Quebec at the time. So off I went, and my brother Marc joined me the following year. I went back home at Christmas and Easter and for the summer. At the time, people said the academic program there was more rigorous than at the other two schools. The teachers subjected us to an intense schedule packed with literary, social, and athletic activities. That is where I learned to play handball, which is kind of like racquetball, but without a racquet, just bare hands. I loved it. It was lots of fun. Once your hands toughened up.

You can bet the Redemptorists were always trying to recruit new members for their congregation, but their efforts were in vain when it came to my peers and me. I did not like the religious part of school, but I tolerated it just fine. I was never a person of faith, but maybe I should have considered calling on a higher power back then. While I was at the Séminaire, I developed pathological anxiety around exams even though I was always top of my class. That did not change when I went to the Collège Saint-Joseph and the Université de Moncton. At the Collège, I shared a little room with a roommate. During the first year, I remember staying up all night, huddled under the covers or in the closet with a flashlight, rereading my notes.

Around then, my father became an alcoholic, and just like that, my life changed. I found out that he drank every evening and every weekend. He became taciturn and morose in his altered state. He would sit all alone, just thinking. Once so talkative, now he kept his thoughts to himself. Later, he got into the habit of sending me out for chicken at Deluxe Take-Out because he got the munchies when he was drunk. Naturally, his alcoholism caused tension at home because my mother was constantly telling him to stop drinking and refused to attend social events with him. She knew he would embarrass her. He tried to quit drinking several times, but he never managed to stay sober for long. Same with smoking.

There were several reasons for my anxiety. For one thing, I wanted to live up to my mother's expectations for my academic success. For another, my father's alcoholism kept me in a constant state of high alert. I wondered if my parents' relationship would get so bad they would separate, and eventually they did. One day, my mother decided to move out. She packed her bags and bought a train ticket for Québec City. My brothers, my sister, and I got wind of it and persuaded my father to talk her out of it. It worked, and she stayed, but we were still concerned about my father's drinking. I often worried he might be in a car accident on his way home from work. He started drinking at the office after work, before coming home for dinner. Fortunately, we lived near the hospital, which reduced the risk of him being in an accident. My mother regularly asked me to walk to my father's office, take his keys, and bring him home safe and sound. I would also commandeer his keys from time to time when he was at the bar or the Beauséjour Club for an event. He never put up much of a fight.

★★★

It was the 1960s. The Beatles, the Rolling Stones, the Doors, Simon and Garfunkel, and others were a beacon to millions of young people around the world. Tectonic social and cultural shifts were under way. Andy Warhol became a pop art legend with his *Campbell's Soup Cans*. Woodstock captured everyone's imagination, and Beatlemania took America by storm. I was not swept up in the excitement, and I was not impressed when John, Paul, George, and Ringo took the stage on the *Ed Sullivan Show* in 1964. "I Want to Hold Your Hand"? I did not get what all the fuss was about. Fortunately, their music evolved considerably after that.

Sea changes around the world had an impact close to home in New Brunswick. In the United States, the 1964 Free Speech Movement at the University of California, Berkeley, sparked a national and international protest against the Vietnam War. In France, a massive student uprising in May 1968 led to strikes that destabilized the Fifth Republic for two months. Around that time, nationalism and sovereignty were taking hold in Quebec. Students marched for better higher education in French. When Quebec created the CEGEPs in 1967, the number of francophone students rose dramatically. The three francophone universities, Université Laval, the Université de Sherbrooke, and the Université de Montréal, could barely keep up with demand. Jean-Jacques Bertrand's government launched the Université du Québec network in December 1968; the Université du Québec à Trois-Rivières, the Université du Québec à Chicoutimi, and the Université du Québec à Montréal were all founded within months of each other.

I was a student at the Université de Montréal when protests broke out in the city's downtown. On March 28, 1969, some ten thousand nationalists gathered in front of McGill University, demanding that it become a French-speaking institution. The demonstration was organized by the Union générale des étudiants du Québec and separatist groups such as the Mouvement souveraineté-association and the Rassemblement pour l'indépendance nationale. Most of the protesters were students, who marched through downtown shouting "*McGill français*" and "*le Québec aux Québécois.*" I will admit I was a mere spectator. The demonstration left an indelible mark on Montréal and Quebec as a whole. Dozens of people were arrested; some were injured. People threw rocks, shattering shop windows. The event was definitely a factor in the development of Quebec's linguistic policies in the 1970s under René Lévesque.

Meanwhile, Francophones back home in New Brunswick were also waking up and beginning to challenge the powers that be. The anglophone establishment, bent on silencing Acadians, was in for a shock, especially Moncton's anglophone mayor, Leonard Jones, who really had it in for Francophones. It all started on February 12, 1968, when Université de Moncton students voted to strike in response to a tuition fee hike. The next day, students marched on city hall in Moncton, calling for bilingual city services. Their demand for more municipal services in French was quite justified. The city had never seen a demonstration like it before, and it really exposed Mayor Jones's anti-francophone racism. The excellent documentary L'Acadie, l'Acadie!?! covers these events.

That same evening, Mayor Jones insisted that everyone speak English during the councillors' swearing-in ceremony. French was forbidden. In the days that followed, a handful of students delivered a pig's head to Mayor Jones's home. Charges were laid against the students.

I finished my undergraduate arts studies, majoring in economics and sociology, in 1967, so I was no longer in Moncton when that storm hit the city. Even though I was not there, I followed the events closely, and I could hardly contain my joy and satisfaction. The uprising forced Acadians to acknowledge their situation, and it drew the whole country's attention to the hypocrisy that characterized the relationship between the two founding linguistic communities of one of the first four provinces in Confederation. These events were a turning point for the Acadian community.

Joining protests was not my style. I have never marched for anything in my life. This time, though, I thought things had gone so far and Francophones were being subjected to such appalling treatment that something had to give. And did it ever. Then, when people found out that the National Film Board was going to make a movie about it, they talked about how at least the rest of Canada would know we existed, we were not assimilated, and we were not about to disappear anytime soon. The resistance was out in the open.

L'Acadie, l'Acadie!?! really captured the mood of the day, especially the awakening of Acadian youth. I think that was crucial because, back then, all the nationalists were old. Those movements did not have a youth presence. Suddenly they did.

My Acadian nationalism, for want of a better definition, was just a consequence of what I experienced as a teenager in Moncton during a time of open discrimination in hiring, public services, and private services. People could be prevented from speaking French in the workplace, even at federal Crown corporations such as Canadian National. The government could set up a school system designed to bring about linguistic and cultural assimilation and get the enthusiastic support of the anglophone media. It was sickening, but apathy still prevailed and was even tacitly encouraged by some members of our community. Fortunately, I was from a family that did not feel inferior and was not inclined to be content with its lot in life.

Louis J. Robichaud's ascent to power breathed new life into a people who had been stifled by the conservative, Anglo-Saxon majority. Francophones made up nearly thirty-eight percent of the population, but our political power had been all but obliterated since Confederation. Quebec had its Quiet Revolution, but New Brunswick had a revolution of its own, at times decidedly less quiet. Quebec's Premier Lesage and New Brunswick's Robichaud were very close then. Both Liberal leaders won elections in June 1960. Jean Lesage had his *équipe du tonnerre*; Robichaud was backed by the francophone population.

Robichaud's Program for Equal Opportunity would transform not only government institutions, but all of New Brunswick society. At the time, the language issue was not the only problem. Most rural counties were bankrupt. The province had to pay their employees every time the end of the month rolled around. The education system had been floundering for years, and the Conservative government had slapped a premium on health care, the infamous hospital tax. According to several observers, including Premier Robichaud's former political attaché, Robert Pichette, that was the catalyst because people did not want to pay it and could not afford it. That was how P'tit Louis appealed not only to Francophones, but to people in very anglophone counties in southern New Brunswick such as Queens County and even in Saint John. Yes, Francophones were the ones who swept Robichaud to power, but nobody could form a government without the anglophone counties' support.

> Robichaud's Program for Equal Opportunity would transform not only government institutions, but all of New Brunswick society.

The Program for Equal Opportunity was controversial because it coincided with greater provincial government interference in the lives of New Brunswickers. Robichaud's government set out to abolish the county councils in charge of local services (municipalities, basically) and centralize education, health, welfare, and the administration of justice. Its priority was equality and equal access to government services for all. Even though the province was poor, the government made money available to modernize public schools and hospitals all over the province.

Most importantly, for the first time in history, Acadians were taking charge of things. We got our francophone university, the Université de Moncton, in 1963. We wanted equality on the legal front, and we got it in 1969 when the *Official Languages Act* was passed, making English and French the province's official languages. From then on, the government was required by law to provide public services in English and French. The Act was not all that strict—it was actually quite toothless in some ways—but it was such a mighty symbol that it guaranteed us equality in principle, especially since it was adopted unanimously by the Legislative Assembly. Pierre Elliott Trudeau's federal government would go on to pass similar legislation a few months later. The idea had actually been put forward in 1963 by Lester B. Pearson's Liberal government when he created the Royal Commission on Bilingualism and Biculturalism, better known as the Laurendeau-Dunton Commission. The commission was tasked with recommending measures to help Canada advance as a federation based on the principle of equality between its two founding peoples. It focused on the cultural and linguistic issues dividing the country. The work took seven years and resulted in a number of recommendations, one of which was to make French and English the official languages of Canada, New Brunswick, Quebec, and Ontario. In the end, the federal government agreed to make Canada an officially bilingual country, but the notion of founding peoples faded over time with the adoption of multiculturalism.

★★★

Sweeping social reforms ushered in by the Program for Equal Opportunity resulted in political tensions in New Brunswick, but the province's Progressive Conservatives and Liberals were on the same page with the *Official Languages Act*. Reading the writing on the wall, both political parties wanted greater recognition for French in the province. When Prime Minister Lester B. Pearson pulled a rabbit out of his hat by creating the commission, P'tit Louis took that rabbit and ran with it. The Premier tacked official bilingualism on to his Equal Opportunity overhaul, and the little Maritime province sailed along smoothly in the federal government's wake. Université de Moncton founder Father Clément Cormier, who was a member of the national commission, suggested applying the commission's recommendations to the New Brunswick context.

According to Robert Pichette, it became a government priority overnight. One morning, Louis Robichaud walked into his chief of staff's office and said to him, "So, where are we at with the official languages file?" A provincial secretariat was handling the file, and things were not moving very fast. Pichette mumbled some excuse to the Premier, not really knowing how to put it. Eventually, he told him that nothing much was happening.

"What do you mean, 'nothing much'? Get a move on!" thundered Robichaud, according to Pichette. A sense of urgency gripped the Premier's staff. Pichette summoned his assistant, Pierre Vachon, and off they went to see Clément Cormier. They spent almost a whole day together, working non-stop. That evening, Pichette had the makings of a bill that would change the province's history. On April 18, 1969, the Legislative Assembly passed the *New Brunswick Official Languages Act*, a few months ahead of the Trudeau government's act.

The province's act certainly was not as stringent as the one passed by the House of Commons. More than fifty years later, the lawyer Michel Doucet explained that, while both acts made English and French official languages, one for federal institutions and the other for New Brunswick's provincial institutions, they did not have much else in common.

The federal act went much further than the provincial Liberals' act. Ottawa's version recognized language of work and created the Office of the Commissioner of Official Languages to serve as the federal government watchdog. Pursuant to the Act, the executive branch had to ensure the equal status of both languages. New Brunswick did not have a commissioner or impose any requirements on public servants. It was little more than symbolic, but it was an extremely important symbol. It goes without saying that, from my perspective, it was one of the most important milestones in our country's history. To me, that legislation sent a clear message: Anglophones and Francophones were equal and were to be treated equally. I have never forgotten that.

★★★

It was the height of summer at the end of the 1960s when I set out from my parents' house for Alma, on the Bay of Fundy. I drove through the little fishing village in my super-fast Ford Galaxie, which had a huge V8 engine. Let me tell you, for three summers, everyone in town and everyone I worked with was well aware of my presence. The sun would just be peeking over the horizon when I parked my car and joined the road crew. My dears, I was a lumberjack, and my job was to chop down the forest to make way for a road through Fundy National Park. Believe it or not, your dad knows how to handle a chainsaw and an axe! I was part of a crew of about five young people overseen by Mac McGinnis, a six-foot-five, three-hundred-pound giant from Cape Breton. That guy was awesome. He could lift a Volkswagen all by himself! Work in the park was pretty dangerous. Some of the people I worked with hurt themselves quite badly with chainsaws. It was hard work, with the flies and the sweltering summer heat.

One of my duties was to go around the campsites in the evening. Famous people hardly ever came to the park, but I once saw Yvette Mimieux, an actress from producer George Pal's *The Time Machine*, which had come out a few years before.

Imagine how proud I was to tell my friends that story! I guess I still tell it. Too bad I did not have a camera to capture the moment. They had to take my word for it.

Physical labour suited me well. As a young man, in addition to cutting trees down in Fundy, I spent other summers driving a refrigerated truck between Moncton and Charlottetown. A few years later, I did kind of the same thing, picking up milk cans from farms around Shediac and Barachois. I also had a job as a vehicle safety inspector on roads in southeast New Brunswick. In the winter, I sold clothes at Rubens and encyclopedias door to door. I did not find any of those jobs particularly difficult, except maybe selling encyclopedias. I actually liked hanging out with blue-collar workers during my college and university years.

I also began to feel more comfortable socially. I started chasing girls, though "chasing" is a bit of an exaggeration. I was no Don Juan, but I finally found myself a girlfriend in Moncton. Her name was Suzanne, and she was very pretty. Once, she even modelled for magazines. She was that pretty! I remember she had an unfortunate accident while doing some kind of snow sport and was in a cast for many months. I might have been eighteen or nineteen, and Suzanne was my first flame. We dated for about two years, maybe less. I was not really in love with her, but I liked being with her, mainly because she was so beautiful. I did not like the fact that we did not have much in common. She had no intention of going to college or university, so I decided to break up with her. I told her, "In five years, we won't have anything left to say to each other. I will have changed, but you won't."

> My greatest success in love came soon after that. As a matter of fact, it was not just a success, it was a triumph. It was the greatest achievement of my life.

My greatest success in love came soon after that. As a matter of fact, it was not just a success, it was a triumph. It was the greatest achievement of my life. It was during the second half of the 1960s, some time after I started at the Université de Moncton. I was single, with no prospects. I spent my time alone, happily listening to Elvis Presley. I skipped dances and events featuring Beatles tunes. I asked a tall redhead from Madawaska County if she would like to go out with me some evening. She rejected my advances. My dears, I admit I was not too happy about that.

I was afraid, afraid that other girls would turn me down. My confidence was shaken. I decided I was done. I would never ask anyone out again. My relationship strike lasted a year, and that was just fine by me.

Then I met Ginette Gagné, a girl in my class. She was great, but she had a boyfriend. On principle, I did not ask her out, but Ginette liked me a lot, and we talked often. She was from Grand-Sault, New Brunswick, and was renting an apartment in Moncton with some other girls. One day, she sat down next to me in class and announced that she had set up a date with a girl named Yolande Martin. I did not know Yolande, but we might well have crossed paths at the Université de Moncton. There were not many buildings on campus at the time, and all the students crossed paths at some point. Ginette told me, "Yolande doesn't go out with anyone, and she needs to go out. You have to go out too, so you're going to go out together."

The big event took place at Fundy Park during a student party. Yolande was studious, like me, but she took a break from her studies to go to the party that evening. That is how we met. It was 1967, and the Rolling Stones, the Supremes, and the Doors topped the Billboard 100. We had our whole lives ahead of us. From that first night, I knew she was an extraordinary young woman. She was an arts student minoring in science and biology. She was from Caraquet, on the Acadian Peninsula, and I was from Moncton. She was from a family of three; I, a family of four. Our mothers had both worked before becoming homemakers. Her father was a travelling salesman, mine a pathologist. I was from the city; she was from the country. During her studies, she developed a passion for literature and genetics. She was a thoughtful, earnest woman, and I wanted to spend as much time with her as possible.

> From that first night, I knew she was an extraordinary young woman.

So there we were relaxing on a couch one day, my head in her lap. Right then, I knew that we could build a life together. There is no explaining that kind of thing. It was not rational. Our love was a gift, a discovery, and we have shared it ever since. We were inseparable then, and we are inseparable now. We got married a year later, in Caraquet. She wanted to wait a few years, but I was in a hurry.

3

Stand Up

I HAD JUST COMPLETED MY STUDIES IN ECONOMICS AND SOCIOLOGY at the Université de Moncton, and I wanted to be a teacher. I just wanted to share my knowledge and shape the next generation, and I would have been happy to do that at either a university or a school. I loved children, so a career in education made sense. My favourite subjects were the soft sciences, the social sciences. Back in those days, I had no idea I would someday become a lawyer, let alone a judge.

I have always been uncertain and anxious about my career choices, though. To this day, I ask myself a million questions before accepting or turning down a job. It pretty much took me a lifetime to find a job I was happy with. When I graduated from the Université de Moncton, the Société Radio-Canada was recruiting summer news readers in Moncton. Journalism? Why not? I went to the audition, but was told I did not have "the right accent" or a "radiophonic" voice. So much for that. I abandoned the idea and focused on teaching. Even though I could picture myself as a teacher, I could not make up my mind. I had nagging doubts. One day, my father could see that I was tormented. He sensed my anxiety.

Ever since early childhood, I had been top of my class. Every subject came easily to me. "Of course you don't know what you want," he told me. That was not particularly helpful. My father generally gave solid advice. He was dynamic, funny, and entertaining by nature, but he also had a way of really tuning in to you and telling you what you needed to hear. It was hard to describe. He and I talked for a few minutes. It was not a particularly deep or formal conversation, but it was one of the most important ones of my life. My father wanted to know what my life goals were, what I wanted to accomplish. He did not want to know what job I had my heart set on; he wanted to know my mission. Why was I on this earth? My father would never have understood if I had told him I wanted to put in minimal effort to hold down a good job and live a comfortable life. He would never have accepted that. Deep down, just between you and me, I felt the same way. I mulled his question over. I knew that what I truly wanted was to make a meaningful contribution to society, and that is what I told him, just like that, sincerely. "Law," was his immediate response. As he saw it, if my main interest was the social sciences, I should consider studying law. He explained that the law was the most demanding discipline of all and that it would open the most doors. I smiled. My father became a pathologist because his health could not sustain the country doctor lifestyle. He had always had a special interest in the law and was often called to serve as an expert witness to explain his autopsy results, especially in murder cases. He then trained to be a medical examiner and become one of the most prominent experts in the Maritimes, so his suggestion was not surprising. It made sense. Law? Why not? I was not interested in defending bad guys, but I wanted to help people and be there for those who did not have the wherewithal or luck to keep themselves out of trouble.

Law? Why not?

Over time, I grew to love the law and became devoted to justice in general and social justice in particular. Society had become overly legalistic because of the decline of factors contributing to community solidarity, so I felt it was important for people in the legal sphere to bring compassion to their work. That would become my definition of justice. Over the years, I also learned that a multidisciplinary approach is vital in most fields, and I have found it very rewarding to work with experts in other domains.

★★★

When I first arrived in Montréal, I had no inkling that I was about to experience the most formative years of my life. I would go on to do a lot of different jobs in my life, and my studies in Montréal prepared me for every one of them. I improved my spoken and written French along with my ability to analyze texts and express my thoughts clearly. I never did master the language to the degree I would have liked, and I still admire professors I had later at the Université de Nice for their extensive vocabularies. At the Université de Montréal, I enjoyed the atmosphere on campus and being surrounded by French. Just French. As you can imagine, given my background, there was no way I was going to pursue my studies in the language of Shakespeare. At the time, the only law programs in the Maritimes were at Dalhousie University, in Halifax, and the University of New Brunswick (UNB), in Fredericton. In 1967, New Brunswick had no French law faculty. The Université de Moncton's Faculty of Law, which I helped set up, was not launched until the late

1970s. It was actually the first French-language common law faculty in the world. Anyway, in 1967, I did not have a lot of options. My priority was to study in French. Laval's law school had a good reputation, as did Montréal's.

So I showed up for the Université de Montréal's entrance exam. The minute I walked into the room, I could tell I would be the only Acadian in the program. Ever the outsider!

Throughout my studies in Montréal, I never really felt included. Maybe it was my fault. There were about 320 students in the first year, including a whole contingent of Collège Brébeuf graduates who were pretty cliquish and tended to take centre stage. They seemed to view all the other students—those from Lac-Saint-Jean, Gaspé, and Beauce, a few Jewish students, a handful of bilingual Anglophones, and me, the little Acadian—as strangers.

My graduating class of 1970 included Louise Arbour, who would become my Supreme Court bench mate thirty years later, and future Quebec premier Pierre Marc Johnson. We had some courses together, but we were not close. I did not have many friends then. I studied a lot and spent most of my spare time with Yvan Bolduc, the smartest kid in class, bar none. Yvan went on to have a brilliant career in civil and commercial litigation. His clients included former Quebec premiers Lucien Bouchard and Jacques Parizeau. Right after graduation, Yvan clerked for the Chief Justice of the Supreme Court of Canada, Gérald Fauteux. I also struck up a friendship with Hélène Dumont, who would later become a vice-dean and the Vice-Rector at the Université de Montréal.

Was I excluded because of my background? I do not think so. Was I even really excluded? I would not say they ignored me, but I never felt a sense of belonging. I did not worry about it too much though because I had excellent relationships with many professors and a few friends. The one inescapable fact was that Yolande was far away and I felt very lonely in Montréal. After I graduated from the Université de Moncton, I left for the big city without my beloved. Yolande went back to Caraquet, on the Acadian Peninsula, to be with her mother after her father died of a heart attack at the age of fifty-six. She taught grade 9 at the regional school. She was just twenty years old, and she was teaching French, history, and religion—essentially a course in values and ethics—to no fewer than eighty-five students in three classes.

Her life was very busy and full. She would say that she did not have time to miss me. Her income supported the household entirely. At first, we planned to have a long-distance relationship the whole time I was studying in Montréal, but I missed her so much after just a few months that I got sick of the arrangement. I waited a year, and then I popped the question. Your mother and I got married in August 1968 in Caraquet. A few weeks later, we moved into a dingy little apartment near the Université de Montréal. Ours was a student lifestyle: no money, no going out. Yolande spent her savings on a used Volkswagen Beetle and was having a hard time finding work. She could not get a job teaching in Quebec because her New Brunswick work experience was not recognized. She applied for lots of jobs, including some in the pharmaceutical industry, but did not get any offers. Our situation was quite unstable because we did not know what I would do after my studies. Would we stay in Quebec? Would we return to our home province? In the end, she stopped searching while I was in school.

The Université de Montréal's Faculty of Law was a much more intellectual environment, and my law studies were very gratifying. I was very partial to the language and methodology associated with the discipline. I had had a penchant for working with clear principles and objectives since childhood, and I was not at all worried when our profs predicted that only about 260 of us would make it to the second year. I was not yet sure that I would practise law, but I felt I was in the right place. I definitely knew I was in a good school, a good community, and a good city, and it was a good time to be there.

My dears, as I write this, I am thinking about how, not that long ago, I was working on a committee tasked with establishing pay for military judges, and I had to choose someone to chair the committee. I chose Jean-Louis Baudoin, one of my professors at the Université de Montréal. He is retired, and he is a little older than me. I will always remember how his father, who also taught us, died all of a sudden as he was wrapping up a class. He had a heart attack, and everyone blamed it on the students because we had been hard on him. He had immigrated from France, and he always taught like a Frenchman. As his student, I knew him to be rigorous with respect to both form and content. His French was impeccable. His son, Jean-Louis, taught us back then too. People liked the son as much as they disliked the father. Both were a big influence on me because I admired their intellectual prowess and it was deeply satisfying to hear people speak French so perfectly.

★★★

Three quarters of the students were separatists. They were members of the Parti Québécois (PQ) or the Mouvement souveraineté-association. I never wanted to join the PQ, and I have to admit that I never voted for the party even though it was progressive in many ways. I have always, without exception, voted Liberal. Always. I have never once voted anything but Liberal, anywhere. At the time, though, I put a PQ sticker on my car to avoid trouble. I was afraid someone would break the windows. It was a time of great upheaval, and the mood in the city was tense. Bad enough that I was not from there, I did not want to take any risks. I finally graduated in the spring of 1970, and the Front de libération du Québec (FLQ) was gaining ground in the lead-up to what came to be known as the October Crisis. A few months later, a British diplomat would be kidnapped and a Quebec government minister assassinated.

I will not get into the details of that time in Quebec's history, but I have to tell you, Émilie and Jean-François, that those events made me heartsick. Students were highly politicized, but in their fervour, many of them, including quite a few at the Université de Montréal's Faculty of Law, sided with the FLQ. Supporting a revolutionary movement is not always problematic, but my classmates' endorsement of the activities of the FLQ, which ended up killing Pierre Laporte, the Minister of Immigration, Labour and Manpower, was disgraceful, rash, and repugnant. When that happened, I could not help but feel sad that the students did not even understand the subject they were studying. They did not grasp the importance of a democratic justice system. To me, what the FLQ did was not only illegal—it amounted to terrorism. Those people were putting bombs in mailboxes. They were not just attacking members of the government, the police, and the army; they were attacking ordinary citizens. Their actions were gratuitous, unforgivable and, ultimately, pointless. They were not constructive. It is not that I disagreed with separatists or hated them. I actually had quite a few PQ friends. I respected those whose allegiance was rooted in a belief that Quebec would never be Canada's equal for political, demographic, cultural, and even economic reasons. I never took issue with that line of thinking. Indeed, I respected that ideology and could argue in favour of it without actually supporting it. However, people who embraced sovereignty because they wanted revenge on the English who beat the French on the Plains of Abraham could never sway me. That, to me, was incomprehensible idiocy, and God knows there were plenty of people who agreed with me at the time.

In October, when Canadian Prime Minister Pierre Trudeau invoked the *War Measures Act*, I was shocked. At first, I was in favour of it, but I was skeptical. I did not know if it was an overreaction to the separatist movement or if it was motivated entirely by the FLQ's actions. I wondered what was really behind that decision. I felt it was an extreme response to what would have to be an extreme threat, but I was not convinced that was actually the case. A man was kidnapped and then freed, and a minister was murdered. The more I learned about what was happening, the more I felt that the Canadian prime minister was attacking the Parti Québécois and the separatist movement. He wanted to crush them, pure and simple, and scare them by throwing them in jail. I was against that. That is not how democracy works. But it was hard to square the person who invoked the incredibly heavy-handed *War Measures Act* and trampled on the individual freedoms of Canadians in Quebec with the person who, a decade later, would enact the *Canadian Charter of Rights and Freedoms*. The two were irreconcilable, and that is why Trudeau's actions seem more like political revenge. I was disappointed in my prime minister.

★★★

Joseph Zénon Daigle was a brilliant man. Originally from Kent County, like my father, he came from nothing and ended up doing great things for New Brunswick, overcoming countless obstacles along the way. The seventh of nine children, he grew up in extreme poverty. They say that his father, a farmer, never had more than ten dollars in his wallet. By dint of hard work, Joe eventually joined a law office in his native region. He attended Collège Saint-Joseph and studied law at UNB before winning a scholarship to do graduate work in law at the Université de Paris in 1958–1959. Upon returning from Europe, he became a close adviser to his long-time friend, Louis J. Robichaud, our newly elected provincial premier. He served as Robichaud's assistant for two years before contracting tuberculosis. He was hospitalized, and it took him months, years even, to get better. Once he recovered, he stayed away from the political jungle of Fredericton for over a decade. He retreated to his hometown, setting up a law office in Richibucto and then in Bouctouche, where he practised criminal law with Guy Richard, who would later become the Chief Justice of the Court of Queen's Bench.

Joe was an excellent lawyer, fluently bilingual, and always self-possessed. As if by magic, he was appointed to the provincial court in 1967. Robichaud was still premier. At thirty-two, Joe became the youngest judge in the province's history. Two years later, he got another call from Premier Robichaud. That call would change my life for some time to come.

***

I was anxious. May was around the corner, and I still did not have plans for summer or even fall. I did not want to practise law in Quebec, so I was not looking for an articling position. I was waffling, weighing various options, none of which was a sure thing. I could study common law at McGill, pursue my career as a teacher, or do a master's. I had no idea what I wanted to do. It was ridiculous because I had made it to the end and had no clear sense of what came next. I should have made a decision sooner, but I felt like an outsider in Montréal. It was hard to network; of course I did not know a single lawyer practising in Quebec. At the time, my classmates had no trouble finding positions in law firms or the public service. My only option was an uncle by marriage in Québec City, Roland Legendre, who was a judge and suggested I contact his former firm, but even that was not guaranteed. Then the phone rang. A guy by the name of Joe Daigle was on the other end of the line. I vaguely recognized his name.

A few weeks later, I met with Daigle in person at the law faculty, and he told me what he wanted to do. He was an eloquent man, not especially tall, but slender and very articulate.

"You were one of few Acadians who studied law in French," he recalled, sitting in his downtown Moncton office in 2017. "You were a brilliant young man, and I wanted you on my team." His "team" was the group responsible for translating and consolidating New Brunswick's statutes, a group created by Premier Robichaud after the *Official Languages Act* was passed a few months before. Maître Daigle was tasked with not only translating the laws, but also cleaning them up and consolidating them. What's consolidating? Well, for example, it means taking an act that was passed in 1950 and amended in 1960, 1966, and 1969 and updating it so people do not have to go digging through all the amendments. In the process, sometimes it makes sense to do a little housekeeping because there might be things that can be taken out or defined differently. The group also wanted to make sure terminology was consistent among departments because there was no real structure. For example, the description of "building" in the *Property Act* might not be the same as in the *Residential Tenancies Act*.

I listened to what he was offering me, and I said, "You know, I just finished my law degree, and I'd like to be able to use it." The project was expected to take two years, and Maître Daigle tried to persuade me, suggesting that it might be useful to join the team and meet some influential people in Fredericton. "It would be a great experience both professionally and personally," he argued. I considered the scope of the job, and let us just say that I could see why he was trying so hard to convince me. Putting together that kind of team is extremely difficult.

"I sought advice," he recollected. "I met with people at the Translation Bureau in Ottawa and soon realized it wouldn't be easy. I knew that, to translate the statutes, I couldn't just go get translators from Ottawa because they didn't have the property law terminology used in New Brunswick's common law. I tried to find someone from here who had training in both common law and translation, but there wasn't anyone, so I went to Ottawa. There was a whole process. I started by hiring translators from Quebec, Quebeckers, and French people, but the best I could do was a guy like Michel, who was finishing his law degree at the Université de Montréal but was from here and had very good English. That was more or less the kind of translator I needed. He wasn't a trained translator, but I knew he had quite an interest in French, so I approached him in April, and he agreed to come."

He also invited other young Francophones such as Fernand and Aldéa Landry, who ended up getting very involved in provincial politics. Fernand went on to become Premier Frank McKenna's chief of staff and strategist, and Aldéa became New Brunswick's first female deputy premier. Aldéa was also the Minister of Intergovernmental Affairs during the Meech Lake Accord negotiations.

It did not take me long to accept the offer, and Yolande and I returned to our native province. There was another problem though: the team was based in Fredericton, where almost everyone was a unilingual Loyalist. Luckily, we had a couple of francophone friends to lean on. The Landrys played an important role in our lives, and we developed a wonderful friendship with them over the years.

***

Yolande understood why we ended up in Fredericton. She understood, but she was not happy about it. It was not exactly a dream destination. Moving there did not mean we would spend the rest of our lives there, but it cast a pall over us. I did not really have a choice because I had not done any job hunting whatsoever, so I wound up trying my hand at legal translation in Fredericton.

My first day on the job, I showed up at the appointed place and was dismayed to see that it was a dark, dingy, old two-storey house close to the main government building on Queen Street, not the government building itself. It was clearly a third-rate building. It occurred to me that our project might not be such a big deal after all. Our team obviously was not a real priority for the government. I mentioned it to Daigle, and he told me nothing else was available. I realized he did not want to make waves because the tide seemed to be turning against Robichaud's Liberals in Fredericton. They had been in power for ten years. The government was tired, the shine had worn off, and on top of that, it had to face a very popular Progressive Conservative challenger. Richard Hatfield became New Brunswick's premier on October 26, 1970, just a few months after I landed in Fredericton. Hatfield, a francophone ally, did not shut down our group. I was relieved I still had a job. The task force had a five-year mandate, and a final report was due in 1974. As the weeks went by, I began to find the work more interesting. I was interested in the language and had to start developing a French common law vocabulary.

There was only one other person on the translation team with legal training. Michel Darras, originally from France and much older than the rest of us, had never practised law. Michel was remarkably energetic and intellectually curious. He had worked in New York and taught at Newfoundland's Memorial University. Michel and I also set up a translation company, Les traductions précises. I was not earning much money from my government job, just over ten thousand dollars per year, and I needed a second income. We got several contracts to translate all kinds of things, especially government reports, such as the Department of Health's annual report. Michel was not great at landing contracts, but he was a superb translator. Initially, he encouraged me to join him, one thing led to another, and our private sector work took off.

He also convinced some other colleagues and me to set up the Corporation of Translators and Interpreters of New Brunswick to boost our profession's credibility. He wanted something more structured and thought translators should have to pass an exam to practise the profession. A professional translators' association would be the only way to ensure decent pay. We were not looking to create a union, but we wanted to establish mandatory standards, so it seemed reasonable and legitimate to expect a translator to pass an exam to obtain professional standing. I wanted our status to be recognized from the get-go, so I went to Montréal to meet with the President of the Association des traducteurs du Québec. She helped me by sharing a number of documents, including their charter, which we copied and adapted to our needs. She also introduced me to some key people who helped me found the association. We got it off the ground a few months later, and it exists to this day. I am still proud to be the first and maybe only honorary member of the Corporation of Translators, Terminologists and Interpreters of New Brunswick (CTINB). My mother was the one who designed the corporation's logo. She was also an artist, working mostly with enamelled copper.

I liked my work in Fredericton even though I knew it would not last forever. The Hatfield government wanted us to work quickly. Daigle met with Justice Minister John Baxter regularly to give him progress reports, but there was no political pressure as such.

"The people we worked with the most were Justice Minister John Baxter and Deputy Minister Gordon Gregory," recalled Daigle. "They were both from Saint John, and I don't think they were really behind the project. But Baxter developed a sudden interest and, in the final year, he insisted we complete the project quickly. He knew there was going to be an election in 1974, and he wanted all the statutes to be done because there was going to be a statement on page one of the volumes and he wanted to be the one to sign it. It was definitely personal. If the statutes were published and adopted by the assembly after the election, he might no longer be the justice minister. As it turned out, he wasn't."

What Minister Baxter wanted was to go down in history. That was his motive. That is why he started putting a lot of pressure on the group after I left. If the Minister wanted the work done fast, it would be done fast.

You see, I wanted job stability, so just a few months after I started working there, I contacted Aurèle Young, the Director of the Université de Moncton's School of Social Sciences, and asked him to consider hiring me as a teacher. I was twenty-three years old, and unfortunately, things did not work out. They could not hire me. I kept working in Fredericton, where I completed my probation without incident on December 1, 1970. The problem was that I was considered a translator, not a jurist, so I was paid seven hundred and eighty-seven dollars per month, which was less than my colleagues who were jurists.

I found out that they did not want to classify me as a jurist because my degree was in civil law, not common law. I was paid much less than the jurists in the unit responsible for consolidating the statutes. It was unfair, and I protested. Judge Daigle said he did not have the power to fix the problem. I arranged a meeting with Rodman Logan, the Provincial Secretary and Minister of Labour. Logan was a unilingual anglophone lawyer from Saint John, and he was uncompromising. In his early twenties, Logan had crossed the Atlantic to fight in the Second World War. Despite being wounded twice in battle, he went on serving his country. The man before me had the look of a soldier.

Our meeting was memorable. He greeted me coldly and told me to get right to the point. He was a "what do you want" kind of person. He was seated at his large wooden desk; behind him was a big Orange Lodge banner. The stage was set. Boldly, I told him I was a jurist and wanted the same pay as my friends whose university education was similar to mine. They had common law degrees from UNB, and I had a civil law degree from the Université de Montréal. I did not see much of a difference. He looked at me incredulously and told me I did not have the same qualifications as them. I was ready to debate the issue. I argued that my colleagues did not have my expertise either. I spoke both of the province's official languages perfectly, my writing was better, and I was one of the only ones, if not the only one, who had completed a law degree in French. I pointed out that that was exactly why his government had come to Montréal to recruit me. Clearly annoyed, he asked me brusquely why he should do me a favour. His exact words were, "Why should I do anything special for you, because you're a Frenchman?"

Without missing a beat, I replied that he would not have to stoop that low. "You won't have to do me any favours; I'm leaving right now," I told him. I had just told the Minister I was resigning. I spun on my heel and left his office. He did not try to stop me, change my mind, or convince me to stay and discuss the matter. Swiftly and calmly, I made my way to the miserable old house on Queen Street. I marched into Daigle's office and immediately notified him I was leaving.

On July 19, 1971, I sent my letter of resignation to H. H. D. Cochrane, Deputy Minister of the Provincial Secretariat. I was furious, going so far as to say in my letter that, "Under the circumstances, I have come to the conclusion that there is no likelihood of advancement in store for me here, nor am I liable to have any guarantee in the matter of salary raises."

When I received the Deputy Minister's response the next day, I knew that my decision to go back to university to study for a master's degree was the right one.

"I do not recall at any time agreeing to any reclassification and salary increase to be effective April 1, 1971 [...] Considering the length of your service I do not feel you have been mistreated, salary wise or in any other way," wrote Deputy Minister Cochrane.

Even now, forty years later, Daigle maintains that I was treated fairly.

"Mr. Bastarache received the salary he asked for. It was about fourteen thousand or fifteen thousand dollars. That was what I was paying my translators," he said. I respect his opinion, but I disagree. He hired me because I had just completed my civil law studies. I may not have been a member of the bar, but I had a degree. I was technically a lawyer, but they chose not to recognize that. Anyway, I left my job and decided I would get to know France, much to Yolande's delight.

4
Activist

THERE IS NO PLACE LIKE THE CÔTE D'AZUR. The beauty of that part of the world, where the Tyrrhenian Sea meets the Balearic Sea with views of Corsica and the Italian Boot off in the distance, is almost impossible to describe. The Côte d'Azur is Cannes. It is Monaco. It is paradise. We discovered France not as tourists do, by visiting museums and monuments, but by getting to know French culture, the people's customs and traditions, community life, their government, their police, and especially the students.

Yolande was taking a film history class, and the professor assigned several movies a week. That was the kind of thing you could do in Nice because it was the French capital of the seventh art. We spent many hours watching movies in theatres that specialized in screening foreign and classic films.

When we arrived in Nice, we rented a basement apartment in the *Maison rose*, a large house on the very narrow Avenue de la Clua belonging to the elderly Madame Maugé, who had asked the Université de Nice to send her only Canadian students as renters. Madame Maugé had lived in Canada some time before and trusted us. Why? No idea.

The university was spread out around the city. Many of the faculties, including mine and Yolande's, were quite some distance apart.

From the *Maison rose*, we had to drive my Renault 4 about ten kilometres to get to our classes. Every morning, I dropped your mother off at the Faculty of Arts, where she took history classes, and then continued on to the Faculty of Law and Economics.

Yolande's faculty had some trouble scheduling two of her classes, which overlapped for an hour each week. Desperate times call for desperate measures. I attended one of her classes and took notes for her. Trouble was, in Nice, the professors always took attendance. In as feminine a voice as possible, I would say "Here" when the professor called Yolande's name. Every single time, the professor would look at me as though this were the first time, hesitate, and say, "You're not Yolande Bastarache!" At first, I tried to explain why I was there, but he refused to listen. After that, I just said, "No, I'm taking notes for her." He just shrugged and moved on to the next name.

I have wonderful memories of my time studying in France; on the Avenue de la Clua in Nice in 1971.
Source: Collection of Michel Bastarache.

***

This was just after everything transpired in Fredericton. Right after leaving the city, I decided to go back to school. In short order, I secured a scholarship through the French consulate in Moncton and enrolled in graduate studies in public law at the Université de Nice. Yolande signed up for a master's in history. I opted for international and constitutional law because it was pointless for a New Brunswicker like me, who already had a civil law degree, to do a master's in civil law. I still did not know what kind of career I would pursue following my two-year European adventure or where I would go next. I was thinking along the lines of teaching at a university or working in diplomacy. The French consulate sent me to Nice. That was not my choice. We do not choose our destination. Friends of ours had their hearts set on Paris and ended up in Montpellier or Strasbourg. What luck that we found ourselves on the Côte d'Azur. We adored it there.

Our arrival in Nice in 1971 coincided with all kinds of notable twentieth-century events, such as François Mitterrand becoming the leader of France's socialist party; the death of the Doors co-founder Jim Morrison in his Paris apartment; and the hijacking of a Pakistan International Airlines flight in December. *Lycéens*, secondary school students, were still restive, and university students were on edge, primed for strike action. In France, the memory of May 1968 was still fresh, the reverberations still palpable.

Nice was nothing like Moncton, Fredericton, or Montréal. It was lovely, and the weather was just wonderful. I was fortunate to have René-Jean Dupuy as my thesis director and main professor. Professor Dupuy was an extraordinary man from another time, my mother's time. Originally from Tunisia, he began studying law in Algiers in 1942 before joining the Allied Forces. The U.S. Army awarded him a Bronze Star Medal in recognition of his military service and integrity. After the Second World War, he resumed his law studies in Paris, where he befriended Boutros Boutros-Ghali, who went on to serve as secretary general of the United Nations and the Organisation internationale de la Francophonie. In 1962, Professor Dupuy became one of the first professors at the Université de Nice, where he founded the Institut du droit de la paix et du développement. As an aside, Boutros Boutros-Ghali agreed to write the preface to an edition of my book on language rights in Canada.

Professor Dupuy's routine was always the same. He came into class with a huge bundle of documents, set it on the table, tilted his head back, and put a few drops in his eyes. He wiped his face and began his class. He hardly ever opened his notes, but he spoke as clearly as though he were reading a text. He answered every question on the spot, even my questions about Canadian constitutional provisions. He was a rigorous teacher, and under his guidance I had to get used to writing lots of papers without much intervention on his part.

I also had a thesis to write. Professor Dupuy focused on treaty law, and in 1970, the UN adopted the *Declaration of Principles Governing the Sea-Bed and the Ocean Floor, and the Subsoil Thereof, beyond the Limits of National Jurisdiction*. That led to the 1972 United Nations Conference on the Environment in Stockholm, Sweden, and the creation of the United Nations Environment Programme (UNEP). My thesis director told me he wanted me to explore a subject related to the law of the sea.

I remember looking at him incredulously, racking my brain. Finally, it hit me: my thesis topic would be pollution in the Canadian Arctic and the Gulf of St. Lawrence.

I'm not bragging at all when I say that I was well ahead of my time, because that became an extremely important international issue in the twenty-first century. Back then though, it was one of the first theses on the subject. Prime Minister Pierre Elliott Trudeau had just made Jack Davis Canada's very first environment minister in 1971. Under the circumstances, finding the documentation I needed was no easy feat.

I wrote to the Department of External Affairs and every other department I could think of in Canada asking for boxes of documents. I could not believe the response: no documents were available. My request was denied. So I went to see Professor Dupuy in hopes of changing the subject of my thesis.

That hope was short-lived. Not beating around the bush, he said, "The Americans have all that, and they'll help you. Get in touch with the U.S. Department of State." Those were the Nixon years, and his secretary of state was William P. Rogers. It was a few months before the legendary Henry Kissinger was put in charge of U.S. foreign affairs. I wrote a letter to the State Department, in Washington. Imagine that, children, a young Canadian student in Nice casting a line and reeling it back in a few weeks later with a massive box containing all the documentation I could imagine. I was like a kid in a candy store for sure.

I completed my master's thesis, but I was not ready to take on a PhD. I had done the coursework, but not the thesis. I had my graduate degree, my *diplôme d'études supérieures*, and that was enough.

★★★

The end was near, and I was feeling the heat. Europe was a dead end for me. As much as I loved my life there, I knew full well that I would have to find a job when I got back to Canada. Still at the *Maison rose*, I tried to land a teaching position, ideally teaching law in a francophone institution. I reached out to Université Laval and the Université de Montréal but had no luck. I realized right away that Laval had no interest in anyone but a *pure laine*, true-blue Quebecois or someone who was actually from France. My CV did not matter, and neither did my areas of specialization. Unlike Laval, Montréal was more open. I was offered a one-year position teaching service courses in other faculties. Let us just say it was not exactly the homecoming I had pictured.

As the weeks went by, I started thinking a public service career with the Ministry of Intergovernmental Affairs in Québec City or Foreign Affairs in Ottawa would help me gain relevant experience. I really wanted to put the theory I had learned in Nice into practice.

I ended up at the Université de Moncton. Helmut Schweiger, the Vice-Rector, Academic, offered me a three-hour weekly introductory political science course in May 1973, and I accepted. I spent my last few months in France travelling around Europe. One day, I got in touch with my father and my brother Marc. I needed cash.

"He asked me to send him money because he wanted to come back from Nice [via Antwerp] with a BMW," recalls Marc. I had struck a good deal when I picked up a BMW 2002 on credit for duty-free import six months before going back to Canada. It was quite a purchase, but eventually I wondered if it was really worth the trouble. For one thing, the owner of the *Maison rose*, Madame Maugé, did not hide her dismay when I turned up at her place with my new wheels. She berated me for buying a German car. Like many French people of her generation who had lived through the Second World War, she did not like Germans.

I had to ship my car to Halifax, Canada, from Antwerp, Belgium. To save space, I packed it full of clothing and other souvenirs of my two years abroad. When I got to the Port of Halifax, I opened the trunk and saw that it was all gone. Everything I had brought back had been stolen. Luckily, I still had the BMW.

★★★

Soon after I began my career as a professor, I realized I would have to adapt. One of my students, Michel Doucet, remembers my class that year: "I'll never forget it. There were students from every faculty, and I think there were about a hundred of us who took that first exam. When he handed back our papers, only six people had passed, and the highest grade was a C. He had to adjust his expectations because people were crying and yelling!" If I am not mistaken, Michel, now a jurist, was one of the students who got that C.

In addition to part-time teaching, I ended up working for the Société nationale des Acadiens (SNA). The year before, I had written a long letter to a friend of the family, Hector Cormier, Secretary General of the SNA, to express my interest in working to advance the rights of Acadians. When I got back from Europe, Hector was having some health issues, so he asked me to help him out and then replace him as secretary general a few months later. That is how I came to take on yet another unfamiliar role as a kind of social worker. The SNA had a team of community liaisons in the regions whose activities complemented the secretariat's advocacy work.

Lots of people I knew were surprised when I went to work for the SNA. Some had a hard time believing I could head up pressure groups like the SNA and the Société de l'Acadie du Nouveau-Brunswick (SANB).

"I wasn't surprised that he had become an advocate for Acadians. I did wonder if he would stay at that level. I pictured him in a more high-profile role because he was such a hard worker. When he went to the SNA and the SANB, I personally hoped he wouldn't be there for long because I could see his potential," said my cousin, Bertin LeBlanc.

One great thing about being president of the SNA from 1974 to 1977 was that it really prepared me for what was to come. Without that experience, I might never have argued a case in court, let alone made it to the Supreme Court of Canada. It was time for me to put everything I had learned over the years into practice. It was a perfect opportunity to demonstrate my lawyerly chops and fight for our rights, whatever it took. It was a golden opportunity.

★★★

My arrival at the SNA was in no way spectacular. I did not have the soul of an ardent activist or nationalist, but I was to be a crusader nonetheless. The organization's key demands were the creation of school boards specifically for Acadians, adequate Acadian representation in the provincial public service, and bilingualism at city hall in Moncton. Nothing revolutionary about that.

Years later, as editor-in-chief of Égalité, the magazine I co-founded, I wrote, "equality is the pursuit of recognition and justice." That was my mission. I soon realized I wanted Acadia to have a solid network of institutions that would be the envy of other minority groups in Canada. Above all, I wanted the federal government to protect our rights.

At the time, Prime Minister Pierre Elliott Trudeau was passionately committed to patriating Canada's constitutional powers from London in Great Britain. New

Brunswick Premier Richard Hatfield and Prime Minister Trudeau believed that language rights should be guaranteed in the constitution and minimum national standards established. I heartily agreed. Even now, minorities must be assured of some level of cultural security. Quebec's unique situation, and that of other provinces with quite a small linguistic minority, could not be allowed to hinder efforts to institute robust measures.

I truly believe that, by agreeing to be part of the Canadian federation, Quebec, along with the other provinces, agreed to certain limits on their freedoms and powers. Francophone minorities across the country could not look to their provincial governments to protect their most basic language rights, so everyone would have to agree on bare minimum rights applicable across Canada. It was urgent, and we could not afford to lose ground nationally. Plus, Quebec was no great ally. We were increasingly on our own.

★★★

A few years earlier, the Estates General of French Canada had a deep and lasting impact on francophone communities from one end of the country to the other. The Estates General was a series of gatherings from 1966 to 1969 during which participants reflected on the Francophone experience in North America. The November 1967 national conferences were truly a turning point. Over a thousand delegates from Quebec, a hundred or so people representing networks of associations, and some 360 Francophones from outside Quebec gathered in Montréal for the occasion.

It was an extraordinary confluence of events. Quebec was in the midst of the Quiet Revolution; it was Canada's centennial year; Montréal was welcoming the world to the International and Universal Exposition, Expo 67; and Charles de Gaulle made his surprise appearance on the balcony of Montréal City Hall, delivering what was to become a historic speech. His "Vive le Québec libre!" (Long live a free Quebec) still resonates with separatists to this day. But it was the rise of the Rassemblement pour l'indépendance nationale (RIN) and the FLQ, René Lévesque's stunning split with the Liberal Party of Quebec, and the crystallization of the separatist movement that kept people on tenterhooks. My dears, it was a very different time, an exhilarating time in many ways.

York University historian Marcel Martel has studied the Estates General in great detail. He believes that the November 1967 national conference was when the relationship between francophone communities in Canada fell apart. Early in the debates, the voices of Francophones from outside Quebec, who made up less than a quarter of the participants, were drowned out by Quebec nationalists asserting that the former could discuss only problems that concerned them. In other words, not Quebec issues.

Then there was the resolution about francophone Quebeckers' right to self-determination, which raised the ire of Ontario Francophones and divided the delegates. HEC Montréal economics professor François-Albert Angers proposed a three-part resolution, as recorded in *Les États généraux du Canada français* (1968): "French Canadians constitute a nation"; "Quebec constitutes the national territory and fundamental polity of this nation"; and "The French-Canadian nation has the right to self-determination and to freely choose the political regime by which it wishes to be governed."

"Delegates from Quebec encouraged those from minority communities to support their Quebec compatriots' push for emancipation because their future now depended on focusing everyone's energy on Quebec," wrote Marcel Martel in *Le deuil d'un pays imaginé*. Only five delegates from outside Quebec participated in the debate, and it was clear the two sides were poles apart.

Of course, Quebeckers supported the resolution almost unanimously (ninety-eight percent), while Ontario was deeply divided (fifty-five percent of the one hundred and eighty-eight delegates voted against the resolution). Francophones from the western provinces split their vote, with similar numbers voting for, voting against, and abstaining, while fifty-two percent of the delegates from the Maritimes supported it fully or "with reservations."

"Delegates from other provinces rejected the proposals that would have entitled Quebec, as the nation-state of French Canada, to the full powers of a quasi-sovereign state, thereby giving it the best chance of survival," continued Marcel Martel.

Ontario Francophones had had enough. They clearly expressed their opposition by scaling back their participation. The later conferences did not have the same impact. French Canadians felt betrayed by Quebecois. It was like a divorce.

From then on, French Canadians from Quebec were called Quebecois. Acadians remained Acadians, which was fine with us, but our brothers and sisters in Ontario and the West felt isolated, abandoned even. Francophones from coast to coast felt that Quebec thought of us as assimilated or about to be. Others said we should forge our own identity independently of Quebec. Although some Quebeckers at the federal level sometimes did things that benefited us indirectly, Quebec was not making any effort to help us. A national association and several provincial ones were created to advocate for Francophones in minority communities. I personally had nothing against Quebecois in general, but I did disagree with some members of the Parti Québécois. The PQ was developing its position on the right of Francophones from other provinces to settle in Quebec. Tensions grew when the PQ took power and chose to go after Francophones outside Quebec in the courts.

★★★

It was a perfect storm. I started at the Société nationale l'Assomption (SNA) after the Estates General, after the Parti Acadien was founded, and after the release of *L'Acadie, l'Acadie!?!*, the film that exposed everything I had experienced during my childhood and my university days as a Francophone in a minority setting. Now the whole country was aware of the Acadian reality. It was an instant awakening at home and everywhere in Canada. I got down to business right away, and the first thing I did at the SNA was establish very close ties with the youth movement, the Activité Jeunesse association. I went to their meetings and invited them to ours. Before long, I had become good friends with their president, Yvon Fontaine, an excellent leader. A few years later, I even taught him international law and property law at the Université de Moncton. We remain friends to this day.

I tried to organize projects we could all get involved in because I wanted young people to understand the principles underpinning the issues. I wanted them to see that their group had a higher purpose than just fun. I wanted everyone in the SNA to benefit from their exuberance. That approach really panned out. Acadian activism was revitalized. People demanded control over their schools, French television in the regions, and more and more services in their language.

Then a second opportunity arose: the Société de l'Acadie du Nouveau-Brunswick (SANB). You see, the SNA, which was founded in 1881 as the Société nationale l'Assomption, held meetings from time to time to debate issues of interest to the Acadian people, issues such as education, colonization, the media, depopulation, and agriculture. It was solely focused on New Brunswick. In 1957, for the first time, the Société nationale des Acadiens began to advocate for French life in Acadia, which included all three maritime provinces. However, the SNA's presence as an advocate for Francophones faded in the wake of the Laurendeau-Dunton Commission even as Nova Scotia's Fédération acadienne de la Nouvelle-Écosse (FANE), which was founded in 1967, and Prince Edward Island's Société Saint-Thomas-d'Aquin began to play an increasingly important role. Our goal was to diversify our activities and make inroads

> Now the whole country was aware of the Acadian reality. It was an instant awakening at home and everywhere in Canada.

nationally and internationally, especially by cultivating ties with France. Our local representation declined as a matter of course, and funds were very tight. We were getting less money from provincial governments and had to ask Ottawa for more resources. We soon realized the solution was to become a federation. In 1974, the FANE, the Société Saint-Thomas-d'Aquin and the SANB, which was founded around the same time in New Brunswick, joined forces as a whole new SNA.

All things considered, I believe the SANB has grown and matured over time, although I am not really up on the latest news. While I admire its progress, I have come to believe that there is a fundamental problem with Acadian associations: there are too many associations, too much politics, and too many voices. A province as small as New Brunswick and lacking a critical mass of Francophones cannot really support dozens and dozens of associations, such as the Association acadienne des artistes professionnel.le.s du Nouveau-Brunswick, the Société des enseignantes et enseignants retraités francophones, the Fédération des femmes acadiennes et francophones du Nouveau-Brunswick, and so on. There has been such a proliferation of organizations that the SANB and the SNA cannot do a proper job of representing all those great people.

Turning the SANB into a federation of organizations meant that individuals no longer felt their advocacy association represented them. Dividing members up into individuals and associations was a pretty bad idea, and the SANB's return in recent years to a more traditional structure and a member-centred mission is a more promising direction. The damage may have been done, however. Acadian representation has suffered, and the course correction was too long in coming. The ship may have sailed. That is the unfortunate thing.

Dead Ducks

ÉMILIE AND JEAN-FRANÇOIS, divorce proceedings with the Quebeckers dragged on through the mid-1970s. The Estates General had taken place over five years before, but the future of minority francophone communities was my primary concern. We were dealing with some challenges at home in Acadia, but the deepening divide between us and Quebec forced us to strengthen alliances with Canada's other francophone communities. It was around that time that I met Hubert Gauthier, an extraordinary Franco-Manitoban who was active in the Western Canadian francophone space and in his home province in particular. He was the director of the Société franco-manitobaine and a board member for what was then called the Fédération des francophones de l'Ouest. I was president of the SNA, and he and I met fairly frequently. We did not yet have a national umbrella organization for all minority Francophones, but we met under the auspices of the Association canadienne d'éducation de langue française, better known as the ACELF, which was doing its level best to unite all Canadian Francophones, including those in Quebec.

At one point, Hubert and I found out that the ACELF had put in a request on behalf of its members for federal money to fund a round table for Francophones outside Quebec. That is when my new friend and I started "plotting," as he would put it. We decided to join the round table even though we thought it was inappropriate for the ACELF, which was essentially a Quebec organization, to be representing us. We thought it would be better to set up an umbrella organization for francophone organizations outside Quebec that would enable us to develop some degree of autonomy. Although it was many years in the making, we eventually inaugurated the Fédération des francophones hors Québec (FFHQ).

From then on, Acadians could meet with our friends from the West and caucus, often in secret. Over time, our relationship with our counterparts became one of frank camaraderie and sincere friendship. At just twenty-seven or twenty-eight years old, we were leading our respective organizations. We were a determined new generation, forging ahead, no filter, no fear. Our older, more experienced colleagues sometimes eyed us with concern. They thought we were young revolutionaries. It was the 1970s, and Pierre Elliott Trudeau represented a golden opportunity to create something that belonged to us. We could make a difference in our society, not only in Acadia or the West, but across the country.

Hubert and I enlisted collaborators in our respective regions. Ontario was reluctant at first because its representatives were in Ottawa and it behooved them to maintain good relations with the federal government there. We ourselves were well outside decision-making circles. As we progressed toward creating the organization, Ontario felt obliged to get on board. We managed to convince them. Imagine that: Francophones from the biggest Canadian province joining us. That was when we knew we were making history.

In 1975, we participated in the ACELF's first biennial meeting of the Canadian Francophonie, which focused on exploring various facets of our reality as Francophones, and it took place in Chicoutimi, of all places. After the Estates General, some Quebecois had indicated they could not be bothered to include us, their lesser cousins from English Canada. They told us there was no need for national associations. Hubert Gauthier and I were members of the ACELF committee of Francophones from outside Quebec, and when we got all the non-Quebec Francophones on side, we announced our intention to leave the organization and distance ourselves from Quebecois.

"We felt that Quebeckers had a different goal and that there wasn't really room for us. In a way, we should be grateful to them because we wouldn't have begun to join forces and talk to each other without them," explained Hubert Gauthier during an interview with TFO forty years after the FFHQ was founded.

We decided very early on that Hubert would be the new federation's president and executive director. I would still be somewhat involved with the SNA, but my main responsibility would be to serve as Hubert's strategic adviser. Hubert was a true populist and remarkably efficient. He had a knack for taking complicated concepts and explaining them in such a way that ordinary people could not only understand them but also be persuaded to support his cause. We were banking on Ottawa transferring the money it had been giving the ACELF to us instead.

Divorce was no longer a theory or even a goal. It was happening. It was real. We spoke on our behalf; Quebecois spoke on theirs. We were ready to fight not only for money but for a political cause. We did not need Quebec Francophones to advocate on behalf of Francophones from outside Quebec. Their approach had never been particularly effective anyway.

Within a few months, the FFHQ had mindshare. Our media presence was ten times greater than the ACELF's, and our influence grew by leaps and bounds. In 1991, the FFHQ became the Fédération des communautés francophones et acadiennes (FCFA) du Canada. The ACELF is still around, but its mission and scope have changed a lot. I feel it was the PQ that killed the ACELF by positioning itself as the Quebecois' champion.

★★★

One day, I called Hubert up and suggested we draft a manifesto, a document outlining our demands and our action plan. Prime Minister Pierre Elliott Trudeau built up the *Official Languages Act* as the solution to all the problems and the key to ensuring the vitality of minority Francophones. I personally thought he was overselling it. Trudeau's beloved Act all but ignored assimilation, education, communities' economic development, and the demographic weight of minority language communities. Hubert put together a little group of lawyers and activists in Ottawa, and together we drafted our manifesto, which we called *Les héritiers de Lord Durham*, Lord Durham's heirs.

The manifesto was unveiled just a few months after the election of the Parti Québécois in November 1976. I was quite concerned about the election results. During my years in Montréal, I had witnessed the founding of the Mouvement souveraineté-association and the Parti Québécois in the 1960s. I felt uncomfortable about the party because it positioned itself as Quebec's champion. A political party that would be in power a number of times and whose goal, election after election, was to be in charge of the *Belle Province* would now be speaking on behalf of Quebecois. Really? That was not only difficult to understand, but difficult to accept. How could the Parti Québécois, headed up by René Lévesque, be its own critic? With all the internal strife the party would go on to experience, time would tell. For those of us outside Quebec, the PQ victory was bad news. The French Quebec–English Canada divide was palpable. After all, René Lévesque, the newly elected premier, had called Western Canadian Francophones "dead ducks" in a *Twenty Million Questions* interview on CBC in 1968. How could a Quebec politician—one born in Campbellton, New Brunswick, no less—tell us we were doomed to assimilation? Hubert was more open with respect to Quebec though.

"It seemed to me that Francophones outside Quebec needed an ally like Quebec one way or another. Michel never really trusted the PQ or Quebeckers in general. He was much more suspicious than me. We found a middle ground where we could get things done. I felt that Trudeau took Francophones outside Quebec for granted, and I saw the need for a counterweight. That meant we had to talk to Quebec. Then Lévesque was elected in 1976," explained Hubert Gauthier.

The FFHQ reaction to the Parti Québécois win was positive. There were certainly big debates among the various organizations across the country, but ultimately, I came on side with the consensus: we had our interests, but we also had to cultivate our relationship with Quebec. The PQ was Quebec's legitimately elected government. We had to have an open, respectful dialogue with it. There was a lot of pressure. Our peers and the federal government explicitly asked us not to talk to the Quebec separatists. Strategically, though, we had to publicly request meetings with the Prime Minister of Canada and the Premier of Quebec.

Ultimately, we delivered the manifesto to both governments so each could see where we stood. "Our dreams are broken. We are experiencing a profound and acute crisis, perhaps one that is being deliberately and consciously perpetuated. As Francophones outside Quebec, we are like a family standing before our burned-down house. We are homeless, eyes fixed on a few scattered belongings. But we are still alive," was the gist of the opening pages of the manifesto, which addressed legislation governing official languages, education, and the role of the media.

Our meeting with Prime Minister Trudeau was memorable because he seemed particularly irritated that we were not openly supporting him. Just a few minutes into the encounter, he accused us of being ungrateful and chastised us for criticizing him publicly. If memory serves, he even called us "mean" during our exchange. I should point out that Hubert found a way to win over the media and get them interested in our cause. He crisscrossed the country representing the FFHQ and held press conferences everywhere. Reporters' interest seemed to stem from the fact that we were young and had nothing to lose. We were acting independently, and neither Trudeau nor Lévesque could claim we were on their side. We figured out how to play with both parties. Politicians in Ottawa hated our flirtation with the separatists. During one meeting, we told them we were engaging with the Government of Quebec, which had been democratically elected and did indeed have nationalist, sovereignist aims. We had our own specific goal though, and we needed help from all sides.

"I was meeting with Société Saint-Jean-Baptiste (SSJB) branches everywhere, and the Secretary of State was threatening to cut our funding if I kept giving speeches. Some of the SSJB members were federalist, some were nationalist, and some, like in Montréal, were completely separatist," said Hubert. We worked on our strategies together, informally. Then we went to meet René Lévesque. We were so young then. Nobody in the group was even thirty yet. Our strategy was to show René Lévesque that he was wrong when he said assimilation was the only possible outcome for us. We were bitter about his "dead ducks" comment.

Lévesque was a true democrat, and we knew our passion would convince him to help us in our struggle to make living in French possible in the vast English sea.

As Hubert Gauthier remembers it, "Right in the middle of the meeting, Lévesque told us—Bastarache was there too—'I can't be against the kind of energy I'm seeing here.' He put it out there just like that. We told him we wanted him to stop saying we were dead. We were right there in front of him. We told him that, like it or not, the same phenomena were at play within Quebec as for Francophones outside Quebec. We knew assimilation was happening; we didn't claim to be flourishing. On the contrary, we feared for our survival. We were the front line, and when the ships landed, we would be the first to fall in combat. Quebeckers would be next."

We hit a nerve.

★★★

That meeting, like all subsequent meetings during the PQ's first term in office, was very cordial. We quickly realized that Quebec's elected officials and bureaucrats were genuinely listening to us. A few times over the years, I met with Claude Morin, the Minister of Intergovernmental Affairs whose portfolio included relations with Canadian francophone communities. Often, the meetings included his chief of staff, Louise Beaudoin, an intelligent woman who went on to become a member of the National Assembly and a minister. The main topic during our meetings was the francophone struggle for education. The FFHQ wanted official status for francophone school boards in Alberta, Manitoba, Ontario, and British Columbia in particular. The Lévesque government was fairly sympathetic to Francophones outside Quebec, but its attention was fleeting. Let us just say that what we were asking for was not exactly on their list of priorities. Unfortunately, they tended to sabotage us more often than not, probably because they thought we were destined for assimilation. I tried to persuade them to do no harm. I was not expecting their unconditional support; I just did not want them to make things harder for us.

"Look, I get that you have your party, you're fighting your fight, and you want to separate. I get all that, but that doesn't mean you shouldn't have positive relationships with Francophones elsewhere and foster collaboration in areas like post-secondary education and culture," I told them during one meeting. It was obvious to me that Quebec had to open up to the world and especially to its closest neighbours. I reiterated that Quebec artists put on shows in Moncton, Caraquet, Campbellton, Ottawa, Saint-Boniface, and Edmonton. That meant more revenue for them. If the Government of Quebec did not support us, it was by the same token not supporting its own artists. The argument resonated with Morin, and he was sympathetic, but as soon as things got political, he would not budge.

We had conflict around the PQ's opposition to enhanced rights for Francophones outside Quebec, especially after the party passed Bill 101. One of Lévesque's Cabinet ministers even told us, "If the feds help you legislatively and so on, whatever Francophones outside Quebec get is what the English in Quebec will want. And we don't want to give the English here anything."

That argument was flawed because anglophone Quebeckers had everything they needed. They had their hospitals, their schools, their universities. We wanted control over our school boards. We had not even started talking about health care, which they had had for ages. Plus, Bill 101, the *Charter of the French Language* passed in 1977, would do even more to protect French in Quebec. So what was the problem? As Claude Morin put it, "The problem is that we want the right to take all that away." He wanted to protect Quebec's jurisdiction over education at all costs.

***

The goal was not to take away some or all the anglophone minority's rights; the PQ wanted to use Bill 101 to circumscribe their linguistic and cultural rights. The conflict arose from the fact that the federal government, much to my delight, wanted to help minorities, including Quebec Anglophones. PQ members, *péquistes*, were furious and tried to defeat us in court numerous times. I was neither angry nor insulted. Frankly, I was not surprised by their approach, but I was disappointed in them for being so petty. "I don't understand what you're afraid of," I told them. More than forty years after our discussions took place, Claude Morin still claims that was never the Lévesque government's true intention.

"I remember talking about that, but I always said we weren't going to abandon Francophones outside Quebec at all. People assumed we were trying to shut them out, but that's not at all true. We had relationships with other countries, so I didn't see why we wouldn't have had a relationship with Francophones outside Quebec. When I was minister, I actually gave funding to francophone associations outside Quebec," explained the eighty-eight-year-old man on the other end of the line. He reiterated that his government never wanted to hurt Francophones in minority communities or even Anglophones in Quebec; it just wanted to protect and strengthen the French language in the province. How he went from there to fighting us over schools in court is a mystery to me.

Interestingly, on two occasions in the barristers' lounge at the Supreme Court of Canada, Government of Quebec lawyers told me they absolutely did not support the position they were arguing for; they were just following orders. I had always thought the government's position did not reflect popular opinion, and now I had proof.

Still, we were not really adversaries and certainly not enemies. It was just politics. One day, I had the pleasure of going out for a drink with Claude Morin and

Camille Laurin at a restaurant in Québec City. Laurin leaned over to me and said, "You know, Michel, I get that you want to be Francophone and that French culture is important to you. Just between us though, the only way to do that is to move to Quebec." I just about choked on my wine. Another disappointment.

Camille Laurin was calm, cool, and collected, and I had a lot of respect for him. He was a statesman and a true democrat, which is why I found comments like that such a letdown. I could not believe that such brilliant men would say such crazy things. Years later, Jean Samson, their lead counsel and a man I have always liked, came up to me and said:

"Michel, you come here and we talk, but you know you're those guys' worst enemy."

"Oh yeah, why's that? Am I that bad?"

"No! You're proof that they're wrong when they say you can't keep your language and culture unless you live in Quebec. It's so irritating."

I've always respected people who want Quebec independence for the right reasons. I know, children, that is hard to believe coming from me. I have always understood those who want to build their own country so they can have their own institutions for cultural, linguistic, and economic reasons. Had I lived in Quebec my whole life, I might feel the same. Fundamentally, I was not in conflict with people like Lévesque (despite the "dead ducks" incident), Morin, Laurin, and Johnson. But the negative and downright mean mindset of many separatists was definitely aggravating. And then there were those who wanted independence for Quebec because they wanted to get back at the English for the Plains of Abraham and other historic events that took place two centuries ago. Theirs was obviously not a valid perspective. Turn the page. Move on. Fight for the present and the future.

★★★

Early on in the constitutional renewal talks that led to the passage of the Constitution Act, 1982, francophones outside Quebec did everything in their power to make their voices heard. You see, sections 16 to 22 of the Charter are about official languages, but section 15, equality rights, often plays an important role in that realm too. Anyway, the main section that my advocacy work hung on, and that of minority Francophones across the country, was section 23, which covers minority language instruction. The section is divided into three parts. Subsection 23 (1) is about language of instruction; 23 (2) is about continuity of language instruction; and 23 (3) is about application where numbers warrant. That last part is the reason Francophones have spent so much time in court. Here's how that section reads:

> (3) The right of citizens of Canada under subsections (1) and (2) to have their children receive primary and secondary school instruction in the language of the English or French linguistic minority population of a province
>   a. applies whenever in the province the number of children of citizens who have such a right is sufficient to warrant the provision to them out of public funds of minority language instruction; and
>   b. includes, where the number of those children so warrants, the right to have them receive that instruction in minority language educational facilities provided out of public funds.

> Generally speaking, for Francophones outside Quebec, I think the goal is to ensure an interpretation of the Constitution establishing that minority educational facilities are reserved for them, governed by them, and distinct from schools that promote bilingualism through immersion.

Generally speaking, for Francophones outside Quebec, I think the goal is to ensure an interpretation of the Constitution establishing that minority educational facilities are reserved for them, governed by them, and distinct from schools that promote bilingualism through immersion. The only real protection the *Constitution Act* offers communities is section 23 of the Charter, and that guarantee is by far the most important one for the future of linguistic minorities.

During the constitutional talks, we wanted to make sure section 23 truly gave us the protection we needed. My francophone colleagues and I penned a manifesto entitled "Pour ne plus être sans pays." It was a political statement, designed to shock people and force the media to include us in the constitutional debate. I appeared before the parliamentary committee, I gave interviews, I participated in press conferences and symposia. We were doing the groundwork to convince people to give us constitutional protection. We had done everything we could. All that was missing was meaningful dialogue with the people drafting the bill. Even sections 16 to 23 of the *Canadian Charter of Rights and Freedoms* were written with other interests in mind. Section 23 was modelled on Quebec legislation. The main thing I fought for at the time was to amend section 23 of the Charter to include control over school governance, but my proposal was rejected. Read the section closely though, and you will pick up on a subtlety that would end up serving us well. Here is the French:

> 23(3) Le droit reconnu aux citoyens canadiens par les paragraphes (1) et (2) de faire instruire leurs enfants, aux niveaux primaire et secondaire, dans la langue de la minorité francophone ou anglophone d'une province : [...]
> > (b) comprend, lorsque le nombre de ces enfants le justifie, le droit de les faire instruire dans des établissements d'enseignement **de** la minorité linguistique financés sur les fonds publics.

It all hinges on the "de." In English, it reads "of." In French, it is "de," not "pour." That is an important nuance, a nuance that makes all the difference. If it read "pour la minorité," that would mean anglophone school boards could govern French schools even if they did not necessarily have a proper understanding of the community's needs. That wording, "de la minorité," gives the minority control over its educational facilities. To my great satisfaction, that meant the courts could interpret the law in our favour.

Even though I was representing Francophones outside Quebec, New Brunswick Premier Richard Hatfield retained my services as constitutional adviser during final negotiations for the Constitution Act, 1982. We had a small team, seven or eight people, while Quebec had about twenty, I would guess. I had a chance to tell Claude Morin that, even though he had more people, he was getting bad advice because all his people had the same training, the same opinion, and zero experience with the other provincial delegates. I was told none of them had ever lived outside Quebec. My conversations with some of them revealed that they had no idea what Premier Hatfield was thinking.

Children, I would like to tell you a little story. The night before the final session of the constitutional talks, I was in a bar in the basement of the Château Laurier. I was sitting with Premier Hatfield and three members of our delegation, including our leader, Barry Toole. There were also people from the Saskatchewan delegation and maybe some others—I do not remember. At one point, Roger Tassé, the federal government's deputy justice minister, walked into the bar and came to our table. He said he had been told to let us know that there was a meeting in the Ontario delegation's suite. Provincial delegates were invited to attend in hopes of finding a way out of the impasse. Negotiations had stalled at that point. Roger asked us to send someone from New Brunswick. We had all noticed Claude Charron and Louise Beaudoin at another table. Roger asked me to let them know about the invitation because I knew Louise quite well. I went over to talk to her, but the Quebec delegates told me they were not mandated to participate. I suggested they call Lévesque or Morin, but they did not want to bother them. I stressed the importance of the meeting. We agreed to an alternative: we would meet very early the next morning so everyone could be up to speed on the negotiations and the Quebec delegates would have time to talk to Lévesque and Morin. Charron and Beaudoin agreed. The next morning, we were waiting for our friends from Quebec, but there was no sign of them. They did not show up for our meeting.

In the hours and days that followed, the legend of the night of the long knives took hold. It was said that the English provinces plotted against Quebec that night. That political fiction endures despite the likes of Chrétien and Hatfield denying it, and I certainly agree with them.

Several years later, while I was waiting for a plane at the Halifax airport, Premier Hatfield, who was quite ill by then, came over to sit with me. We knew each other quite well, and we talked for almost an hour. During our conversation, he told me that he most likely would not have a chance to write his memoirs because his illness was terminal. He said he truly regretted the fact that he would never have the opportunity to put the lie to the myth of the night of the long knives. He told me he wanted to talk to me about it so I could set the record straight myself. I have done so several times, and I am doing it again now.

I find it most unfortunate that separatist propaganda has taken hold in Quebec's universities, CEGEPs, and schools. There is no need to lie to explain what happened during the constitutional negotiations or justify Quebec's refusal to endorse the agreement. It is easy to understand why the various parties did what they did and see what happened. How strange that Quebec officials were so suspicious.

★★★

That said, it was not just the separatists who made my life difficult in Quebec. Following the Meech Lake negotiations in the 1980s, members of Robert Bourassa's government made me sweat bullets.

Because Quebec did not sign the "new" 1982 Constitution, Brian Mulroney's Progressive Conservative government decided to do everything it could to reconcile Canada and Quebec. In 1986, it launched another round of negotiations in an attempt to get Quebec to sign the 1982 Constitution. That was the Meech Lake Accord.

The negotiations did not go smoothly. The Bourassa government had some very rigid conditions for signing on to Mulroney's proposal. There were five conditions, to be precise: recognition of Quebec as a distinct society; constitutionally guaranteed control over immigration; entrenchment of Quebec's entitlement to three Supreme Court of Canada justices; the right to opt out with compensation of any program the federal government created in areas under Quebec's jurisdiction; and a veto over constitutional amendments and the right to opt out of any agreement with compensation in order to protect its status as a distinct society.

I was against that. I thought the Bourassa government was going too far. My francophone compatriots from across the country thought so too. The concept of a distinct society is extremely difficult to accept for Francophones who are not the majority in their province. Although I was not directly involved in the Meech Lake negotiations, I gave some advice to Yvon Fontaine, who was president of the FFHQ at the time.

Around then, I was involved in a number of section 23 cases, including the Mahé case in Alberta. The Government of Quebec regularly intervened against me. Canada's only officially francophone province intervened against Western Francophones. I was not going to stand for that, so I told the government and the Minister of Education, Claude Ryan, that although I did not expect them to come on side, I would appreciate it if they just stayed home and left us alone. I wanted Quebec to stop hurting our cause and leave us be so we could do what we needed to do to get control over our schools. Quebec's Liberal government should have been ashamed of itself for trying to get in our way!

I made lots of phone calls and had lots of candid conversations with Ryan and the Minister of Intergovernmental Affairs, Gil Rémillard. One day, we arranged to meet with members of the Bourassa government to discuss our respective positions on the Meech Lake Accord. Quebec had about fifteen representatives on their side of the table. We had three. A few minutes before the meeting, Gil Rémillard approached me and said, "Your French is really good for a Francophone from outside Quebec."

Things were sure off to a great start. I am not sure if he was aware then that we were both University of Ottawa alumni and that we had been at the Université de Nice almost at the same time. I was not impressed. "Yes, Mr. Rémillard, I'm so glad you mentioned that because I was just going to point out that there are some grammatical errors in the document you circulated."

That set the tone. Thirty years later, Rémillard maintained that our relationship was never hostile, and I tend to agree with him on that. I have always had a lot of respect for him as a politician. His contribution to the Meech Lake negotiations is practically legendary. I recognize that he is a man of conviction, just like me. Even so, his claim that Quebec did not intervene against Francophones in either the Mahé case or in Meech is false. He does not seem to understand how insulting it was for him to go to Fredericton and tell the Legislative Assembly of New Brunswick that it was not entitled to change a single word of the Meech Lake Accord. His message was rejected in any case. Gil Rémillard would not budge on minority education rights.

"It was Claude Ryan's file, not mine, but as I recall, we wanted minorities to have the right to govern their facilities as well as the right to instruction in their language in facilities they didn't necessarily govern because there are places where the numbers don't warrant them having their own schools. They could still have classes though. There was that kind of nuance," said Rémillard. In fact, Ryan told me that he was sympathetic to my demands but Rémillard was not and had obtained the support of Cabinet.

Over the years, the Government of Quebec had bragged about its meaningful relationship with francophone communities outside the province. Oh, there were investments, plenty of lip service and gestures of support, but Quebec's ulterior motive was always to preserve its special status within the Canadian federation no matter what. Its actions may have been intended to keep Quebec's anglophone community at bay, but they ended up penalizing and even harming Francophones from coast to coast. The Quebec government's intervention in the Mahé case concerning Franco-Albertans' right to education and to the governance of educational facilities was unjustified. The minority won, and, quite frankly, Quebec lost all credibility when the Supreme Court of Canada ruled in that historic case.

"No. I was the attorney general, and from what I remember, everyone was fine with that," countered Rémillard. "As I recall, when Mahé happened, I personally thought it was just fine." The newspaper clippings do not lie though. The Government of Quebec was labelled a traitor. Things got so messy that Minister Ryan dispatched the Government of Quebec's language policy secretary, Jean-Claude Rondeau, to Western Canada on a cross-country mission to meet with francophone communities. Marcel Adam nailed the reason for the tour in his December 5, 1989, article in La Presse: "To justify Quebec's unexpected behaviour in the Mahé case and to tell them the Government of Quebec was not against the right of Francophones outside Quebec to school governance." According to Adam, the emissary said that, "The reason Quebec did not clearly support Francophones outside Quebec in the case was that it was protective of its exclusive jurisdiction over education and did not want to violate that principle by getting involved in other provinces' affairs."

A decade later, in a document about language rights prepared for the Quebec Bar, Claude Ryan himself wrote that, in Quebec, the majority existed as and perceived itself to be a minority within the broader context of Canada and North America, and endeavoured to protect itself accordingly. He said that explained why majority linguistic rights were of prime importance in the *Charter of the French Language* and why the Charter tended to curtail minority rights. That says it all.

★★★

In the 2010s, Philippe Couillard's Liberal government made overtures to the other provinces in an attempt to reunite the great Canadian family. Simultaneously, however, he opposed the Yukon Francophone School Board, Education Area #23's action against Yukon's Attorney General for failing to meet its minority language education obligations under section 23 of the Charter and Yukon's *Education Act* and *Languages Act*.

The case went all the way to the Supreme Court of Canada. In her factum, Quebec's Attorney General opposed any interpretation of section 23 of the Charter that would give more governance powers to the anglophone minority. According to the factum, because English exerts a powerful attraction over Francophones and Allophones in Quebec, allowing anglophone minority representatives greater control over and management of schools would have a significant negative impact on the protection of the French language and the organization of the education system. It would also undermine the fragile equilibrium of Quebec's linguistic dynamic and efforts to protect the French language, whose vitality benefits not only Quebecois but all Francophones in Canada. For the government to say that kind of thing to the Court, then turn around and launch its manifesto, *Quebecers, Our Way of Being Canadian: Policy on Québec Affirmation and Canadian Relations*, with great fanfare was absolutely ridiculous. In its June 2017 manifesto, the government tried to convince itself to be a steadfast ally to Francophones outside Quebec.

The nearly two-hundred-page document reads:

> Québec has concluded cooperation and exchange agreements on the Canadian Francophonie with all the provincial and territorial governments. We wish to increase cooperation with these governments and increasingly work with community associations in establishing priorities for action. In this way, Québec will be fully committed to promoting the Canadian Francophonie, as it has done in the past, particularly by signing declarations with many provinces and territories respecting the Canadian Francophonie, and by renewing its cooperation agreements.

I will just point out that the FCFA had spent years condemning most provincial and territorial governments for not honouring their obligations to support minority language education pursuant to agreements with the federal government, so what are interprovincial agreements really worth?

What of Acadia?

OCTOBER 1979, EDMUNDSTON. Émilie, you were a newborn, and it was a tumultuous time in our province, especially for Acadians. Tensions peaked at the Convention d'orientation nationale de l'Acadie, where 1,200 delegates gathered to debate francophone issues. It was the sixteenth such convention and the first in nearly a century to bring together that many participants. The idea was to give Acadians an opportunity to have their say on Acadia's political future and a defining Acadian undertaking.

Every New Brunswick Acadian was invited, and I seized the opportunity to attend, partly because I had helped create the Société de l'Acadie du Nouveau-Brunswick a few years earlier and partly because, as vice-dean of the Université de Moncton's School of Law, I felt somewhat obligated to participate. The gathering lasted three days and included workshops and plenaries. It was the perfect setting for what would become at times some rather passionate debates.

As soon as I got there on October 6, I sensed that something was afoot. There was an energy in the room, and I soon figured out why: the Parti Acadien (PA) had packed the place.

★★★

Bernard Richard was in his early twenties, and he was quite active in the Greater Moncton community. Originally from Cap-Pelé, he was a social worker with New Brunswick's Department of Social Development. He was driven, and he believed at the time that he could help his part of the province by getting involved in politics.

"As far back as 1974, I was interested in the societal side of things, in social policy. The pursuit of equality, equal opportunity. The Parti Acadien was all about that," he said in an interview in the early 2010s with L'Étoile, a weekly paper published in New Brunswick. Richard accurately described the Parti Acadien as similar to the New Democratic Party (NDP) in terms of its social policy, but when it came to language policy, the PA had a nationalistic bent the NDP never would.

Founded in 1972, the PA was mostly made up of union leaders and francophone intellectuals who felt overlooked by the traditional political parties. Late

1960s linguistic conflicts and the rise of the Parti Québécois inspired many young Acadians to take action. In January 1971, a teacher in Petit-Rocher, André Dumont, brought together six other people in northeastern New Brunswick, and the seven of them explored the possibility of creating a new political party. Some advocated for an Acadian national territory, while others were more interested in defending the province's Francophones. As it turned out, the seven-member committee never managed to reach a consensus on which direction they should take. In November 1972, the PA held its founding convention, and 125 activists acclaimed Euclide Chiasson as their leader. Party membership never exceeded one thousand.

In the 1974 election, Bernard Richard ran for the Parti Acadian in the riding of Shediac. He had his work cut out for him because Shediac was a blood-red riding ruled by the Liberal Party for generations. It was a losing battle. The Cap-Pelé Richard family at the time were known as staunch Conservative supporters, so when young Bernard ran for the PA, his chances of success were minute. He got 283 votes, coming in well behind Liberal Azor LeBlanc with 4,404 votes. He was not last though; fourth place went to the NDP candidate with 206 votes.

Bernard was not elected, obviously. He went on to become a lawyer and then a Liberal Party MLA for years. He was Minister of Justice and Minister of Education under Frank McKenna and Camille Thériault and then served as the party's interim leader. He did a lot for our province, and Progressive Conservative (PC) Premier Bernard Lord recognized his contribution by making him the provincial ombudsman in the early 2000s even though he was a Liberal.

Bernard is a man of integrity. He accepted the Premier's mandate, giving up his seat in the Legislative Assembly and alienating the New Brunswick Liberal family. The Liberals could not believe one of their own would accept an appointment from a PC premier even though the ombudsman is important to democratic life in our province. He did amazing work in that position, especially as New Brunswick's child and youth advocate. A few years later, the Government of British Columbia asked him to be its representative for children and youth out West.

At the time, I told myself that Bernard was not a bad guy and that his intentions were honourable. The Parti Acadien he joined was much more moderate than it would be four years later. It was nationalistic for sure, but it was not yet separatist. I believe it was naiveté that led Bernard to run for such a party. He himself admitted that his involvement with the PA was more or less accidental.

"Friends invited me to a meeting to choose a PA candidate, and there were about ten of us there. In the end, we drew straws, and I was the one who had to run," he recalled in the interview for L'Étoile. That gives you a sense of just how serious the party was.

Two years after it was founded, the PA attracted just 12 candidates and received 3,607 votes in the 1974 election. That was about 1,200 more votes than the number of spoiled ballots that year. There were not many good candidates. Other than Bernard Richard, there was Jean-Marie Nadeau, the Acadian activists' activist, and Gilles Thériault, a union leader and key player in the New Brunswick fisheries. Gilles is the brother of Camille Thériault, who was premier of New Brunswick for a year in the late 1990s, and a first cousin to the wife of future federal Liberal Minister Dominic LeBlanc.

The Progressive Conservative Party got the fright of its life in that election because, just four years after coming to power, it got two thousand fewer votes than the Liberal Party. Even so, it managed to hold on to a majority of the seats in the Legislative Assembly. Just like that, the Parti Acadian became a deciding factor in the election.

According to political scientist Roger Ouellette, "In 1974, a guy by the name of Jean-Pierre Ouellette ran for the Conservatives and was elected by a margin of 95 votes. Another guy by the name of Jean-Marie Nadeau, the PA candidate, got 99 votes. Jean-Pierre Ouellette won because of Nadeau. That's why, even though the PA didn't meet the criteria for party status, the government amended the law to recognize it because it suited them."

In no time at all, along came the 1978 election. Two years earlier, the PA had adopted a decidedly nationalistic agenda, calling for the division of New Brunswick and the creation of an Acadian national state, a state that could either become the eleventh province or annex itself to a sovereign Quebec. The party changed, but so did the people. In the summer of 1982, I wrote in Égalité:

> New Brunswick's bilingualism regime is based on the concept of personality and designed to enable individuals to function in both languages anywhere in the province, thereby ensuring the equal status of both official languages. It's clear that, for some Francophones in the northeast in particular, this philosophy represents the government's desire to unify New Brunswick by denying Acadians' sense of belonging to a region even though that appears to be key to maintaining the cultural and linguistic cohesiveness of the francophone community.

Politically, the PA saw an opportunity to gain ground, especially in the northern part of the province. Euclide Chiasson stepped down as party leader, and Jean-Pierre Lanteigne, a Bathurst physician, took his place. PA members were divided into two factions: those who wanted to split up New Brunswick and create an Acadian province, and those who wanted to split up New Brunswick and annex the northern part to Quebec. I was vehemently opposed to both options. I thought it was an absolutely ridiculous, pie-in-the-sky idea with no real merit. In 1977, the party organized another convention—with fifty delegates this time!—to shed its far-left wing and adopt a clear separatist agenda. The idea of an Acadian province became central to the party's platform just before the election.

The PA's 1978 election results were a windfall. It fielded 23 candidates and got 11,562 votes—four times more than in the previous election. Father Armand Plourde came close to winning in Restigouche West, garnering close to forty percent of the votes in the riding that included Saint-Quentin and Kedgwick, his hometown. It was odd because most people in northwestern New Brunswick considered themselves to be only part-time Acadians, whenever it suited them, such as during the 2014 Acadian World Congress. Even Armand Plourde considered himself both a *Brayon* (a resident of the greater Madawaska area, basically) and an Acadian. Jean-Pierre Lanteigne resigned a few months after the election, disappointed that he was not able to get a single candidate elected despite the door being wide open, as he saw it.

★★★

There were hundreds of them. When I got to Edmundston, I expected PA people would be there, but I had no idea there would be so many. The SANB had organized the three-day convention to give Acadians a say about their political future. The big debate and vote were scheduled for Monday, October 8, 1979. PA people packed the place, and it soon became obvious that the idea of creating an Acadian province would divide the delegates. Backroom dealings got underway, and the end result was astounding: forty-eight percent of the participants believed that Acadians' first priority should be the creation of an Acadian province. I could not believe it.

"When I was in Mr. Bastarache's workshop in 1979, he said something that really made an impression on me. At the time, there was a lot of talk about creating an Acadian province, and he said that, if he could make one wish, it would be for Acadia to be a country. I don't think he was in favour of an Acadian province. He didn't think it was possible, but if it were possible, that would be his wish. That's what he said in 1979," recalled historian Maurice Basque, who was then a student at the Université de Moncton. He was there. He remembers. But I do not think he understood the context of that statement. What I said during that workshop was that, even if we do not have a choice and have to collaborate, we can still dream. As long as we are dreaming, we might as well dream up an imaginary country, not a complex territorial organization.

I will tell it like it is: we had other fish to fry back then. PA members thought they were for real, but their bitter battles over the territorial question caused us to lose sight of the key issue. Our goal was to amplify our voice in Fredericton and achieve equality for both linguistic communities. As Francophones and

Acadians, we wanted meaningful representation in government. In my workshop and during the whole convention, I told participants that it was pointless to talk about Acadia separating because we did not have the land base, the population, or the resources to succeed.

The fact is, we had nothing at all. We could not even say that the northern part of New Brunswick was Francophone and the southern part Anglophone, because that was a common misconception. Bathurst, the biggest city in the northeast, was fifty-three percent Francophone. Campbellton? The same! Many people pointed to the fact that Caraquet was practically 99.9999 percent Francophone, which was true, but there were not actually a lot of people there. That was the problem. There was no economy either. In *La question du pouvoir en Acadie*, Léon Thériault pointed out that, based on 1976 statistics, the Acadian province would be sixty-one percent Francophone and thirty-seven percent Anglophone. How could we possibly convince one in three Anglophones to vote in favour of separating a small geographic and demographic area of the province at a time when Anglophones across the country were furious about Quebec separatists?

I witnessed the stunning debut of the PQ, a brand-new party whose popularity in the polls was meteoric. Here is what you need to know about the PQ: at the time, it had an actual political agenda. It was not just a dream; it was a possibility, it was achievable.

My relationship with people in the PA was extremely fraught, tense, and personal. Jean-Pierre Lanteigne was one of the most offensive people I have ever met. It was impossible to have an intelligent conversation with him because he would automatically accuse you of being a traitor. Every time I opened my mouth, he would interrupt me, and he frequently used incendiary language to intimidate people, which brought nothing positive to the debate, so I just did not engage. Ultimately, he was screaming into the void. The relationship was too hostile. Too few PA partisans were capable of intelligent discussion. That is why the party never really stood a chance. Frankly, that kind of PA has no real place in New Brunswick.

The worst part is that we found ourselves in conflict with the government and the anglophone press, and we ended up stoking our differences rather than looking for common ground where we could make progress. I think the whole debate set us back rather than moving us forward.

Instead of creating the PA, Acadians should have looked to people like Bernard Richard who were willing to speak up within the traditional parties and force them to adopt more audacious positions across the board. Just as I was coming to that conclusion, people in government risked their careers by handing me not one, but two opportunities. Émilie and Jean-François, what happened next is fascinating.

7
Duality, Eh!

HIS NAME WAS RICHARD HATFIELD. The son of Heber Hatfield, former mayor of Hartland and federal member of Parliament from 1940 to 1952, Richard Hatfield could certainly be said to have come by politics honestly—virtually from his birth in 1931 in the very rural town of Woodstock, New Brunswick, in fact. Young Richard attended the best schools in the Maritimes, starting with Rothesay Collegiate School near Saint John and then Acadia University in Nova Scotia before going to Dalhousie University to study law. His roommate at the time was none other than Alex Campbell, who would go on to become the longest-serving premier of Canada's smallest province, Prince Edward Island, from 1966 to 1978. Campbell was also Canada's youngest twentieth-century premier, taking office at thirty-two years of age.

After practising law in Nova Scotia for six months, Hatfield became an assistant to Canada's Minister of Trade and Commerce, Gordon Churchill. That was in the late 1950s. Just a year later, Richard left the job to return home to Hartland, where he took up the family business his father left him. Some time before he died, in 1952, the elder Hatfield advised his son not to go into politics, but in 1961 Richard Hatfield announced that he would be running for a provincial seat in the riding of Carleton, the seat former premier Hugh John Flemming resigned after he lost to Louis Robichaud. Why did Richard get into politics? "For the people," he said later. Five years after entering politics, Dick, as most people called him, ran for the leadership of the Progressive Conservative Party against a dyed-in-the-wool Conservative, J. C. "Charlie" Van Horne.

Deep down, Richard was a liberal, or at least much more inclined toward the progressive end of the Progressive Conservative spectrum. Vicious attacks by Van Horne, whom political pundits said was on the payroll of the wealthy Irving family, gave Hatfield an easy win. Van Horne also failed to keep his seat in the 1967 general election, so Richard easily stepped into the official opposition leader role. In 1969, in Saint John, the two politicians once again crossed swords. This time, Richard was ready, and he had an ace up his sleeve: francophone support.

★★★

Hatfield was an eccentric. In those days, Fredericton's Lord Beaverbrook Hotel was the epicentre of political decision-making, and the Premier treated his inner circle like royalty. He barely slept, and everyone knew he liked to party. In government, people close to him talked about how remarkably open-minded he was.

Brenda Robertson was the first female MLA in Fredericton, first for the riding of Albert in 1967 and then for Riverview; she was also the first female Cabinet minister. She was only rarely invited to those social gatherings attended by leading politicians and other influential members of Fredericton's elite. "I drank my own Scotch," she said in an interview with *L'Étoile*.

One night, when she was hardly expecting a 2 a.m. wake-up call from the premier, she was summoned to Hatfield's house near the Saint John River in Fredericton. As she was parking her car, a francophone colleague from the Edmundston area also came up the drive. The premier had convened two strikingly different allies.

The same thing happened another night: the three of them met through the wee hours until six in the morning. Again and again, they met secretly at the premier's house one night a week for three years. They covered everything, developed parliamentary and media strategies, solved problems, and analyzed upcoming events.

That is how the premier chose to meet with his only female minister, who was the member for one of the most anglophone ridings in the province, which was also among the most staunchly opposed to bilingualism, and Jean-Maurice Simard, the leading francophone voice whose star was on the rise.

★★★

People just called him Jean-Maurice. You could not even make up a character like him. Jean-Maurice was a political animal to the core. He was pragmatism personified. Actions produced results. A Quebecker from Rivière-Bleue in the Bas-Saint-Laurent, he studied commerce at the University of Ottawa and became an accountant. He spent a few years with the firm of Riddell, Stead, Graham & Hutchison. Then he set up shop in Edmundston and expanded to Grand-Sault. He first got involved in politics in the 1960s, seeing in the Progressive Conservative Party an alternative to the Liberals, whom he thought were taking the province's francophones for granted. He joined the local Progressive Conservative riding association and ran for a federal seat. He failed, but that did not slow him down. It actually gave him wings. He made his way to Saint John, where he decided to help Richard Hatfield win the party leadership in 1969. The two of them were true progressives. Hatfield knew he needed Francophone support to defeat Van Horne, an Anglophone who wanted to challenge the progressive gains brought about by Louis J. Robichaud's Equal Opportunity Program. Virtually from the moment they met, Hatfield and Simard realized their political futures would be inextricably linked. That is exactly how it played out. Jean-Maurice was elected in 1970 and did not leave the crew until 1985, when Prime Minister Brian Mulroney appointed him to the Senate of Canada.

In 2001, Brenda Robertson, who also became a senator following her time in New Brunswick politics, paid tribute to her former colleague in Parliament's upper chamber a few months after his death: "Jean-Maurice knew that if he were to effect change, he had to change the very power structures of the government. To do that, he had to first change the face and the attitudes of the PC Party of our province. We were lucky that he had his own champion in our late Senate colleague, Richard Hatfield. In many ways, as we look back, I think it is fair to say that one could not have existed without the other, even if that coexistence was sometimes as intense as the times in which we lived."

During his years in Fredericton, Jean-Maurice was much more than the Premier's francophone political lieutenant. Hatfield wasted no time giving him the Finance portfolio in the Conservatives' first term and later made him Treasury Board president, a key government position. That is where Jean-Maurice won his political freedom. He was not the kind of guy who let people push him around, so let us just say that being in charge of the Treasury Board gave him ample latitude to bring in government policies that would enable the Conservatives to stay in power for a long time. That was his opinion, anyway, though his anglophone colleagues from southern New Brunswick might have disagreed.

A few months after the 1979 Acadian national convention in Edmundston, Jean-Maurice strode into my law school office and, dispensing with niceties, declared, "Michel, we need to talk."

***

In 1980, the Progressive Conservatives were concerned about the political situation. They had been in power for ten years, and voter support was clearly waning. Jean-Maurice was worried about the Parti Acadian stoking francophone and Acadian demands by drawing their attention to things like the lack of government services in French. The 1978 election was way too close for comfort, and it was only because of the Parti Acadien that the PCs clung to power. During that election, Joe Daigle, NB Liberal Party leader, made the biggest mistake of his life. He tried to stay on the Anglophones' good side and avoid getting them up in arms while promising nothing of substance to Francophones. He ended up with nothing.

Instinctively, Jean-Maurice sensed a golden opportunity. To ensure an election victory, the party would have to appeal to Francophones while keeping Anglophones happy. Ever since coming to power in 1970, Hatfield's Progressive

Conservatives had borne a striking resemblance to Trudeau's Liberals in Ottawa as well as Louis Robichaud's Liberals. They immediately got the ball rolling on major linguistic initiatives, such as the right to obtain documents in both official languages in the Legislative Assembly, permission to hold trials in English or French, and the creation of francophone school boards. Those were all initiatives that came about in the 1970s.

In the New Brunswick of my childhood, Anglophones and Francophones simply did not mix. They lived separate and apart. That isolation seemed to create a psychological barrier. Premier Hatfield understood that right from the start of his first term and made it a priority to ensure equality between the two official language communities. "No problem we have could require more serious consideration and effort than the need for us to create a just accommodation between the two official language communities of New Brunswick," he declared in his April 1972 budget speech. That balance would be achieved if, and only if, Francophones could play a meaningful role in all aspects of society.

Hatfield went on to say, "Francophones must be involved in the decision-making process if we want to set goals and objectives of achievement that reflect the aspirations of all New Brunswickers. Otherwise, as I indicated earlier, we will not, I repeat, we will not be able to achieve our self realization as a province."

Hatfield was betting big. Did he realize it? Probably. Louis J. Robichaud's dream, the Acadian dream, was becoming reality slowly but surely. An Anglophone from Woodstock had just announced that he would fight to ensure equality between Francophones and Anglophones.

"New Brunswick wants to respond positively to the challenge of establishing mutual understanding within our provincial boundaries. New Brunswickers want to know each other better, they are willing to establish together common goals which can meet the aspirations of both linguistic communities," said the Premier.

It was a major challenge. Jean-Maurice, a Quebecker by birth, was not well loved by New Brunswick's Bible belt loyalists. The anglophone vote was not a sure thing in 1982 because the government had gone to such great lengths to win over Francophones. All his efforts may well have amounted to nothing. Not only was the Parti Acadien making noise, but all the anglophone papers were blasting the government for being too accommodating of the French fact. Jean-Maurice came to see me, and I got the feeling he needed my help.

"We can't fix this by amending the *Official Languages Act*. There's too much opposition in Cabinet," he told me. The government wanted to update the *Official Languages Act* the Liberals passed in 1969, but it did not know how. The idea of a commission to recommend amendments to the Act came up. A commission would probably result in little things like a language of work policy and bilingual positions in the public service, but it was sure to divide Anglophones and Francophones. The fact remained that the government had to modernize the Act.

Jean-Maurice did not think it was a big enough political move to win the election. It probably was, but Jean-Maurice wanted something more because his priority was winning the election thanks to the francophone vote. For Richard Hatfield, the question was always, "Is it enduring?" Hatfield and I met many times to talk about those things, and I always got the impression that his top priority was the common good. The longevity of any policy being contemplated was always the prime consideration.

Hatfield and I always got along well. He did not talk much, and when he did, it was often to ask a question. Anyone conversing with him could tell that he was a very attentive listener. If nothing else, you could count on him to listen. That is one aspect of his personality I always admired. One day, he asked me to set up a meeting with Acadian leaders, so I invited him to the house, where a small group of people from various sectors gathered to discuss francophone issues with him. The conversation went on until three in the morning, and he must have drunk at least twenty cups of coffee that night.

I was at my office in the Adrien-Cormier building when the Hatfield government's language issues point man came to ask me if there was any way an act could be passed that would guarantee the equality of both linguistic communities—not just languages, but communities.

"Can it be done?" asked Jean-Maurice Simard, eyes wide open. I was surprised. I had never really thought about it. I did not even know if there was any precedent anywhere in the world. I told him I figured it would be a first, and a complicated venture. I wondered whether I, as dean, could take it on, and I quickly found my answer. The faculty's purpose was to train people who would go on to defend linguistic rights, so contributing to this kind of bill was crucial. That is why I decided to dive in.

★★★

> I drafted principles and guarantees for Anglophones, Francophones, and Acadians, all of which would be complemented by a new official languages act. We would have one law for linguistic communities and another for languages.

Here is how I went about it: I drafted principles and guarantees for Anglophones, Francophones, and Acadians, all of which would be complemented by a new official languages act. We would have one law for linguistic communities and another for languages. That is an important distinction because the scope of the first was much broader. The main idea was to ensure that both communities were equal—Anglophones had no more rights than Francophones. Both were equal and entitled to access to education not only in their own language, but in their own schools. They would have their own community centres for social and cultural activities. That was extremely important. The *Official Languages Act* was important too, but the main thing it did was give people the right to speak both languages and obligate the government to provide services. It's worth remembering that, historically, Francophones have always been oriented more toward collective rights, while Anglophones have tended to favour individual rights.

My starting point was a painstakingly thorough study of acts passed by the Canadian Parliament, federal acts that might include principles similar to those I was looking for. That approach did not work. Digging deeper, the only useful reference I found was Belgium's state reform, an attempt to set up a system in which the country's major ethnic groups, the Walloons and the Flemish, could exercise a certain degree of autonomy.

The deeper I dug, the more it became clear to me that New Brunswick's situation was not at all conducive to the side-by-side existence of both communities. Our two cultures had different realities, and a major contextual study needed to happen as soon as possible. Such a study could lead to the creation and implementation of a unique multifunctional administrative map for the province. The map would make it possible to decentralize power, transferring it to new or existing local governments. I thought that if the "equality of the founding peoples" bill did not create administrative regions, subsequent regional authority legislation would have to be passed. Parliamentary reform would also have to happen. If that was how we chose to proceed, we could write our principles into provisions that, taken together, would comprise a substantive provincial constitution. That would endow them with significant symbolic and educational value.

When I sent the first version of my bill to Jean-Maurice Simard, I told him in writing that Acadian nationalists would probably criticize the bill if it did not include provisions for some degree of Acadian autonomy or at least the concept of an Acadian territory.

As I saw it, any legislation purporting to guarantee the rights of ethnic groups had to accomplish two key objectives: protection from discrimination—formal equality—including free use of the mother tongue and respect for civil and political rights; and, second, protection from assimilation—substantive equality—including collective rights such as the right to separate educational, cultural, and social institutions the government is obligated to support. The important thing was ensuring the greatest possible autonomy for both communities.

Children, the Act that was passed was not the one I drafted. Mine was four pages long and contained lots of different things. The one passed by the Legislative Assembly, Bill 88, had three clauses. In a nutshell, its purpose was to (1) strengthen the province's unique character by recognizing the two linguistic communities and their equality of status and equal rights and privileges; (2) guarantee that the provincial government would ensure protection of the equality of the two communities by recognizing their right to distinct cultural, economic, educational, and social institutions; and (3) stipulate that the provincial government would allocate resources to its departments and agencies to create programs promoting the cultural, economic, educational, and social development of the official linguistic communities.

That is what I affectionately call a "summary." It is a summary because my initial proposal contained seven rather more detailed clauses. For example, clause 2 read: "The Government of New Brunswick commits to protecting the communities' rights and to the equitable distribution of benefits and monies allocated from public funds." That is not exactly what Bill 88 said. Clause 4 was particularly meaty because it included subclauses (c), the maintenance of "a separate school system for each of the two

> The important thing was ensuring the greatest possible autonomy for both communities.

official linguistic communities and the governance of the school system by each community," and (d), take positive actions to guarantee "comparable economic development in various regions occupied by the two official linguistic communities by ensuring balanced industrial, commercial, and agricultural development in all parts of the province." I also added that the government had to "ensure that both linguistic communities are represented equitably at all levels of the public service."

Of course, my bill also included the right of any individual or any social or cultural organization belonging to either of the two communities to turn to the courts to enforce the law. That was clause 5.

Finally, dissenters would see clause 6 as the last straw because it would have given the act precedence over all other laws and required the approval of three quarters of MLAs to make any changes. It was all supposed to come into effect on July 1, 1980. Needless to say, that is not at all what happened.

★★★

Jean-Maurice was in favour of it all, of course, but I told him myself that there were plenty of things in the bill the government would never go for. He was in for some particularly lively cabinet meetings. Some of the anglophone ministers would never agree to a bill like this because it went too far. The first version of the bill was sent to a handful of senior bureaucrats and influential ministers. In no time at all, there was a palpable sense of panic.

In a letter to Jean-Maurice Simard, Alan D. Reid, the New Brunswick Minister of Justice's legislative counsel, wrote:

> Section 5 is a matter of key importance, since it attempts to provide for the implementation of the propositions and directives contained in the earlier sections. It would give an authority to courts that is unprecedented, to my knowledge, in this Province and probably elsewhere in this country. The courts would be required to issue directives that would have a direct bearing on government spending, and would in fact be making policy decisions in areas that to date have generally been regarded as prerogatives of the elected governmental party.

In his note, Reid expressed concern about the influence of the courts on the democratic process and the development of public policy. But you see, I would rather start big and scale back than start small and get no for an answer. Jean-Maurice agreed with my approach and asked me to present my bill to Hatfield. I went to his office and showed him my work, expecting a reaction. Hatfield read it over quickly, and here is what he said, word for word: "Oh my God, Michel, I'll never be able to convince Cabinet to go for this." What the premier had in mind was a new official languages act, and he figured his government would look good because it would be an improvement over what his predecessor had done. That was his goal at first, but now things were not looking quite so straightforward. Modernizing the 1969 *Official Languages Act was* going to be a lot trickier than he expected. He anticipated failure on that front but saw the two linguistic communities bill as his salvation. Most importantly, this bill would have a much wider scope than a language law.

Quietly, the Premier considered his options. He wanted to get the bill passed anyway, but he would have to talk to some people about it.

"Let me call a couple of guys," he said.

Those two guys were Bruce Hatfield, his nephew and a well-known lawyer in Fredericton who was very involved in the party, and Roger Savoie, another lawyer, who was later appointed to the Court of Queen's Bench in Moncton. I have to admit I found that strange. I did not know either of them.

"My uncle and I mostly talked politics," said Bruce Hatfield during a phone call in 2017. They took my draft bill, analyzed it, and told me several parts would have to be cut. I was not too keen on that. Two unelected lawyers, whose only credentials were that they had the ear of the premier, had just thrown a wrench in the works.

Bruce Hatfield was extremely averse to the idea of collective rights. He was involved in paring down the bill, especially clause 5 on the role of the courts. In a confidential letter to Jean-Maurice Simard, he wrote, "I am in agreement with the principles expressed in sections 2–4 of it. I believe such principles should guide the policy of any Government of New Brunswick. However, I think it would be unwise to try to turn these principles of policy into propositions, of enforceable law, which would be the effect of sections 5 and 6 of the Bill."

He felt that such a law would "drastically" change the fact that it is up to the government and democratically elected representatives to spend taxpayers' money and implement public policy.

He claimed it would transfer significant powers from elected members of government in their day-to-day business to judges and the courts. I agreed that it was an ambitious bill.

Bruce then said that neither Cabinet nor the province's Anglophones would agree to it. More than thirty-five years later, he conceded that Bill 88 was extremely important for the province and for the Progressive Conservative Party.

In 2017, Bruce Hatfield said, "I don't remember ever talking to [Mr. Bastarache] or Jean-Maurice Simard about it. I'm not saying I didn't, but I don't recall that. I do remember talking to Lowell Murray about it. He would have been the senior person in the premier's office. His question was legal. As to how the Court would handle it. What that would mean legally. I also remember talking to my uncle about it from a political point of view. There was a lot of concerns in the party at the time. This Bill 88, the political response was good. As it turned out, in the 1982 election, we had our best success ever. Jean-Maurice Simard was the driving force behind this."

In December, Simard told me he would go see his people and decide what to do next. I was totally exhausted. I was dean of the School of Law and teaching two courses per session, and every evening I would come home to Yolande and you, Émilie, but I knew it was a unique opportunity to advance the cause of the francophone minority. There was too much at stake for me to drop out.

Simard called me back a few weeks later, and at his request, I rewrote the bill so it would not look too chopped up when it was introduced. He also asked my opinion on the development of the bill, which people were starting to get excited about. I replied even though I did not think my comments would be useful. It was a good bill, but nobody really knew that because the message was not getting out there. The general public just did not understand what the bill was about. I thought a debate about New Brunswick's political evolution, and duality in particular, was absolutely essential in 1980. Unfortunately, people did not want to have that debate. I identified three reasons why the two official language communities reacted as they did:

1) Acadian representatives failed to mobilize, which was hard to fathom given that the bill was primarily intended for that community.
2) Media attention was minimal and mostly negative in its analysis of the bill and its impact.
3) The only person advocating for the bill was Jean-Maurice, the most controversial character in New Brunswick politics.

I found the lack of support for this bill from the Acadian establishment bizarre. By "establishment," I mean L'*Évangéline*, the community's daily paper; the Université de Moncton; Acadian caisses populaires, or credit unions; Assomption, the life insurance company; the Association des enseignants francophones du Nouveau-Brunswick; and other weekly papers and cultural groups. Thought leaders such as Roger Savoie, Rino Volpé, Jean-Guy Finn, Claude Bourque, Jean-Guy Rioux, Donatien Gaudet, and Hector Cormier had little or nothing to say about it. I could not believe it. Were they skeptical? Indifferent? Was there some kind of conspiracy? Were they against it? I had no idea, and that bothered me.

In time, the bill was introduced, and after months of debate and divisiveness, especially on the anglophone side, it was passed and went down in history as Bill 88, *Loi* 88.

The eighteen-month ordeal finally came to an end, and I have to say I was very satisfied with the outcome. Yes, my initial proposal was watered down, but it was still the first time, as far as I knew, that a bill on the equality of communities had been passed in any country. This was not just about linguistic equality. I told myself that you, my children, would grow up in a province where both communities were equal. That was clearly an accomplishment. I was particularly pleased with the section about the right to distinct cultural institutions. I stood my ground with the government bigwigs, and I got my way. I believed there was no going back; nobody was going to take away our school boards. I wanted health care to be in there too, but the response from those in the upper echelons of government was a categorical "no."

The government was able to keep everything pertaining to culture in the bill because it could sell the people on its justification for language and culture. All government laws and programs had to guarantee access to distinct cultural and educational institutions for both linguistic communities. I suspect that provision made it through because Department of Justice officials probably told the politicians it would be meaningless in court and amounted to nothing more than a political statement.

I recognized its value though. I knew Pierre Elliott Trudeau's federal government was just months away from passing the *Canadian Charter of Rights and Freedoms*. Deep down, I knew a lot of people, including jurists, would be worried the courts might apply a liberal, progressive interpretation. It strongly resembled section 15 of the *Canadian Charter of Rights and Freedoms*, which says, "Every individual is equal before and under the law and has the right to the equal protection and equal benefit of the law without discrimination and, in particular, without discrimination based on race, national or ethnic origin, colour, religion, sex, age or mental or physical disability." That is why I thought the Act would be interpreted in its broadest sense. The two texts were similar in nature.

Remember, children, the Act was not at all constitutional at the time. Essentially, it was a bill like any other, one that resembled the *Official Languages Act*, even. However, it was a quasi-constitutional statute, and that would affect its interpretation. What I mean is that anyone attempting to abolish it or amend it in any significant way would have to be awfully clever. Politically, the Act would become explosive, untouchable except by those seeking to expand its scope. A few zealous politicians, populists who thought they could divide and conquer, gave it a try, but they failed. I was enormously proud back then because I had just won a political and legal jousting match.

Later, in the 1990s, there was a push to incorporate the Act into the *Canadian Charter of Rights and Freedoms*. Vindication! In 1993, section 16.1 was added to the Charter, confirming that "the English linguistic community and the French linguistic community in New Brunswick have equality of status and equal rights and privileges, including the right to distinct educational institutions and such distinct cultural institutions as are necessary for the preservation and promotion of those communities."

The Charter also recognized that the "role of the legislature and government of New Brunswick [is] to preserve and promote the status, rights and privileges" of the two communities. New Brunswick's Acadians and Francophones owe Fernand Landry a debt of gratitude for working so hard to get that amendment passed. Still, we must render unto Caesar that which is Caesar's. Brian Mulroney's government had the political will and courage to make that constitutional amendment. I was not privy to the details of the political debates that must have taken place behind the scenes at the federal level, nor do I know who the key players were. Some people say the member for Madawaska-Victoria, Bernard Valcourt, played an important role. I could not say for sure. What I do know is that the province could not go it alone. It needed an ally in Ottawa, especially with a new premier in charge, an unsympathetic man who, ironically in retrospect, gets all the credit: Frank McKenna.

The Task Force That Would Change Everything

IN 1967, a fellow by the name of Bernard Poirier was hired by Premier Louis J. Robichaud to clean up government, although "clean up" might not be the right way to put it. Essentially, the Premier wanted to create structures for the Equal Opportunity Program, but the priority was introducing an obligation to maintain francophone staffing in the province's public service, which was overwhelmingly dominated by Anglophones. I had met Bernard a few times, but he was better acquainted with my father and especially my brother Marc, the journalist. Bernard was a reporter with the daily paper L'Évangéline and would eventually become its chief editorialist and editor-in-chief. One day, he announced to his wife that he was going to Fredericton and changing careers. He started working on francophone files and was involved in the development of Service New Brunswick, and he quickly rose through the ranks. Three years later, the Progressive Conservatives were elected, and Premier Richard Hatfield certainly was not about to turn his back on a skilled Francophone in the public service.

In 1975, the Premier asked Bernard to serve as director general of the Official Languages Branch, which was then under the Secretariat of the Council of Ministers. Hatfield wanted to take Bernard under his wing and, slowly but surely, make the Acadian into a kind of official languages commissioner. The position was not yet an officer of the Legislative Assembly, as it would become in the 2000s. That is an important distinction. Government employees' hands are tied when they criticize the executive. They have to be prudent and diplomatic. A commissioner, on the other hand, is accountable to elected representatives and, through them, to the people.

Bernard took up the post five years after the *Official Languages Act* came into force, and he says that was when he first talked to Premier Hatfield about a major study of the status of bilingualism in New Brunswick to mark the Act's tenth anniversary.

"I suggested it, and it eventually got approved. I'm not sure Premier Hatfield even read the whole mandate! Anyway, we were mostly working with Jean-Maurice Simard, and he was convinced it was a good idea," said Bernard.

The Premier wanted to amend the *Official Languages Act*, but he did not know exactly how to go about it. Jean-Maurice Simard was already talking about the Bill 88 mandate when he approached me in 1980 to discuss modernizing the Act and making it more effective. A few weeks later, I was discussing the matter with the Premier in Fredericton. He wanted ideas. I explained to him that one of the most important things the 1969 Act did not cover was people's right to work in their own language in New Brunswick. The Act offered no formal statement about that. His expression told me right away that it would be a hard sell. Not that he did not like the idea—in fact, he seemed quite receptive—but he had doubts about the feasibility of such a proposal.

"You'd have to have bilingual supervisors and lots of bilingual positions," he said, musing. "Is it really feasible? Does it work in Ottawa?" He did not have answers to those questions. He did not know, and neither did Jean-Maurice. But Jean-Maurice, clever politician that he was, suggested, "What if we create a task force and give everyone a say? That'll give us legitimacy. Give us ideas that are doable, and we'll do them." Before making any changes to the historic Act, the government had to understand the current state of affairs. We decided to carry out a very broad study of linguistic issues, prepare a report, and present it to the Legislative Assembly. The MLAs could analyze the report and then amend the Act. At least that is what we thought at the time. That is how the Poirier-Bastarache task force was born.

★★★

We wasted no time. First order of business: appointing task force members. The Premier and his francophone lieutenant wanted me to head up the task force, but they wanted me to have a co-chair from the public service. I was told the government did not want the working group's documents to be accessible under the *Right to Information Act* passed a few years before. It was a kind of internal task force, and secrecy mattered. That is why Bernard Poirier, in his capacity as director general of official languages, was included. Bernard was tremendously useful to our work. For one thing, he knew everyone in Fredericton, and for another, he knew the system. He was highly respected among the province's senior bureaucrats, and his opinion was invaluable.

On May 23, 1980, the Premier's office authorized Poirier, a public servant named Martin Thériault, and me to begin our work. On June 26, the Premier signed a confidential Cabinet Secretariat order authorizing a budget of thirty thousand dollars for our work, which would take about a year. We soon realized the job would take an extra year and cost more. The Premier and other top people in government were not too happy to hear that. If the report was delayed, that could have consequences because there was going to be an election in 1982.

The Cabinet order read:

> The Official Languages Act has now been adopted for over ten years. As with all other legislation the need for review and adjustment is always present because of the constant evolution of the New Brunswick Society. The progress made by the government in the area of service to the public indicates that the priority should start shifting toward other aspects of the Act implied in section 2 which mentions the equality of status and privileges of the two official languages groups in New Brunswick. This revision will also take into account the concerns and ideas of groups and individuals whose goals it is to promote the development of the two linguistics communities of the province.

Most of the time, Bernard chaired the meetings and I focused on drafting documents. Our approach was quite simple. I would write something, and all the members would sit down together to discuss it. We talked about whether the recommendations were realistic and how likely the government was to accept them because, ultimately, the government would decide what to do with our report. I knew from the start what I wanted to put in the report, but I was not sure how we would get Premier Hatfield to accept all our recommendations. Should we lobby deputy ministers? That is where Bernard's skill set came in very handy. He knew the machine like the back of his hand.

***

Where to begin? We had to put together a report that was several hundred pages long, and we had about a year to do it. At the outset, I divided it up into four main objectives. The first was to gain acceptance for bilingualism as an asset for New Brunswick. Bilingualism distinguished us in a positive way and could be leveraged to stimulate the province's development. We had to show how New Brunswick stood out from other provinces so the federal government would be more inclined to send funding our way.

The second objective was public sector jobs for francophones. I know, children, I bring that up a lot, but it is so important. With Francophones providing government services, Acadians and Francophones in the rest of the province would have greater access to and confidence in government, as well as better-quality services, of course. If I had a nickel for every time I heard someone in the southeast part of New Brunswick talk about the Anglos' government or "those people" in Fredericton over the years. We had to find a way for Francophones to get hired in the public service. I knew from experience that the main obstacles were geographic and demographic. Francophones did not want to go live in Fredericton and work for Anglophones. No two ways about it, Fredericton was an anglophone city. French would have to become a language of work in the public service, but that could not happen if a unilingual Anglophone was in charge of a group of Francophones. That is why we came up with the idea of legislating or regulating the creation of francophone work units.

The third objective was about decentralization. A significant proportion of the population considered Fredericton to be the centre of the universe. The government was not really present elsewhere, except for some relatively unimportant outposts in the regions. For example, why not manage a big chunk of the Fisheries Department out of Caraquet or Shippagan? That is where people fish, after all. There and in the Bay of Fundy, of course. People hundreds of kilometres away from the ocean were making decisions about how to manage the fisheries.

Services had to be offered to everyone by everyone in both official language communities. That was the inspiration behind my controversial map of administrative regions. I tried to picture how the government could go about imposing bilingualism across New Brunswick without creating all kinds of problems. I did not think bilingualism would just magically take root in every region of the province. A law stating that services were available everywhere was already on the books. We could implement that by making services available everywhere but without necessarily setting up offices everywhere. For example, there was no real need to have both francophone and anglophone public servants in Caraquet, where everyone was Francophone. We could offer services in English using technology such as phone and fax and, now, the internet.

For a region to be declared bilingual, it had to have a certain percentage of members of both linguistic communities. That is where I came up with the "20 percent" idea. I figured that if twenty percent of the population belonged to the minority, that was enough to justify the presence of representatives able to communicate in both official languages. In an average-sized New Brunswick city, twenty percent was about five thousand people. If the minority linguistic group's population accounted for less than twenty percent, government staff would speak the majority language, and there would be ad hoc services for the minority. We also had to set the boundaries of these regions. Each region needed a critical mass, and we had to divide things up without cutting the province in two. The idea of a francophone north and an anglophone south was a misrepresentation of reality. Case in point: Bathurst, a statistically bilingual city. Where exactly would we draw the dividing line for that region? On which street? We had to come up with a different approach and focus on the goal: providing quality government services. That was the idea.

The fourth and last objective was to increase individual bilingualism by changing the education system. The idea was to get professional associations to declare themselves bilingual or for us to declare them bilingual, and to require English schools to teach French. French schools were already teaching English. What I really wanted was to encourage immersion in unilingual anglophone areas, such as Chatham, St. Stephen, and St. Andrews.

★★★

I was determined to get the job done quickly. I was still dean of the Université de Moncton's School of Law, teaching two courses per session and publishing as many articles as any other faculty member. Life at home was tough. Émilie, sweetheart, you were very sick, and we could not get a diagnosis.

On July 21, 1980, Bernard Poirier, Martin Thériault, and I decided to commission three studies: legal, political, and sociological. We contacted a number of experts, such as sociologist René-Jean Ravault, and asked them to do the studies we needed.

During our July 1980 meeting, we were determined to cover a lot of ground. We identified key people in the federal government and the Government of Quebec, people such as Jean-Denis Gendron, Pierre Coulombe, and Dr. Camille Laurin, whom I knew through the FFHQ. Martin Thériault, the task force's secretary, got in touch with Paul Ponjaert at the Belgian embassy in Ottawa so we could learn more about how the Belgians handled official languages issues. We also invited Robert Kerr, an anglophone law professor from Ontario's University of Windsor, to join our working group. Big mistake! Our bilingualism task force was made up of three Acadians and an Ontarian. Worse still, people definitely saw us as militants because of our approach. In hindsight, Bernard Poirier and I realized we should have done things differently.

"I think we got off on the wrong foot. When they appointed the task force members, they should maybe have had two Anglophones and two Francophones. At least two out of five should have been Anglophones. Plus, our Anglophone was from Ontario! He might have had roots in New Brunswick, but lots of people who were antagonistic to the whole undertaking thought we were just a gang of

Francophones because that's all they saw all the time," said Bernard, thirty-five years later.

From August 11 to 14, 1980, Robert Kerr, Martin Thériault, and I went to Ottawa and Québec City to see how the federal government developed, maintained, and applied its *Official Languages Act* and how Quebec applied its *Charter of the French Language*. People at the Official Languages Branch of the Treasury Board Secretariat advised us to stick to general principles in legislation and use policies and regulations to get into the specifics. For example, the policy on language of work in the public service could be included in the bill. Identifying language requirements for positions was essentially the basis for any Treasury Board linguistic policy. Above all, bilingual bonuses to reward bilingual employees were to be avoided at all costs.

The next day, we went to the Office of the Commissioner of Official Languages to meet with Gilles Lalande, Stuart Beaty, and Steven Acker, senior public servants who were working closely with then-Commissioner Maxwell Yalden. That conversation, too, had a lot to do with enshrining a language of work policy in future legislation to the extent possible. The gentlemen told us that, by and large, departments had paid very little attention to official languages since the Act had come into force. They felt that a standard definition of the bilingualism requirement was needed across all government departments and agencies.

In Québec City, officers of the Conseil de la langue française suggested opening the debate up to the public and calling for submissions once we had a draft proposal. The idea had its appeal because the final version of Quebec's *Charter of the French Language* was based in large part on the demands of lobby groups such as the Mouvement Québec français. I was especially pleased to hear them say that territorial boundaries were of crucial importance in our case because of our demographic and linguistic situation. Of course people had to have the right to remain unilingual, and the government had to ensure there were mechanisms in place that enabled them to pursue and advance in their chosen career. That is when we really grasped the importance of symbolic gestures, such as French signage, because those things helped establish and maintain a relationship between language and identity.

On the last day of our tour, I met with Dr. Camille Laurin, the father of Bill 101, a man I already knew. Laurin laid his cards on the table right away. The situation in Quebec when Bill 101 passed in 1977 was not the same as the situation in New Brunswick three years later. He thought the political risk in Quebec had been much lower than it would be for the Hatfield government. After all, the *Charter of the French Language* was not your everyday law. We understood that we would be under a lot of pressure. The concept of drawing boundaries to create anglophone and francophone zones, as well as bilingual ones, was on the agenda again. I was more convinced than ever that we needed a map.

Laurin strongly recommended that we address the private sector, especially as regards the thorny issue of language of service. Even in the twentieth century, imposing any such policy on private enterprise could lead to extreme tension in New Brunswick. Minister Laurin was very courteous and helpful. He and his colleagues invited us to reach out and consult them anytime we needed something. He also floated the possibility of someone from Quebec helping us with our work. Laurin stressed the importance of both linguistic groups being treated equally within government and of making sure both Anglophones and Francophones could pursue public service careers without necessarily having to become bilingual.

We returned home with a lot of information to ponder. Our work was off to a good start.

★★★

In October 1980, we were in Premier Hatfield's office explaining the scope of our undertaking. Our plan to analyze language legislation in four European nations and in Canada was shot down.

"There's no need to go all over the country. It would be pointless because New Brunswick is unique," he declared. We explained the importance of studying the legal and linguistic issues relevant to professional associations, Crown corporations, and municipalities. "I'm not sure New Brunswick is ready to impose linguistic policies on municipalities and businesses. I don't want this imposed on municipalities, but I do think it should apply to Crown corporations," replied Hatfield.

As soon as we told him about the surveys we wanted to do on attitudes toward bilingualism, the premier got straight to the point. "Protect both languages," he said. "Try to give the government guidelines. In other domains, such as business and municipalities, you can offer suggestions. The law must give people a choice, not an obligation." Most importantly, he said, "I'm against surveys, and you know it, so I don't want to hear that word, and I don't want you doing any surveys."

That was vital to our work though. If we wanted to understand the impact and implications of the *Official Languages Act*, we had to find out what people thought about it. Instead of using the term "surveys," we would use the terms "studies" and "analyses." We wanted an analysis of the language of justice and of language policy oversight and implementation mechanisms. We made plans for one study on bilingualism in the public service and education and another more general demolinguistic and sociolinguistic study of New Brunswick. It was the sociological analysis of attitudes toward bilingualism that garnered the most attention. That, children, was what would change our lives.

***

René-Jean Ravault and I had previously crossed paths without really realizing it. In 1967, he was teaching at the Université de Moncton as I was completing my studies there. Ravault was a sociologist and an expert in mass communication working as a consultant and researcher when my team reached out to him. I knew René-Jean could help us with the most sensitive part of our work because he had experienced the student movement in Moncton in the late 1960s first-hand. He understood the complex and sometimes explosive relationship between the province's two linguistic communities. I had confidence in him. We asked him to do the sociological study on both official language communities' perception of bilingualism. In all, we spent over twenty-five thousand dollars on the study, and it proved fatal to our task force.

In the summer of 1981, René-Jean sent us his first impressions after conducting dozens of interviews with Anglophones and Francophones across the province. "There are lots of subtleties to analyze. I'll make sure my final report is as diplomatic and judicious as possible," he wrote.

In the first part of his report, he wrote that, to the extent that establishing the equal status of Francophones and Anglophones would be promoted by the Government of New Brunswick, it seemed clear that the most radical and militant elements of the francophone population would not have a significant influence on the province's francophone and Acadian populations as a whole. I could already picture the smile on Jean-Maurice Simard's face. Francophones were unanimous in their desire for real and symbolic bilingualism in Fredericton and the decentralization of certain departments. Substantive bilingualism of the public service and expansion of the duality principle to departments other than the Department of Education were other issues that came up in our meetings with René-Jean. I was also pleased to see that Francophones wanted well-defined linguistic regions.

Things were more complicated on the anglophone side, especially among older Anglophones. The old, backward way of thinking was alive and well. That fringe element of society felt the government had already gone too far with its *Official Languages Act*. They felt that Canada and New Brunswick had always been and should always be English.

"Bilingualism is a huge waste of money because English is the international language of business. Bilingualism and duality in education are just dividing the country and the province. This is all the fault of de Gaulle, French Power in Ottawa, René Lévesque, Quebecois who came to Moncton at the end of the 1960s, and Jean-Maurice Simard," wrote René-Jean Ravault in his report.

René-Jean concluded in no uncertain terms that it was a hot-button issue among Anglophones. Some people refused to be interviewed even on condition of anonymity. When our 1,020-page report was submitted to the Premier's office on May 7, 1982, we humbly thought that our ninety-six recommendations would make headlines within weeks. As it turned out, that particular study was what raised people's ire, even years later. Anglophones saw that section as a direct attack on the part of Francophones, who, it seemed to them, wanted to take power away from the majority. It was chaos. The anglophone media got involved, and our report ended up being worthless.

"I got calls and letters, anonymous threats that I forwarded to the RCMP. There were unflattering cartoons. But that was part of our work, and we had to take risks. I took a risk when I went to Fredericton, and I took risks in everything I ever chose to do. Plus, we had no choice. Once we opted to do a study and read what was in the consultants' reports and put that in our report, we knew it would get people angry," recalled Bernard Poirier.

Like Bernard, I got some rather unkind messages, including one death threat. It was all so weird. It started off with anonymous phone calls at home. Then I started getting written threats. When that happened, I did not do anything because I did not want to worry Yolande. There was a lot of pressure though. The anglophone community must have decided I was an enemy. After a while, I showed the letters to Bernard Poirier, and he immediately told me to notify the police, which I eventually did. Their response was surprising, to say the least. I was told that kind of thing happened a lot and there was no real danger because the threats were not serious.

One day, I got a call that was a bit different. Brusquely, the person on the other end of the line informed me that he was going to put a bomb in my car. That got me worried, and I notified the RCMP. The RCMP did absolutely nothing. Zip, zilch, zero. I had a wife and child, and the police were refusing to keep us safe. I knew nothing about RCMP policy and had no idea if this kind of thing happened a lot with task forces. I was not too worried because I never seriously believed that anyone would kill me for heading up a task force. Plus, the subject was so academic.

★★★

The task force took almost two years and cost the provincial government hundreds of thousands of dollars. To be honest, I saw very little of that money, most of which paid for the studies we commissioned, supplies, and a bit of travel. We went through some tough times because of the task force, but it was also deeply stimulating intellectually. I wrote the whole report from beginning to end, but that document would never have existed without the help of my three colleagues. Despite everything that happened, I felt we had accomplished something important for the province's future.

Our recommendations were clear and precise, and they were based on extremely rigorous studies. We called for a complete overhaul of the province's linguistic policy, whose goal going forward should be to provide services of equal quality in both official languages. All New Brunswickers would benefit. We wanted to make sure that all citizens had reasonable access to public service jobs regardless of which official language they spoke, and we also wanted to ensure the equitable participation of both Anglophones and Francophones in government. Finally, we wanted to recognize the regional identity of linguistic communities and support the growth and vitality of both linguistic communities on a regional basis.

As such, we recommended that the government recognize linguistic duality within the public administration and move toward the administrative regionalization of government services on a linguistic basis. Duality would give public servants and citizens the freedom to use the language of their choice in their everyday lives. That would make it possible to offer all services in both official languages. In our conclusions, we also noted that linguistic duality would not result in the duplication of government functions or the immediate appointment of two deputy ministers for each department. Our vision was of a major administrative reorganization to create anglophone and francophone work units. Fundamentally, duality is the delivery of services based on the specific needs of both linguistic communities.

Administrative regionalization was the centrepiece of our report. We rejected the concept of territoriality, but we argued in favour of recognition of regional identity in order to protect the linguistic homogeneity of francophone areas in particular. Ultimately, we gave Premier Hatfield a recommendation for a new piece of legislation to replace the existing *Official Languages Act* entirely. In our view, Louis J. Robichaud's Act was out of date. In addition, the new linguistic policy would be implemented by a new official languages office.

The reaction was dismaying. For one thing, the government kept our report quiet for the months leading up to the October 1982 election.

"I don't remember Poirier-Bastarache being a primary concern pre-1982. In my mind, the big issue was support for the repatriation of the constitution and the Bill 88. But later, the backlash was certainly great and those concerns came after with the hearings and the report of Poirier-Bastarache," recalled Bruce Hatfield, the Premier's nephew and Conservative strategist during the election.

In the end, both the government and the official opposition rejected all our recommendations. We could not believe it. The report was meticulously shelved, and it was the francophones' turn to express their discontent in the ensuing months and years. The pressure was so intense that the government was forced to establish the Guérette-Smith committee, which, over the course of more than 150 hours of public hearings, gave people a chance to vent about our report. It was a "big success" because there were numerous outbursts during the hearings. There was violence, there were insults, there was everything but an honest debate. That happened in 1985, and it irrefutably confirmed the analysis in our report from three years earlier. Their conclusions were eerily similar to ours. To be honest, at times, it was pretty hard to distinguish between that committee's point of view and the one put forward by our group, which had been convened three or four years before. The Guérette-Smith report was tabled in the Legislative Assembly in 1986, and Richard Hatfield proceeded to shelve that one too. Clearly, New Brunswick had not progressed since 1969. Then Frank McKenna's Liberals swept every seat in the Legislative Assembly in 1987. Had the Progressive Conservatives seen that coming, they would have adopted our report in 1983 after the election, and all our work would not have been in vain. Despite the fiasco, the Law Society of New Brunswick asked me to co-chair a working group tasked with proposing a linguistic policy for the organization. That led to the Barry-Bastarache report, which was partially adopted and kick-started cooperation between lawyers from both of New Brunswick's linguistic communities.

★★★

I knew from the start that the Poirier-Bastarache report could be either accepted or rejected. I thought that if it was accepted, the government would adopt all kinds of internal policies to implement our recommendations. I even pictured myself helping them do that. How naive! I had no idea it would be summarily rejected. I never imagined the study on people's attitudes would get the reaction it got. Everyone criticized me for including it in the final report because I was the one who wanted it there. I thought it was vital to understand how people felt about such an important issue. It was about identity. How could anyone solve a problem unless they knew what the problem was? What exactly were we trying to convince the Anglophones of? If we wanted to convince them of anything, we had to know what they thought. I thought Ravault's questions were objective. His questionnaire was not meant to rile people up, but all of a sudden, we found ourselves on the receiving end of incendiary comments, such as "Well, you lost the war, so you should go back to France." Honestly, how was I supposed to see that kind of reaction coming? I anticipated some backlash, but not from such a large number of Anglophones. No, I did not expect that at all.

The hardest part was that we had devoted so much energy to the work and had nothing to show for it. I lost track of how many times I travelled from Moncton to Fredericton to meet with my colleagues. I was back home every evening because I did not want to leave you and your mother alone, Émilie. Once at home, I would write a chapter and send it off to my colleagues a few days later. I often got up at night to write because I could not sleep. I would go to bed, and then I would think of things I needed to flesh out. So I would get up, go to my office and make notes so as not to forget my thoughts the next day. Then I would go back to bed.

I do not regret all that hard work, but if I had a chance to do it over again, knowing how negatively people would react, knowing the report would be rejected, knowing about the threats and the bad press, I would change my approach. Had we done things differently, we might have ended up with a better *Official Languages Act*, and the province might have made some progress. I was so disappointed that I was not able to help my province at that moment in time. If I could do it over, I would not commission the study on attitudes. I am not saying that because I have an issue with the quality of René-Jean's work. It was good work, and it was useful, but it compromised the outcome. I would have been better off skipping the study and trusting my own impression of what the two linguistic communities thought of bilingualism. I could also have opted to do the study and not make the results public. I have a sneaking suspicion that, either way, our recommendations would have been rejected.

The Dream

TRACY WAS TWELVE YEARS OLD and suffered from a severe form of cerebral palsy. She was quadriplegic, and her physical condition rendered her immobile and bedridden for much of the time. Her condition was a permanent one, caused by neurological damage at the time of her birth. She was completely dependent on others for her care. She had to be spoon-fed, and her lack of nutrients caused weight loss. Tracy was said to have the mental capacity of a four-month-old baby, and she could communicate only by means of facial expressions, laughter, and crying.

The little girl from Wilkie, Saskatchewan, appeared to exhibit her own kind of joie de vivre. Tracy loved music, the circus, and her family. She laughed uproariously when her father made a campfire at the family farm. Tracy could apparently recognize family members and would express joy at seeing them. She also loved being gently rocked by her parents.

However, she suffered seizures despite the medication she took. Her parents and doctors believed her suffering to be extreme and her pain unrelieved by the medicine she was given. Tracy experienced five to six epileptic seizures every day. Her disabilities were severe, but her life was not in its final stages. Her doctors anticipated that she would have to undergo repeated surgeries, and that is what happened. She went under the knife in 1990 to balance the muscles around her pelvis and again in 1992 to correct the abnormal curvature in her back.

Little Tracy was also scheduled to undergo surgery to deal with her dislocated hip and, doctors hoped, lessen her constant pain. The surgery was scheduled for November 19, 1993. In the meantime, her family placed her in a group home in North Battleford, some fifty kilometres from the family farm. She lived there between July and October of 1993 while her mother was pregnant with a fourth child, Lee. One day, Laura confided to her husband that the November 1993 surgery would probably be too much. She perceived it as mutilation.

Tracy's father could not stand the idea of her continuing to live like that. He decided to end her life. He considered a number of possibilities, such as an overdose of Valium or shooting her in the head. On Sunday, October 24, 1993, while his wife and other children were at church, Robert Latimer carried Tracy to his pickup truck, seated her in the cab, and inserted a hose from the truck's exhaust pipe into the cab. When Laura returned home from church, she found Tracy dead in her bed.

***

Émilie, the day you were born was the happiest day of my life. And you too, of course, Jean-François. On that day, Émilie, there was nothing in the world I wanted more than a daughter. Yolande and I had started talking about children when we returned from Europe in 1973. We both wanted a big family. Yolande wanted four kids, and although I had pictured three, I was not opposed to the idea of four. I grew up in a family of four, and Yolande, a family of three. We both came from big families with lots of cousins. Your mother was working toward her bachelor of science at the Université de Moncton and finally got pregnant during her last year, 1978. I was finishing up my common law studies at the University of Ottawa and on my way back to New Brunswick to begin my career as a prof at the Université de Moncton's School of Law. I had landed a good job as an assistant professor in March, so we were fine financially. Yolande was planning to complete her studies and begin her career. We were living the dream.

All in all, your mother's pregnancy was normal. She kept attending classes and was just as ambitious as ever. She fully intended to do a master's in history or literature. Then, just a few weeks before the end of term, she quit everything. She did not talk about it much, but she was anxious. That whole final year of her science degree, she was apprehensive about something. Nothing alarming, just a persistent sense that something might not be quite right.

"It's like I knew it was going to happen. People say that kind of thing, but nobody really believes it. I didn't even believe it. There was something though. Before Émilie was born, I had a nagging feeling something was going to happen," said your mother.

One day, she calmly informed me that we had to be prepared in case our children were sick. That startled me. I did not understand what she was trying to tell me right away, but it is true: a new parent has to be ready for anything.

The great day arrived. Émilie, you were born on July 28, 1979, in Moncton, and you were in perfect health. Nothing out of the ordinary at all. Yolande had been worried for nothing. We spent the first three months adapting. We were thirty-two years old, and I had a career. I would become dean of the School of Law a few months later. I was even playing hockey with law students and racquetball with friends from other faculties. Things were moving fast, and I was not home much, but Yolande was taking good care of you. Bit by bit, though, a sense of worry was creeping up on her. Little by little, she was getting more and more worried.

When you were two months old, she took you to see my father. "There's something wrong with Émilie," she told him. Fred, your grandfather, examined you right away. He did not detect anything wrong. But Yolande knew something was off because she noticed you would freeze. You would be playing with your toys, and suddenly, you would go completely still for a few seconds. We were getting quite worried, but we could never have imagined what was to come. As my mother said, "Oh, you two don't smoke, you don't drink, your lives have been easy and safe. What kind of problems could you possibly have?" She was right. We were both well behaved, not prone to excess. There was no reason to worry. But still...

Yolande said that with genetics, you could never be sure because anything was possible. She had spent too much time studying science to think otherwise. Émilie, you cried and cried and cried. You were inconsolable. Even so, the doctors told us that until you hit three months, there was nothing we could do to help you. I did not want to overreact, but I was starting to ask myself some serious questions. What if our little girl, who was such a ray of sunshine in our lives, was sick? I did not even want to think about it.

★★★

We were in a state of shock. We did not think there was anything we could do. You were three months old and convulsing. We were terrified. Together at the Georges-Dumont Hospital in Moncton, we fought to overcome the panic that gripped us. I paced the halls. We clung to the hope that the doctors would do something, would stop the seizures, and figure out how to prevent it from happening again. We could not believe it. We desperately hoped it was just a terrible nightmare. Alas, it was all too real, and the doctors in Moncton could not do anything. Fine, we would go to Halifax, where the IWK Hospital for Children had a good reputation.

They spent two weeks trying to identify the cause of the convulsions. They did everything in their power. They managed to calm you a bit, but you were stubborn like your father. You did not really respond to medication because it was not just a minor episode. The convulsions were happening over and over.

Reluctantly, I had to leave Halifax and go back to work, where the files had piled up on my desk at the School of Law. Yolande was by your bedside every day, keeping a constant eye on you. Some francophone parents had to leave their children at the hospital. They had no choice; they did not have the means to do otherwise. There was no children's hospital in New Brunswick. All the staff in Halifax were unilingual Anglophones, and when those children heard your mother speak French, they flocked to her and started following her everywhere all day. Many of them were afraid of the adults who tried talking to them in English. Some years later, I raised funds for the hospital foundation to enable it to offer children's services in French.

One evening, everything was dead calm on the ward. Yolande was there, sitting near you. A doctor we had never seen before came into the room. She appeared to be replacing our doctor that evening. She was familiar with your file. "When we can't easily control the convulsions, there's nothing we can do," she told Yolande. That was another shock.

The whole family tried to figure out what you had. My father reviewed the scientific literature. We asked the doctors all kinds of questions, but none of them could point to the cause. What bothered them was that if it were a genetic problem, you would have had a number of signs and symptoms. But Émilie, you had just the one symptom. There was nothing else. Your body was developing normally for a baby your age. It made no sense. Over time, you grew as big as a ten-year-old. I always wondered what was going on in your head. I knew you were conscious, aware of what was going on, even though you were bedridden and a prisoner of your body and your nervous system, which denied you the right to live freely. That was the hardest part: you were a prisoner.

We never found an answer to our biggest question: What disease did you have? It was so rare that specialists had no idea what it was. They came up with various names, but that did not get us very far. Basically, it was as if someone told me, "Mr. Bastarache, you have cancer." What kind of cancer? "We don't know." A researcher in Ottawa thought the problem might have to do with mitochondria because that is the body's source of energy. Maybe your mitochondria were not producing energy normally, so perhaps secondary components in the cells were trying to compensate. That is why the doctors told us all your tests were normal. Maybe your brain did not have enough energy though. It takes a lot of energy to keep the body's engine running, and that's what was not working. That was all we knew.

***

We did not really talk about having a second child. Our plans for a big family had not changed, but we were overwhelmed at home. In the blink of an eye, Yolande the student had become Yolande the new mom and Yolande the nurse. I was busy shaping and defining the new School of Law following the premature departure of the Dean, Pierre Patenaude. In addition to my work as head of the school, I agreed to be part of the task force on official languages in New Brunswick, better known as the Poirier-Bastarache task force. I was sometimes away from home for several days at a time, but I always tried to get back as quickly as possible. And I was writing, and writing, and writing. I published law articles, I wrote journal articles, I prepared legal memos. I was constantly working. I have no idea how many of those documents were written by your bedside, Émilie.

Then, out of the blue, Yolande got pregnant again. We were very worried about our second child. We had no idea what you had, Émilie, and we did not know if Jean-François would have the same thing. Nobody knew what the problem was. Doctors tried to figure out the probability of our second child being sick too. Given the fact that the disease was so rare it did not even have a name, chances were very slim. We were told we might have another child with the same problem. Or not.

"You could have four children who are fine or four who all have the same problem. It's all the luck of the draw," said a medical geneticist at the Montreal Children's Hospital.

Yolande put it best: "It was all a blur." We had absolutely no idea what the coming months and years had in store for us. Your mother wanted to keep her child, of course. Despite the looks of concern and pity friends and relatives sent our way, we had always wanted lots of children. When you were born, in 1981, Jean-François, your grandfather heaved a sigh of relief. You were a boy, so it seemed quite unlikely you would have the same disease as Émilie.

***

Jean-François, you were born six weeks early, and we spent the first three months of your life on tenterhooks. Would you start having convulsions like your sister? Or would you be the child we saw in our future as we drove around the Côte d'Azur a few years before? Alas, when you were exactly three months old, the convulsions started. It was just like with your sister.

"They were on Prince Edward Island," recalled my good friend Yvon Fontaine. "It was summer, they had rented a cottage, and we were supposed to go join them the next day. We got a call from Michel, who said, 'Don't come. Jean-François is having the same convulsions Émilie had at that age. We have to go home right away.' It was a terrible shock for them."

I had so many dreams for my wife, my children, my family. I could not accept the fact that my children were so sick. I did not know what to do or think. "It makes no sense," I said to Yolande. "What are we going to do? How is this going to work?" She was incredibly strong. Calmly, she replied, "No problem. We'll figure it out. We'll put them both in the same room. We'll deal with it. We'll do what needs to be done."

From then on, our life changed completely. Yolande gave up her dream of a scientific and literary career to focus on the two of you full time. You were her whole world. Completely cut off from the outside world, she devoted all her energy to you. One thing we absolutely did not want was to be the parents of hopeless cases like the ones we had seen so many of in hospital. We never wanted to abandon you and let you waste away far from home. For us, our children's well-being was our priority. We would not let you suffer. We would not let you be in pain. Over time, Yolande learned how to run an infirmary, and our house became like a hospital.

"I just couldn't abandon my children. They were my children, and I adored them both," she said. I adored you too. Even though I was away a lot, the agony I felt was intense. To cope, I threw myself into my work. Every time we got bad news, I just worked even harder. I could not save you, but maybe I could save someone else. I fled the reality of my everyday life. It was too hard to bear.

You were both afflicted with an incurable neurological disease, one that would leave you totally disabled and result in your premature death. The sense of powerlessness that inhabits any parent in that kind of situation was so overpowering that I lost sleep. I had to take action. I had to do everything in my power to get a definitive diagnosis so we could explore all the treatment options. In situations like this, all parents react in their own way.

It became our mission. Would we be able to get a diagnosis? Was there a treatment? Looking ahead, was the disease congenital and likely to afflict all our children? We did everything we could to find answers to those questions. We consulted specialists in Halifax, Montréal, Toronto, Ottawa, and even Johns Hopkins Hospital in Baltimore. The interesting thing about our trip to Baltimore was that New Brunswick's health insurance refused to pay for the consultation, so the U.S. Department of Health covered everything. The American specialists got funding because your case, Émilie, was particularly interesting from a scientific standpoint. A friend put us in touch with a Canadian doctor in Boston, who followed up with the top U.S. specialists in Baltimore. It was a time of incredible upheaval. Uncertainty, worry, and physical and emotional fatigue wore your mother and me out.

"When Michel was alone, you could distract him," recalled my brother Marc. "You could get him to talk about other things and concentrate on other things. Intelligence is a wonderful thing. You had to talk to him about something other than his family. Yolande was unbearably sad. She was white as a sheet. She lost the will to live. He tried to distract her. He took her on trips. He managed to focus entirely on his career and not think so much about that stuff, which was so messed up."

And you, my beautiful little girl, you survived for seventeen years when your life expectancy, according to various specialists, was a year or two or three or four. Seventeen years of intensive care at home, right up until the day you died in my arms.

★★★

There was one bright spot in the whole ordeal: the wonderful relationship that developed between the two of you over time until Jean-François died. Doctors said otherwise, but you communicated regularly in your own way. We knew you were living the fullest lives possible under the circumstances. You looked at each other, smiled at each other, made little sounds from time to time. Even in bed, with the nasogastric tubes Yolande inserted, you had your routine with your mother and you figured out how to communicate with each other.

When we went to the hospital, Émilie, you sat with Yolande, swinging your legs. The doctors examining you said it was a tic, but we knew you were doing it on purpose. How were you doing it? We do not know because you never told us! When we put the two of you in one bed to change the sheets on the other, we could clearly see your hands creeping toward each other and eventually touching. Never any fighting, just an affectionate touch. Still, you were a little boy, Jean-François, so there were times when you were very vocal. Your mother said you and I were alike, both of us impatient, apparently. She remembers the day she left the two of you in your room and went to the kitchen. Hearing your small cries, she turned right back around.

"I went into the room and said, 'Jean-François, what's going on? What's wrong?' Émilie had vomited, and he was calling me. I could see they had a truly symbiotic relationship," said Yolande. And Émilie, when I took you out of the bath and was drying your hair, I knew you were happy. I just knew it. You communicated without words.

Yolande was with you around the clock six days a week. She took Saturdays off. We often left the house in the morning and came back around five o'clock. We left you in the care of one of the few nurses who would agree to come look after you. It is not that you were difficult children, but some nurses were afraid you would die in their arms, so they turned down the job.

As five o'clock approached, however, all worries disappeared and you came alive, expressing joy and pleasure at the prospect of seeing your mother. We knew this because the nurses and family members who helped us told us all about it.

***

To avoid thinking about my problems, I drowned myself in work. I often worked sixty hours a week, and when I got home at night, I was so tired I would fall asleep. I did think of you, children, but most of the time I was too wrapped up in my work, too absorbed. When we were told your disease was incurable, that felt like rock bottom. It was worse than if you had died because it meant contemplating your death over and over again. Mentally, I steeled myself, thinking we would have to face your death in a year. A year passed, and another, and another. In your case, Émilie, it took seventeen years. The specialists in Baltimore, in the United States, were the best in the world, and they told us it would be four years at the most. More than that, forget it. Well, they were wrong.

Now I feel guilty for seeking refuge in my work during that time. I should have found a way to take better care of Yolande, but I did not know how. She was deeply depressed, always tired because it was so much work. I did not know what to do. I knew we needed a break. In the 1980s, I took more and more cases across the country. Mahé in Alberta and Mercure in Saskatchewan were my biggest cases. That whole time, Yolande ran the infirmary expertly. We needed to stop and take time for ourselves though. The doctor, a Dr. Léger, even forced Yolande to step back for a bit.

"If you don't go right now, if you don't take some time off, you're going to get sick and you won't be able to look after them," he said. He succeeded where I had so often failed. He convinced her to take a break. Later on, when I was the president of Assumption Life, we visited a little piece of paradise in the Caribbean. Émilie, you were in hospital and you were constantly on my mind. We also took a big trip to Singapore, and just before we were scheduled to come back, my mother sent us a message to let us know that you had developed pneumonia. I do not really know why, but every time we left you at the hospital, you ended up with pneumonia. That is exactly why your mother hated leaving. She got to rest, but afterward she had to work twice as hard.

My sister, Monique, was such a big help with you two. As she remembers, "I went to the hospital with Mom to see her, and we spent the afternoon. We would hold her arm and try to pretend we were Yolande. As soon as Yolande arrived, she changed. It was like she woke up, like she knew Yolande was there. Even if she had severe pneumonia and could barely breathe, as soon as she saw her mother, everything was fine and she went back home."

The doctors and nurses always expected you to die of pneumonia, but you kept living. We brought you back home, and Yolande healed you.

***

A few months after my father died in 1984, your health started declining, Jean-François. You had trouble keeping food down, and we tried to stabilize you and come up with new techniques. This time, though, Yolande was exhausted, truly exhausted. Things were tougher than ever. I was working at Lang Michener, and I spent most of my time in airports and courts out West. Your mother had to care for both of you and turn you in your beds at night so you could get back to sleep and avoid developing bedsores. The situation was so critical that Yolande started having panic attacks. She would fall asleep and then wake abruptly, feeling like she was being suffocated. One doctor suggested she see a specialist, but instead of following that advice, she went home and lay down for an afternoon nap. Suddenly, she sensed that you, Jean-François, had taken a turn for the worse, but she did not realize how serious things were. She took you to the hospital. I was not there, of course; I was too busy fighting for Francophones in Alberta and Manitoba.

While you were at the hospital, a nurse dropped you on the terrazzo. Both of your legs shattered on impact. You already had pneumonia, and a little three-year-old baby just cannot withstand that kind of trauma.

A young doctor from Nova Scotia sat down with Yolande and tried to tell her you would not make it. He could not make her understand.

"I looked at the doctor and asked him, 'When can I bring him home? When will it stop?' He couldn't tell me Jean-François was going to die. We lost him two days later. It was hard. It was terribly, terribly hard," she said.

***

After you died, Jean-François, we noticed that your sister was having a hard time coping with the loss. It was Yolande's routine to look after you both every morning at ten o'clock, but for a week, Émilie, you would call your mother with a sound you did not usually make. You were missing something, someone. Your little brother, of course. We rocked you and comforted you, but there was nothing we could do. We could not bring him back. From one devastating blow to the next, our impotence darkened our outlook on life in general. Losing a child is the worst tragedy a parent can experience. Losing one child and knowing the other will also die eventually, but not knowing exactly when, is torture. We searched for meaning in our lives. We tried to find the energy to keep fighting with you, Émilie. I even sought solace in spirituality—though only briefly—which is saying something because I was essentially an atheist. Well, I say I was an atheist because I could not believe even though I wished I could. I was not anti-religious or rebelling against the fact that I grew up in a community dominated by the Catholic Church. I do not think people can force themselves to believe. Pascal's wager does not work in practice.

To be honest, I find talking about religion tedious. My parents were Catholic, but we never talked about religion at home. They stopped practising in the 1960s, once we kids were grown up. I think I preferred to avoid the subject because of the three-year indoctrination I was subjected to at the Séminaire Notre-Dame-du-Perpétuel-Secours. No doubt I believed at the time without really understanding why. At any rate, I stopped practising in the 1960s and eventually stopped believing. When you were hospitalized in Toronto, Émilie, Yolande and I went to church. It is true: desperate people turn to religion. In a way, I wished I could be a believer because it would have provided comfort during my time of trial, but as soon as the priest started talking, as soon as I heard the reading from the gospel, I was done. I do not begrudge believers their faith, but I could not force myself to believe.

When misfortune strikes so cruelly, you feel totally lost and utterly alone in the universe. The doctors could not help us, and our family and friends were at a loss. The greater spiritual family and what we were taught when we were children became a kind of safety net. You were baptized for your protection. I am sure we figured that when you died, you would be taken into that spiritual family and we would not lose you to who knows what. We did not really want to think about it. It was another way to protect you. At the time, it was not really a rational decision, more of an instinctive response. Did it bring us a sense of peace? Maybe so.

What really brought me comfort was the people close to me. Yolande and I were fortunate to have amazing friends and family members who helped us during that difficult time. We also had great pediatricians in Moncton, Halifax, Toronto, Baltimore, and Ottawa.

That said, no words of mine could ever do justice to your mother's extraordinary devotion over those seventeen years. I often sank into a state of heartache and pain, but she lifted me out of my misery. Her support was steadfast, and I could never have abandoned her. When I accepted a job as director of promotion of official languages in Ottawa, doctors told us we would have to take great care to protect our marriage. Apparently, eight-five percent of couples in situations like ours divorced. Not us. Divorce and separation from our children was never an option. You belonged to us, not to doctors and nurses. Our family was united.

Your incurable and totally debilitating illness caused unfathomable and ever-present sorrow that suffused our whole world. It banished joy and any prospect of happiness. What made things even worse was seeing that sorrow on your mother's face every day. I will see it until the day we die.

I will always remember one particular doctor who cared for you, Émilie, and who wanted to understand how your mother and I managed to cope with our tragedy. He asked me plainly, "Are you finding any joy in life, in what you do and see, or have you lost interest in everything?" I think he hit the nail right on the head. Still, I cannot be certain the tragedy we experienced was the sole cause of my mental anguish. I can still picture my father, lost in thought in the living room, the epitome of a man dissatisfied with his life. I do know that the pain of losing my children was immense, indelible, and permanent, and that it transformed my life. It was true: I had a very hard time feeling joy and wonder. Yolande said I was the only person in the world who was not impressed by Niagara Falls.

***

When Robert Latimer's case reached the Supreme Court of Canada in 1999, I did not know what to do. Latimer had been accused of first-degree murder, and a jury convicted him of second-degree murder, on November 16, 1994. The judge gave him the mandatory minimum sentence, life in prison with no eligibility of parole for ten years. He appealed. The Court of Appeal for Saskatchewan upheld the trial judge's ruling. Robert Latimer was tenacious though. He petitioned the Supreme Court of Canada to hear his case. He claimed that, at the time of his arrest, he was not told that he had the right to call a lawyer. Latimer's defence team also claimed that the prosecutor had interfered with the jury selection process and the jury's work.

In February 1997, the Supreme Court of Canada ordered a new trial and found in his favour. The Court stated that the Crown prosecutor's interference in the jury selection process was an abuse of process and obstruction of justice. Latimer's second trial began on October 22 of that year. The judge and jury seemed sympathetic to his case, but he was nevertheless convicted of second-degree murder. At the time, the *Criminal Code* did not contain a provision for clemency in cases of mercy killing. From the start, Latimer argued that he had acted out of compassion for his sick daughter.

The judge in the second trial found that the initial sentence was "grossly disproportionate." In his decision, he granted a constitutional exemption from the mandatory minimum sentence. Robert Latimer was sentenced to one year of imprisonment and one year on probation, to be spent confined on his farm. The Crown appealed, and the Saskatchewan Court of Appeal reversed the sentence, imposing the initial ten-year sentence. Robert Latimer once again asked the Supreme Court of Canada to rule. The Saskatchewan farmer argued that the Crown had fabricated evidence. He appealed the sentence as well as the conviction. The Crown supported his petition to the Supreme Court on the grounds that it might at last demystify constitutional exemptions in the case of minimum sentences. The Court had to answer this question: "Would the imposition of the mandatory minimum sentence for second-degree murder constitute cruel and unusual punishment, contrary to s. 12 of the Charter, in this particular case?"

This all happened when I had been a justice of the highest court in the land for three years. I had not missed a single case. I read the documents in preparation for the hearing and was struck by the similarity between you, Émilie, and Tracy Latimer. You were almost the same age in 1993. I pored over the file and saw that Tracy's medications were the same ones we had been giving you your whole life. Her chair was the same as yours. I sat there in my office, unsure what to do. Over the years, I had talked to colleagues and friends about you. In interviews, I had mentioned that my children were ill, but I had never gotten into the details. That was private. Who would know that I knew better than anyone what the Latimers were going through? My fellow justices were well aware, but they were the only ones. I told myself that it made no real difference and that I could hear the case impartially, but I was still hesitant. I talked to your mother about it, and I waited a while before deciding whether I should recuse myself from the case.

"We knew about his children," recalled Beverley McLachlin, who was just beginning her tenure as chief justice. I discussed the situation at length with her. "He didn't talk about it much, but we sympathized with him and his wife. Unlike with linguistic cases, he felt he was too close to the subject, so he told me he didn't feel comfortable participating," she said.

In January 2001, seven of my colleagues rendered a unanimous verdict. They upheld Robert Latimer's life sentence with no parole eligibility for ten years. My colleagues wrote: "[...] the minimum mandatory sentence is not grossly disproportionate in this case. We cannot find that any aspect of the particular circumstances of the case or the offender diminishes the degree of criminal responsibility borne by Mr. Latimer." He had to go back to prison for the most serious crime of all: murder.

★★★

It is very complicated. If a child is suffering terribly, you can understand a parent's desire to relieve that suffering, but the law was what it was then. If the sick child is not suffering, that is a whole different story.

Is it mercy to end your child's life? It is agonizing. I can understand someone choosing to do that, but I could never have done it. How could I have? I was certainly suffering, but you were not. Émilie, you recognized your father and your mother. When Yolande came into your room, you smiled at her. You recognized her. You did not smile when a nurse came in. Your mother swore to me that, every day, when I came home and the garage door opened, you reacted. You knew I was home! How can anyone know their child wants to die? There is a whole debate on legislation around ending life under certain circumstances, but I would rather not get involved. It is all too painful.

The Battle of Alberta

IN THE EARLY 1980s, Paul Dubé took his son to kindergarten every day. The boy was bright, enthusiastic, and energetic. Two weeks after school started, it became virtually impossible to coax him out of bed. He was bored to death. Driving around in their Beetle, father and son chatted about this and that, always in French. Suddenly, the child exclaimed to his father: "*Regarde papa, t'as vu la bleue voiture?*" What was so strange about that? Well, in French we say "*la voiture bleue*," so saying "*la bleue voiture*" would be like saying "the car blue" in English.

"I couldn't believe it. He'd never made a mistake like that," said Dubé, more than thirty years later. It was immersion school at work. Paul and his wife were not simply going to let it slide. "They let kids talk and just hope they'll learn correct syntax, but suddenly he was making mistakes like that," he explained emphatically. His desire for change coincided with that of Jean-Claude Mahé and Angéline Martel, two young professionals with great ambitions. Mahé was in communications at the National Film Board in Edmonton, and Martel was a teacher.

Mahé left his hometown of St. Paul, Alberta, in the 1970s to travel and teach abroad. When he returned to Canada in the early 1980s, there was a renewed sense of energy around Prime Minister Pierre Elliott Trudeau, who was fighting to patriate the Canadian Constitution and adopt a charter of rights and freedoms. "I asked myself, 'What does this mean for Alberta? What does it mean for Francophones outside Quebec?'" Mahé said in May 2018 at the Telefilm Canada office in Montréal, where he was the interim executive director. He was just as passionate about education for the Franco-Albertan minority as ever, especially when he talked about how ardently he wanted a robust and widespread French-language school system in the country's most conservative province.

The Mahé-Martel children were regularly called upon to help their anglophone peers learn the French tongue until, one day, the parents woke up to the injustice of the situation. What were their children learning? They wanted a French school in Edmonton, not an immersion school. A public—not Catholic, also known as separate—French school.

"We thought it was great that there were kids in immersion and that anglophone parents wanted their kids to become bilingual," said Jean-Claude Mahé.

"The kicker for me, though, was the fact that the government at the time refused to even listen to us, as did the school boards and the ACFA. That's what spurred us to organize."

At the time, the Association canadienne-française de l'Alberta (ACFA), the Franco-Albertan advocacy organization, had a very cordial relationship with the provincial government, which was made up entirely of Anglophones. To this day, Paul Dubé and Jean-Claude Mahé say that the ACFA was afraid of losing its anglophone friends, who had until then been accommodating of the minority. As Mahé, Martel, and Dubé saw it, the organization considered their proposal to be too revolutionary, while they thought things were not moving fast enough. "We weren't trying to change the world," said Dubé. "We wanted to change our community. We wanted French education. We wanted to save our children. At first, the main reason I wanted to do something to change the system was that I could see what it was doing to my children." In the old house that served as office space for a handful of professors on the University of Alberta's Campus Saint-Jean in Edmonton, Paul Dubé still recalls, down to the last detail, the episode that left an indelible mark on the country's history.

He remembers the time he and his friends managed to set up a meeting with the Minister of Education, David King. There was every indication that the Minister considered it merely a courtesy meeting, but the three friends saw things differently. After the meeting, Jean-Claude Mahé told Minister King that he expected a follow-up meeting in due course, but the Minister never followed up. That was the end of that.

But Mahé was not about to give up. He contacted every francophone lawyer, young and old, in the province. Nobody wanted to represent them, he said. Finally, he hired well-known labour lawyer Brent Gawne, a unilingual Anglophone and a francophile. Gawne was prepared to go to war for his clients. He viewed the case as setting a precedent for all Francophones in Canada.

★★★

The trio's battle ramped up in the early 1980s. There were more and more informal meetings with other members of the community. Support grew, and people pulled out all the stops. At that point, the three of them understood what I had been thinking about and reflecting on way over on the other side of the country. The new *Canadian Charter of Rights and Freedoms* opened up several different options to advance our cause. Our only way forward was through the courts because the legislative parameters were still much too vague. Section 23, the education section, would never be implemented unless governments were taken to court. The purpose of section 23 is to maintain Canada's two official languages as well as the cultures represented by English and French. Furthermore, its intent is to ensure that each language flourishes in provinces where it is not spoken by the majority. Section 23 grants minority language parents the right to education in their language throughout Canada where numbers warrant.

In the mid-1980s, there were several language-focused cases relating to education in Canada. Cases in Ontario, Manitoba, Prince Edward Island, Nova Scotia, and especially Alberta were so numerous that we had to prioritize. We had to figure out which battles would help us win the war and validate our right to instruction and school governance in our language. I occasionally met with jurists in private to discuss the cases and how I could help. "Everyone agreed that the Mahé group was the furthest ahead. That case had the best chance of succeeding, so that was the one we got behind. The others would wait and see how the Mahé decision played out," recalled lawyer and law professor Pierre Foucher, who was present at quite a few of those meetings.

In 1984, the Edmonton Roman Catholic Separate School District No. 7 established a francophone school, École Maurice-Lavallée. It had 242 students from kindergarten to grade 6 the following year and soon doubled its enrollment. At the time, there were over 3,700 children in the Edmonton district.

The Mahé case was exactly what we needed. A solid case in an extremely conservative province with practically perfect protagonists. A formidable trio of young professionals and intellectuals who wanted only to provide their children with a good education in French. It was actually much more than that, however. It was a battle for the children, but it was also for a vision of Canada where linguistic duality is important and recognized, and where culture can be passed on to the next generation. Francophone minorities' war was national in scope, but our battle would be fought in Alberta. And we were ready to do anything to win it.

> It was a battle for the children, but it was also for a vision of Canada where linguistic duality is important and recognized, and where culture can be passed on to the next generation.

★★★

My friend Georges Arès was on the other end of the line. It was 1983, and the Mahé case was picking up steam. "We can't stay neutral. Education in the province is important.

We have to intervene," said Georges, who was heavily involved in francophone struggles with the ACFA. I ended up sending him a legal opinion on the position the association should take in the case. Children, it was pretty straightforward: I told him the ACFA had to join forces with the trio.

Not everyone agreed with my recommendation, however. You see, religion was extremely important to quite a few Albertans, especially in rural areas. Many Francophones wanted Catholic schools, but the trio's proposal was very clear. They wanted a school that respected everyone but was not faith-based.

Personally, I agreed with their position from the start. Dividing people up based on religion was archaic and discriminatory. The system was dominated by a kind of puritanical hypocrisy even though three quarters of the families who enrolled their children in school were not practising. My client, however, felt that maintaining unity among Francophones was crucial and that going the Catholic school route was the best way to bring the most people on board. The debate was already raging in some families, and any mention of the Mahé group's undertaking heightened the tension in various communities. I reiterated to Georges and the others that we would avoid any reference to the religious debate. If the judge raised the issue, we would say that section 23 applied either way and that people could ask for a public or separate school.

At that point, we still could not be sure we had the numbers to back up a solid legal case as far as management of educational facilities went, but the trio would not budge on the religious issue. I approached Gawne and asked him to convince his clients not to push that angle and to keep their statements discreet.

Best to avoid giving the government ammunition. I wanted us to stay as far away from that hot potato as possible and focus on our guiding principles. Why did we need a school? Why did section 23 support the vitality and survival of the community? Why did the community absolutely need the right to management? This was, after all, the first time anyone had tried to secure the right to full management and control, and not just over one school. We had to win this one or risk jeopardizing everything else we were fighting for across the country.

★★★

Shortly before the case went to court, I flew to Edmonton to meet with Brent Gawne and let him know I planned to seek intervener status. I wanted to argue the substance of the case and call witnesses. In court, there is always a complainant and a respondent. The complainant prosecutes and the respondent defends. There are also interveners who can try to make the case go one way or the other. I was sure we had a better chance of winning against the government if I could call witnesses to the stand.

The Government of Alberta was not going to assign a rookie lawyer to the case. There was too much at stake, and it would spare no expense to ensure a win. Years later, in the documentary *Droit comme un F*, which was broadcast on TFO in Ontario, David King, Alberta's Minister of Education from 1979 to 1986, said, "The government was very reluctant to do anything relating to section 23 at that time [...]. Politically, the government wasn't ready to take that kind of initiative."

Jurists and politicians across the country kept close tabs on the Battle of Alberta. Ultimately, there were fifteen interveners when the case reached the Supreme Court. The Government of Alberta and other opposing parties invested significant resources in hopes of winning the case, and Quebec, the province we were counting on for support, was against us. It really was not a fair fight.

Brent Gawne was a good man, but he just was not equipped to take on an army of constitutional lawyers single-handedly. I am not bragging when I say he needed me. By bringing key witnesses to the stand, witnesses he could not afford, I undeniably helped his clients and, most importantly, enabled him to amass evidence.

Unlike other national francophone associations, the ACFA had substantial funds in trust. When it was founded in 1926, the ACFA wanted a way to connect with as many francophones in Alberta as possible. Eventually, it acquired a radio frequency, CHFA. In 1974, Radio-Canada purchased the frequency, and the ACFA placed the proceeds in trust. Like other francophone organizations, the ACFA also received annual funding, and it ran lucrative fundraising campaigns too. Over time, it accumulated quite a healthy nest egg, so it was ready to do battle for the cause.

***

John C. Major was a funny kind of guy. He was born in Mattawa, Ontario, between the two world wars, and he moved about ten times before reaching adulthood. He started out in Mattawa in northwestern Ontario and made his way to Longueuil, formerly known as Ville Jacques-Cartier, on Montréal's South Shore. He spent his childhood living out of a suitcase, moving from town to town with his father, a telegraphist for Canadian Pacific. John, who was also called Jack, did not speak a single word of French at a time when an anglophone Quebecker could get along just fine in English in Quebec. As he tells it with a smile, "I deserve a lot of credit for teaching English to quite a few Francophones because they went to Loyola to learn English and I wasn't smart enough to learn French at the same time."

Those were the days of Maurice "Rocket" Richard and anglophone domination in Maurice Duplessis's Quebec. It was during the depths of the *Grande noirceur*, a socially conservative time when life was dominated by the Church. Like many

Anglophones, Jack saw no need to learn French. He could live his life, get health care, work, and study in English, so why bother learning another language?

In the fall of 1953, Jack was free as a bird and found himself in Toronto, having gained entry into the wonderful world of law. Who could have guessed such a blasé young man would find himself enrolled in Osgoode Hall, one of the country's most prestigious law schools? It was a time when anything was possible, especially for someone as intelligent as Jack. When he finished his studies, he headed for Calgary to article and be admitted to the bar. In time, he got a job at Bennett Jones, a small firm founded by Canada's eleventh Prime Minister, Richard Bedford (R. B.) Bennett, that employed sixteen lawyers.

Jack said he was acquainted with Alberta Premier Peter Lougheed because of his practice. He confided that the Conservatives being in power cleared the way for him to get contracts because the government did not want to use the same lawyers as the Social Credit Party. Was it the Premier who approved his contracts? He did not know, but he got contracts. Jack eventually earned himself a reputation as one of the most feared lawyers in Alberta. In court, he bested opponent after opponent. Sadly for him, I was not one of them!

***

Mahé was the first case I was involved in all the way from the Court of Queen's Bench to the Supreme Court of Canada. As a law professor, I was not a regular litigator, so I was not all that familiar with the rules and procedures of arguing at trial. Appeals I could handle because that was mostly what I did, but going to trial was a new experience. I had to call witnesses to the stand and enter things into evidence. At first, I improvised a little. With practice, I found it was not bad at all. Fortunately, I had another lawyer, Georges Arès, close by, and he gave me advice now and then, whenever he was not on the witness stand.

The Mahé group filed suit against the Government of Alberta to obtain a clear definition of their rights under section 23 of the *Canadian Charter of Rights and Freedoms*. The group asked the judges to find that the number of children in the Edmonton area whose first language was French was sufficient and that they were entitled to publicly funded instruction in their language in institutions managed by the francophone minority. Crucially, the judges also had to find that section 23 of the Charter granted Francophones the right to have their children educated in establishments equivalent to those provided to anglophone children in Alberta.

Enter the great John C. Major. I had heard of him, but did not know much about him. Early in the trial, I was not all that impressed. I thought his argument was simplistic: The right to publicly funded education in the minority language exists only if there is a sufficient number of students in an existing school district.

"I treated it like any other case. The issue was that Mahé wanted more space in his school and more instruction. From the government's perspective, the primary argument was that there weren't enough students to justify that," Major explained.

I could see that Jack had one quality every jurist the world over should have: he was pragmatic. He did not use stalling tactics to buy time or derail the trial. He was forthright and always a gentleman, truly. Thirty years later, Jack seemed to agree with my analysis.

"I'd have to say it was because I was lazy. There were things I didn't think were important, so I didn't pay attention to them. What I thought was important was the interpretation of that section," he said, sitting calmly in a conference room in a Calgary office tower.

I soon grasped his style and how he operated. I saw him as a capable, charismatic, and clever man, but, to be honest, I found his arguments lacking in substance. At first instance, his cross-examinations went no further than stressing the fact that there was not a significant number of Francophones and that École Maurice-Lavallée was adequate for the community. Well, of course Francophones were in the minority! That was the whole point. All he did was state the obvious, so I decided to completely ignore him. I chose a more informative approach, more like a speaker trying to convince an audience of his position. I opted not to respond directly to Jack but to focus on our arguments. I was logical by nature, so I set about constructing a fortress, starting with a foundation, then the ground floor and the second floor. Ultimately, my goal was to erect an indestructible stronghold that would ensure our victory.

My witnesses were my weapons. I called to the stand Dr. Lionel Desjarlais, a professor of education at the University of Ottawa and an internationally recognized expert in education for minority Francophones. One of the things I got him to say was that, "school is a microcosm that provides a level of cultural support that cannot be found outside the school when children are in an Anglo-American environment."

Then I called Stacy Churchill to the stand. Churchill was an expert in educational management and program development who had studied at the London School of Economics in England and the Institut d'Études politiques at the Université de Paris. Churchill was quite an eccentric, and I had been strongly advised to prepare him well. During my examination, Churchill clarified the importance of giving representatives of linguistic minorities the right to manage their own educational establishments. That right is essential to implementing a program of study adapted to the unique needs of francophone families. If the minority does not manage its own school, French will be merely the language of instruction. The entire cultural aspect will be put on the back burner.

As Churchill told the Court, "There is definitely a connection between the nature of the services offered, students belonging to minority communities, their rate of participation in general, and the structures and methods employed to provide those services. That connection has been demonstrated in countries other than Canada. My research shows in part that these kinds of relationships exist across most industrialized countries."

According to my two experts, a school is a cultural milieu. Ultimately, the Court understood that. In his decision, the Chief Justice of the Supreme Court of Canada, Brian Dickson, wrote:

> [...] minority language groups cannot always rely upon the majority to take account of all of their linguistic and cultural concerns. Such neglect is not necessarily intentional: the majority cannot be expected to understand and appreciate all of the diverse ways in which educational practices may influence the language and culture of the minority. [...] If section 23 is to remedy past injustices and ensure that they are not repeated in the future, it is important that minority language groups have a measure of control over the minority language facilities and instruction.

Case closed.

★★★

I was cautiously optimistic. I felt that the language of instruction issue was a done deal, but I was not at all sure we had won on the management question. From the start, I suspected the wording of section 23 of the *Canadian Charter of Rights and Freedoms* would end up hurting our cause. My textual argument was kind of crude, and the more I thought about it, the more I doubted I would be able to persuade an Anglophone with such a simple textual interpretation.

Children, I am sure you remember that part in section 23 of the *Canadian Charter of Rights and Freedoms* that reads, "établissements d'enseignement *de la minorité*." It does not say "*pour la minorité*." In French, there is a distinction between "of the minority" and "for the minority." The English wording says, "minority language educational facilities," which is more open to interpretation. Jack Major did not appreciate the difference, and I was worried the judges would not either. I had to explain it as simply as possible to them. Sitting back in his chair, Jack seemed to think that was irrelevant. Luckily, the judges did not think it was irrelevant. They did not grasp the nuance because their understanding of French was not at that level, but throughout the hearing, the judges listened closely to my argument. Based on their body language alone, I was sure I had gotten my point across.

Still, the consequences were far-reaching. Would they condone something of such significant impact on the strength of an argument based on two words in one section of the *Canadian Charter of Rights and Freedoms*? I hoped so. I was betting heavily on the fact that the federal government had not patriated the Constitution for nothing. Why did the government amend the Constitution? Why did it add a minority language rights provision? Why, if not to change the way everything worked in Canada before the Charter? It was clearly a fundamental change. I hammered the message home, and the judges bought it.

As nice and pragmatic as he was, Jack was still an Anglophone who just was not sensitive to the French fact in a minority context even though his wife was Francophone. Sometimes he and his colleagues were pretty hard on us when our arguments hit the mark. Judges in all three proceedings observed their actions and their arguments and seemed to think their behaviour was mean-spirited. What is wrong with sending one's francophone children to French school? I really focused on that in my arguments, and so did Gawne. At the Court of Appeal, I remember laying it all out and hoping for a home run: "What's the downside? We're looking at the upside, and I have witnesses here who are talking to you about culture, about linguistic continuity, about family unity. Aren't those values we share as Canadians? The other party says, 'We'll just assimilate them because it'll cost less.' Isn't that what they're telling us? Sending francophone children to French school is too expensive!"

I calmly told one of the judges that children have to go to school anyway, but for purely financial reasons, they would be deprived of their culture and prevented from talking to their grandparents. Glancing over at Jack, I could see he was furious. His position would have unfortunate consequences for one of Canada's founding peoples. As I drove my point home, the edifice of his argument crumbled. I could sense the judges thinking to themselves that such an injustice was not okay.

In the end, thanks to the hard work of Brent Gawne and his clients, we won both in the first instance and on appeal. That was not good enough for us though. The judges agreed with our general arguments, but their decisions were not precise enough. The meaning of section 23 was not conclusively defined. Gawne ended up recruiting a brilliant young lawyer, Mary T. Moreau, who argued the case in French before the Supreme Court of Canada and went on to become one of Alberta's most prominent francophone lawyers. Mary's family was well known in the Franco-Albertan community, and her argument before the seven justices is deeply symbolic to Franco-Albertans to this day.

"Brent Gawne said, 'Here we are, we've made it this far, so let's get this done. Let's deal with all of it. Not just the part about whether the numbers warrant a school, but the part about whether the number of Francophones warrants a school board.' Some people said the facts weren't ideal because the numbers in Alberta were too low to establish a school board. As the Supreme Court of Canada saw it, it was precisely in those jurisdictions that the need was greatest because assimilation had already taken a toll and a quick and effective response was called for," said Mary, who was made chief justice of the Alberta Court of Queen's Bench in 2017.

At both the appeal court and the Supreme Court of Canada, Jack Major decided to get a little political. Clever fox that he was, Jack knew that I had appeared before the parliamentary committee on constitutional patriation in the early 1980s, where I proposed amending section 23 to include the minority's right to manage its educational facilities. In court, he stated, "If he himself [meaning me] sought an amendment to have it included, that's because he knew it wasn't there. Back then, he said, 'It's not there, so put it in,' so he can't turn around and say the opposite now."

I was caught off guard, blindsided. I did not know what to say. I had to think about it for a bit. How could I regain the upper hand? Finally, I said, "You know, when I asked them to put that in, it was Jean Chrétien's file. Mr. Chrétien didn't say, 'It's not in there, and I don't want to put it in.' He said, 'It will be up to the courts to decide the ambit of section 23.' So here we are in court, and now the Court will decide the ambit of section 23."

★★★

Émilie and Jean-François, one of the first times I set foot in the Supreme Court of Canada was as defence counsel for a dead man. In November 1980, Father André Mercure got a speeding ticket. He fought the ticket on the grounds that the law did not apply because it was in English only. He demanded a trial in French. He was defeated at trial and on appeal. Things were not working out for the Mercure team. One day, the lawyer representing him, Roger Lepage, called me up and asked me to help him take the appeal to the Supreme Court. I gladly agreed to work with him and argue the case before the highest court in the land. While we were diligently putting together our brief, we got word that Father Mercure was dead. We were dismayed. The Supreme Court would surely hold the case to be inadmissible if the applicant was no longer alive. That is what usually happened in criminal law. This case, however, was of national interest, and under exceptional circumstances, the Court could decide to hear it.

I wrote a letter to the then-Chief Justice Brian Dickson, asking him to sustain the authorization. In his response, Chief Justice Dickson asked us to argue the motion before three Supreme Court justices. The other party, the Government of Saskatchewan, would have an opportunity to argue against the motion. It was my first real appearance before the Supreme Court, and in the end, I was successful. A few months later, the Court notified us that it would hear the case even though André Mercure was dead.

That was just the first round. During argument, I stood there while the justices bombarded me for what seemed like forever. Reliving the event thirty years later,

I can still feel what it was like to be besieged on all sides by the other parties' lawyers. I vividly recall the frostiness in the justices' aggressive tone. I remember Justice Willard Estey's attitude in particular. He was a ruthless man. Seated to the right of Chief Justice Dickson as I addressed the bench, he was almost contemptuous. I found him so intimidating. From my perspective, he did not so much ask me questions as attack me. Then, for no apparent reason, he just stopped listening to me. He flipped through the pages in front of him and talked to his neighbour. He put me on edge and stressed me out.

Also on the bench and just as daunting was Justice Antonio Lamer, but I was well acquainted with Lamer and figured I knew how to win him over. Estey, on the other hand? Nobody could go up against him. In the end, he was the one who wrote the dissenting opinion in Mercure. He wrote: "Saskatchewan, like all provinces, acquired the power to establish its institutions when it was created, including the power to specify the language to be used in their proceedings."

It was only a partial victory though. We established the right to bilingual statutes and trials in French, but that was not a constitutional right and could therefore be withdrawn. The Supreme Court sent the provinces a message: translate your laws. In the same breath, it said that was not constitutionally protected. Naturally, the provinces that had not translated their statutes passed legislation cancelling their obligation to do so.

***

On June 14, 1989, there was no Google, no Facebook, no Twitter. It behooves every lawyer to know something about the judge or judges hearing their case. The basics: their interests and areas of legal expertise, decisions they have rendered in the past that relate to the case at hand. Lawyers need to know things like that to avoid getting caught trapped.

That takes no time at all now. With all the information available instantaneously, people make quick work of figuring out which way the wind is blowing in the Supreme Court of Canada. At the time, you had to spend a fair bit of time digging. In fact, I myself sometimes tried to guess which justice would be most sympathetic to my cause, and then I would try to speak directly to that person because that is who I wanted asking me questions. Being grilled by a cold or antagonistic judge could be unnerving. In the Mahé case, I knew Gérald La Forest was on side, as he had been in Mercure. I also knew it was one of Chief Justice Dickson's last cases and that he would most likely be looking to make up for some of the disastrous decisions his court had rendered in cases involving linguistic rights in previous years. Fortunately, Justices Estey and Beetz were no longer on the bench at that point. Some years before, Jean Beetz had written an extremely restrictive decision concerning language rights in Société des Acadiens, and his presence on the bench would have jeopardized our case.

That said, Justice Lamer, a criminal lawyer from Quebec who later succeeded Brian Dickson as chief justice, was the one who made me grit my teeth. He was such a difficult man! He was the kind of judge who would listen to the evidence and then discombobulate the lawyers by zeroing in on insignificant details. If there had been a car accident and the lawyer said the vehicle involved was blue, he would say something like, "Yes, but what if the car had been red?" If the lawyer managed to answer, he would press the point: "OK, and what if it had been yellow?" He would not let up. He was like a dog with a bone, and the lawyer involved would not be able to make any headway because of his questions.

At the Supreme Court of Canada, it is hard to lay out a whole argument logically because right from the get-go, the justices interrupt the attorneys to ask questions. It is basically a question-and-answer session. One justice asks a question, the lawyer does their best to answer and pick up where they left off, and then another justice asks yet another question. Often, the questions are completely unrelated. One justice might ask about management, another about the issue of where numbers warrant, another about the cultural aspect, and so on and so forth. It is all over the map. The judges are familiar with the case, they have read the briefs, and most importantly, they want to get it over with as quickly as possible. It is total anarchy. Thank goodness the lawyers did not have a one-hour time limit back then.

I spent months preparing to argue the Mahé case. As usual, I was not stressed when I walked into the Court because I was sure I knew the case better than anyone else in the hearing room. My strategy was simple. I planned a very short presentation to ensure I covered enough ground. If I had any time left, I would wing it. I had given some thought to all the questions the justices might ask me and written them down as they occurred to me.

With Dickson, La Forest, L'Heureux-Dubé, Lamer, Wilson, Sopinka, Gonthier, and Cory on the bench, the whole thing was much simpler than expected. According to the court transcripts, not one of the justices interrupted me during my short presentation—not one! That is practically unheard of.

⋆⋆⋆

As Jean-Claude Mahé recalls, on March 15, 1990, "Nobody thought we'd get the decision we got. I think the Supreme Court of Canada went as far as it could." He was right about that! A unanimous decision written by one of the greatest legal minds in Canadian history, a unilingual Anglophone from Manitoba, Brian Dickson.

According to a memo written by Chief Justice Dickson himself and quoted in the biography by Robert J. Sharpe and Kent Roach, "The Court [seemed] to be very much of one view with minor variations" in the Mahé case. The biographers report that Peter Cory spoke first in the deliberations. As an Anglophone from Ontario, Justice Cory had worked quite hard to learn French and told the other justices that he was "in favour of encouraging bilingualism and biculturalism" and giving the francophone minority a significant role in the management of their educational facilities. Justice Gonthier agreed, suggesting that section 23 "is a remedial section which should have a purposive and broad interpretation." Justice Sopinka also agreed with a special approach to section 23. And, as I predicted, Gérard La Forest apparently pushed for a generous interpretation of school management. "The whole system cannot function without giving the minority interest positive say in the management and the education," he reportedly said.

Justice Dickson said in private that Quebec's position had a "divisive" effect. "I felt the action of Mr. Bourassa [...] had done great damage to the attitude of Western Canadians towards encouragement of bilingualism," he said. In reading the decision, it is clear that Justice Dickson chose to encourage bilingualism and biculturalism and to ensure respect for the rights of the francophone minority. In the sociopolitical context of the 1990s, Brian Dickson's decision could hardly have been more favourable.

"I thought the trial judge went too far, but I knew it wasn't far enough for the other side," explained Major in October 2017. "I thought that, in the Supreme Court of Canada decision, the justices wanted to make the decision they made, and I thought they ignored the facts by not accepting answers and evidence for the government's position [in debates concerning the Charter]. I believed their assessment of the government's intentions was close-minded. I thought they told themselves it was a good idea for the country, so they became politicians. I didn't think they were being intellectually honest. I didn't particularly object, but my opinion was that that wasn't what Parliament had said. I thought the Court interpreted the government's intention very broadly."

It is certainly rare for a ruling to have such a significant impact for such a long period of time. Decisions typically fade into obscurity within five or six years. Despite the fact that there have been many, many decisions concerning education rights, even Supreme Court of Canada decisions, the Mahé case is still the most frequently cited one. Children, I think that is due in very large part to Justice Dickson's clarity. Brian Dickson was not only a great jurist but a great intellectual. He wrote extremely well. He grasped the true nature of section 23 and extrapolated what needed to change in Canadian society. I think that is the essence of the Mahé affair.

★★★

Émilie and Jean-François, it is clear that Alberta in the twenty-first century has come a long way in terms of minority education. By 2018, it had four francophone school boards with a total of over forty schools. The Conseil scolaire FrancoSud alone has over 3,300 students attending fourteen francophone schools in southern Alberta. Four of those schools are Catholic, and ten of them are public.

The Conseil scolaire Centre-Nord, which includes schools in Edmonton, where the Mahé case got its start, has nineteen francophone schools and more than 3,300 students. If the Government of Alberta had known just how positive an impact the decision would have on French education in the province, it would no doubt have given Francophones the right to manage their own schools immediately. That is not what happened though. It took four years of intense negotiations between Francophones and the Province to establish a model for those school boards. To this day, the system is fragile, especially in the northwestern part of the province, in part because of demographic decline but mainly because of divisions within the francophone community.

Northwest Alberta went through some tough times when the new schools came into the picture. Some Francophones are still opposed to French-language school for religious, social, linguistic, or even just identity reasons. Petty squabbles have torn families apart because some kids do not go to immersion schools or English-language schools.

More than twenty-five years after the Supreme Court of Canada's decision in Mahé, the biggest barrier to French-language education in Alberta today is not resistance on the part of Anglophones but the attitude of Francophones themselves. From Fahler in Peace River Country to St. Isidore and Grande Prairie, the francophone Conseil scolaire du Nord-Ouest is still grappling with the same issues. The Battle of Alberta against the government was won, but there are still adversaries.

"People were working against us," said Chantal Monfette, a former school board trustee in the northwestern part of the province who spent two decades fighting for northern Alberta Francophones' rights to their own schools. "There were people who didn't believe it was a good thing. The sad thing is that it was often Francophones versus Francophones. I think it would have been easier if we had been united. Sometimes Francophones kicked us out of meetings. Those were tough times."

Teachers and principals in the region have practically worked miracles. They have to shepherd a handful of students from kindergarten to grade 12, teaching eight to ten different courses per year, all under a cloud of uncertainty because of the state of public funding and the division within the francophone community itself.

You see the same problem everywhere. I went to Nova Scotia four or five times over the years to meet with parent groups and assure them they had nothing to worry about. That is actually why I hired an expert by the name of Rodrigue Landry to help me persuade people and publish articles on the topic. He testified in court that going to French school does not prevent kids from learning English. Children, English is like the flu: you catch it by walking down the street and opening doors. I remember going to a meeting in Calgary when people were pushing for a French-language high school even though the majority of Francophones were against it. Why? People thought a bilingual school would enable kids to learn both languages. Landry explained to them that studies show better academic outcomes when a child masters one language before taking up another. Some people you can convince; others you cannot.

Any Francophones opposed to the idea can simply look at the results. They can see what happens to children who went to French school and compare that to those who chose bilingual or French immersion school. I am sure they have done better, and I guarantee you every single one of them can speak proper English.

Children, how dearly I wish I could have fought alongside you to convince Quebecois and the whole world that we are entitled to our place as Francophones in Canada. How fervently I wish I could have awakened our francophone friends to the validity of our existence. If only I could have persuaded them to unite. The war with governments is far from won, but how can a people divided be victorious?

> Children, how dearly I wish I could have fought alongside you to convince Quebecois and the whole world that we are entitled to our place as Francophones in Canada.

11
Salesman, Teacher, Bureaucrat, Lawyer

GILBERT FINN WAS A TITAN OF A MAN, a towering figure in Acadia from the 1960s through the 1980s. Finn was born in 1920 to a poor family in Inkerman on the Acadian Peninsula, and education was available to only a lucky few back then. On his fifteenth birthday, however, he received a scholarship to study at the Petit Séminaire de Chicoutimi, and that probably changed his life. Upon returning to Acadia, he embarked on a tireless war to liberate Acadians from anglophone oppression. In the 1940s and 1950s, he got involved in the Acadian cooperative movement to give Francophones opportunities to thrive economically too. That became his lifelong mission.

Finn was a friend of my father's, and the two of them regularly spent time with Martin J. Légère, the founder of Caisses populaires acadiennes, at gatherings of the Ordre de Jacques-Cartier, also known as La Patente, a secret organization whose goal was to further the interests of Catholic French Canadians.

His career was exceptional. He kept a tight rein on the Assumption Life insurance company, served as president of the Université de Moncton, and founded the Conseil économique du Nouveau-Brunswick. In 1987, he was named lieutenant-governor of New Brunswick. Finn was the son of a fisherman and a devout believer, as he demonstrated in 2008, when Canada's Governor General, Michaëlle Jean, made prominent pro-choice activist Dr. Henry Morgentaler a member of the Order of Canada. Gilbert Finn, an officer of the Order of Canada since 1979, left the order and returned his insignia. His actions were driven by his values.

His motto was simple: Do something! He did not see obstacles; he saw challenges. When I returned from Nice in the 1970s, all I wanted was to practise or teach law. Unfortunately, that did not work out for me right away. One day, feeling a little discouraged, I sat down with my father. I wanted a stimulating job that would give me a chance to put everything I had learned at law school into practice or, failing that for the time being, the kind of work that offered professional development opportunities. Community work did not interest me at all. I would not have minded doing it temporarily, maybe as an executive director developing policy, but travelling all over the place to facilitate local meetings really was not my thing. I needed a job though, a real one. My father simply said, "Go see Gilbert."

Gilbert was certainly an imposing figure. At the time, he was CEO of Assumption Life, an insurance company with deep roots in the Maritimes. The company was founded in 1903 in Waltham, Massachusetts. When Gilbert arrived in 1950, the company had seven million dollars in net assets, having taken thirty-six years to log its first million. The years 1969 to 1979 were the company's glory years. Over the decade, the value of its insurance policies grew by two hundred and fourteen million dollars, reaching eight hundred and fifty million dollars according to Finn, and its assets swelled from thirty million to eighty-four million dollars.

Assumption Life was always considered one of Acadia's most important institutions, one of a triumvirate that included the Fédération des Caisses populaires acadiennes and the Université de Moncton.

Children, I am in no way, shape, or form a salesman. I detest asking for donations, and whenever I find myself having to do so, I feel like a fraud. When I walked into Finn's office, my intention was not to ask him for a job. I was just hoping he could point me in the direction of some good job openings in the area, suggest people I could offer my services to. He looked at me with that trademark seriousness.

Eschewing preliminaries, he said, "Michel, I need you." That took me by surprise. It turned out that one of Assumption's subsidiaries wanted to apply for a cable broadcasting licence for southeastern New Brunswick, so the company was going through the process with the Canadian Radio-television and Telecommunications Commission, the CRTC, and needed a lawyer to prepare the paperwork. "You studied law; you're perfect for this. Will you do it?" asked Finn. I accepted on the spot.

I spent two or three months as project lead, making the necessary representations to the CRTC. Assumption did not get the licence, but I think Finn was satisfied with my work. I do not mean to boast, but I think he saw me as a methodical person who took the time to do things properly and in accordance with the law. When I told him I was leaving, he would not hear of it. Assumption was restructuring, trying to bring in younger people, new blood. He asked me to stay and become his assistant. I did not beat around the bush. As tactfully as possible, I told him that was not a "real" job. He sweetened the pot, asking me if I would like to be the company's sales director. The offer kind of came out of nowhere. I had no experience in that area, and I did not really like sales. I told him I did not know the first thing about it.

"Well, if you become sales director, the three guys in that department will be happy to have you on the team. They have plenty of experience, and they'll help you. They'll teach you everything you need to know. Do it for a year, and then decide," he replied.

I got to work right away, and the other employees did indeed make me feel very welcome, as did the agencies. The following year, Finn restructured the organization and gave me the VP marketing job. I told him things were moving way too fast. I was not even thirty years old, and I was going to be in charge of a whole department at the largest Acadian financial institution? What I did not know then was that Finn was going to be stepping down as CEO in a few months and wanted to make sure his successors were firmly ensconced.

I told him I could not take the job because people at the agency level would object and the Marketing Department would not be happy about it. People like Paul Arseneault, Gérard Marcoux, and Raoul Thériault were much more experienced and deserving of the position. "Look, those guys have been doing this their whole lives, and they know their stuff. They're going to say they should get the job," I said to Mr. Finn. "No, I know them, and they agree with me that we need new blood," he replied, smiling just a little.

Clearly, my career plan was turning out to be of the fly-by-the-seat-of-my-pants variety. I turned my attention to product development, strategic planning, participating in professional association meetings, negotiating with reinsurers, and dealing with the Board of Directors. I also handled negotiations with Canadian and American regulatory agencies as well as other companies and industry representatives. I worked closely with Paul Arseneault, an individual insurance pro. Gérard Marcoux took care of group insurance and did not need supervision. Raoul Thériault left shortly after I arrived to set up his own general insurance company.

Staying at Assumption Life gave me an opportunity to learn from one of the greatest CEOs New Brunswick has ever known. I learned so much from Gilbert Finn. He taught me how to work with a board of directors and how to prepare for meetings. Lots of people said he was an expert backdoor lobbyist, but that is not quite right. Everyone does a little of that, after all. That was not his preferred approach though. The Finn formula was to always be better informed than anyone else at the table and ready to answer any potential question. He had a knack for figuring out what was on people's minds. He also knew the Acadian community and the government. He was an active and well-known Conservative supporter, and most of his undertakings involved some kind of government element, such as regulatory amendments or rezoning. The government, of course, was always in the know before a given proposal was even put to the Board of Directors.

Finn was a consummate professional, a rarity among New Brunswick's businesses and associations. He had a hand in just about everything. He even headed up a group that launched a newspaper to replace L'Évangéline, the Acadian daily that ended up going out of business.

He was probably the only businessman I knew who believed that his community engagement was just as important as his role in the business world. His commitment to society's well-being was hundred percent genuine. I know he has been accused of all kinds of things over the years, especially by those critical of his methods, but his detractors did not know him as well as I did. He was perfectly sincere and never did anything for his own benefit, certainly not financially. Gilbert never earned as much as other insurance company presidents, and he spent his whole life fighting for his community.

Some Acadians thought Finn was a hard man, an iron-fisted boss with a tendency to bully. That was not at all the man I knew. He certainly did not shy away from defending his opinions, though they were not so much opinions as big ideas. He always had big ideas. He always wanted to accomplish things. For example, he was the one who came up with the idea of creating an association of Acadian business people. He thought it was of vital importance. Initially, three quarters of the people did not like the idea. Influential businessmen were afraid Francophones would cut themselves off from Anglophones and be seen as whiners, but he sold them on the value of his proposal. He set up meetings, invited the dissenters, and explained what he was trying to do. He answered every one of their questions. He said, "What are you afraid of? Why are you afraid of the Anglos? Are you worried about not being able to sell to them? Forty percent of Assumption's clients are Anglos even though I talk about Acadian issues on TV all the time." That was Gilbert Finn's brand of strength.

***

What I liked about working at Assumption was the opportunity to spearhead development initiatives. I enjoyed the internal workings of the business, the collegiality, and especially the government relations part, but working with insurance salespeople was not really my cup of tea. Actually, I loathed it. I spent three years travelling around the Maritimes and New England meeting with them, but I lacked any genuine desire to do that job. I was averse to the salespeople's money-grubbing nature, sales contests, and conventions. I really felt like a fish out of water. I spent more and more time thinking about practising law, and I realized I would have to get back to it before it was too late.

I sat down with Finn to explain my dilemma. I told him I wanted to study common law so I could work as a lawyer outside Quebec. That meant resigning from my job at Assumption so I could go study in Ottawa. He said, "I'll help you." I replied that I did not want to be beholden to Assumption. If he helped me, I would have to go back to work for the company. I was not interested in doing that. I wanted to be free. He promised I would not have to commit to anything, and he paid my tuition at the University of Ottawa. Not only that, but he also paid me a salary, and in return, I supervised the Sales Department from a distance and participated in a few important company meetings. I was never under any obligation to go back to the company or reimburse the tuition fees. Finn was a good, kind man. I will always be grateful for what he did for me in 1977.

I wanted to get through the common law program quickly. I had already done my civil law degree, so I figured it would take me a year to get my degree before taking the New Brunswick Bar exam. I applied to the University of New Brunswick, Dalhousie University, and McGill, but none of them wanted to let me do the program on my terms, so I got in touch with the University of Ottawa and went there to meet with the Dean and explain my situation. He agreed to let me do the program in a year and a half, but I said that was not good enough because it was half a year too much. He was not going to give in, so I tried to butter him up and persuade him to let me do it at my own risk. "Look, I'll do the year and a half of coursework, but I'll do it in one calendar year," I said. The problem was that there were two second-year courses that had first-year prerequisites. I told him I would do them both at the same time. The Dean would not hear of it. He told me to go talk to the Rector and see if I could convince him. Father Roger Guindon was the University of Ottawa rector at the time and a living legend in his own right. He held the position from 1964 to 1984, the longest-serving rector in the university's history. Some people thought of him as the University of Ottawa's founding father because he contributed so much to its development.

Off I went to his office to explain my situation. Eyeing me through his heavy black 1970s glasses, a hint of a smile denoting his skepticism, he said, "Do you really think you can handle fifty percent more classes while also working for Assumption Life?" Without missing a beat, I replied, "I sure can!" It was the only answer that gave me a chance to win my bet. He gave me the go-ahead and, children, I will not go into the details, but I was one of the top graduates. I do not know how I did it. I am, by nature, very focused when I am working. I also taught myself how to speed read because I wanted to spend as little time reading as possible. I never really mastered the skill, but I read a book about it, applied some of the techniques, and that helped me read faster. It is funny how so many people told me I would never make it.

When I got to Fredericton to do my bar exam, my friend Fernand Landry came to see me with an interesting proposal. Finally, there was something I could sink my teeth into.

★★★

The Université de Moncton had been looking at setting up a law school for months, years even. The Maritime Provinces Higher Education Commission, which makes recommendations to eastern Canada's four provincial governments, was studying the possibility, about which members of the academic community had strong feelings. It was also a particularly hot topic in the legal community. The Dean of Law at Queen's University, Daniel A. Soberman, was hired to do a feasibility study. In his report, he concluded that the proposal was not viable, more fantasy than reality. Meanwhile, the University of New Brunswick (UNB) was showing some interest in teaching a few courses in French. UNB had always been against Moncton setting up a faculty of law and devoted significant resources to preventing it. It was kind of like what had happened fifteen years before, when UNB vehemently opposed the creation of the Université de Moncton on the grounds that New Brunswick did not have room for a francophone university. In contrast, Mount Allison University "produced an absolutely extraordinary positive submission about how Acadians needed a university," recalled Yvon Fontaine, the Université de Moncton Rector from 2000 to 2012.

I was not at the Université de Moncton at the time, but I paid close attention to the debate. Public meetings were held, and I know some people were worried the faculty might have a negative impact on the university's resources.

"Even Francophones practising law in Moncton didn't believe in it. Even Court of Queen's Bench Justice Adrien Cormier wasn't on board!" said Joe Daigle, who would himself go on to become New Brunswick's chief justice in 1998. Interestingly, the Faculty of Law is actually housed in a building named after, of all people, Adrien-J. Cormier. Anyway... Although the debate was public, much of it took place behind the scenes. I was not directly involved, but in Moncton everyone knew everything. Opponents included Justice Guy A. Richard, a close friend of Justice Cormier, and Roméo LeBlanc, a federal MP and Minister of Fisheries under Pierre Elliott Trudeau.

"At the time, people thought the Université de Moncton wouldn't be able to support a faculty of law and that it would be better for the province to focus on UNB and keep everyone together," said Law Professor Michel Doucet. "I remember talking to lawyers and some judges who said it wouldn't work at Moncton and UNB was the place."

Roméo LeBlanc actually never publicly supported the School of Law. I have been told that Université de Moncton Rector Jean Cadieux was a strong supporter though, and that he asked Joe Daigle to draft a response to the

Soberman report. The assignment was so hush-hush that Joe went to his cottage for a week to write the report, which Jean Cadieux used in his representations to the Maritime Provinces Higher Education Commission. The Commission was powerful, and governments rarely made major changes without its support. It approved the proposal, but then the Hatfield government had to make the necessary funds available. There was a big debate at the provincial level, but in the end it went ahead. Hatfield decided he would do everything in his power to get the faculty off the ground because it would be concrete evidence of New Brunswick's linguistic duality. Some people said that Gilbert Finn, who was close to Hatfield, put pressure on the government. That would not surprise me, but I do not know if it is true. The federal government got involved too, granting the Université de Moncton one million dollars to build the law library.

After all that, people had to move fast to get the school up and running. Jean Cadieux tasked Fernand Landry with finding a dean and professors.

★★★

I ended up spending five very full years at the Université de Moncton's Faculty of Law. We had to start from scratch. For example, I helped develop a French common law lexicon, which was the first of its kind anywhere. We had to prepare courses, recruit professors and students, obtain bar accreditations, and establish relationships with other law schools, the Department of Justice, and the courts. Our core mission was to train socially engaged legal practitioners, always bearing in mind that our main goal was to ensure access to justice for Francophones in general and access to the profession for students. "We knew we needed to create a French common law vocabulary as well as advance linguistic rights," said Michel Doucet. "That was every professor's mission. Everyone knew that was the goal. One area in which we needed to make progress was French legal terminology."

I became dean of the Faculty of Law in its second year. The first dean, a civil lawyer from Sherbrooke by the name of Pierre Patenaude, never got used to the environment. He devoted a lot of energy and hard work to building the school. When he left, he told us it was because of the Anglophones at the Bar and the Department of Justice and their attitude. Nobody believed him.

When I took the job, I was determined to continue teaching a solid course load while running the school without a vice-dean. Resources were tight, and I wanted to bring all my influence to bear on setting up a demanding program even though I expected a number of students to fail. The program had to be tough to be taken seriously. Unfortunately, some of the fifty or so people who signed up had not been in school for a while, so that was a challenge on top of the fact that studying law is inherently difficult. Some of those students were successful anyway; others were not. Some of them thought I was making their lives difficult on purpose, but that was not the case at all. I wanted to help all of them succeed, but I did not want to compromise the quality of the program. Overall, I found the university to be sorely lacking in rigour, though there were some exceptions. There were very few professional programs, and hardly anyone understood their ins and outs. That meant we had to recruit nationally, build a specialized library, and offer attractive compensation to compete with the University of New Brunswick and especially the University of Ottawa, which offered some courses in French. It was a major challenge getting the administration to accept that, even though we did not have a lot of students, some of them were bound to fail.

I think jealousy within the institution itself had a real impact. The Academic Senate wanted to close our library, and that led to a deeply acrimonious internal battle. The university also refused to grant the Law School faculty status. Salary bonuses for lawyer-professors were never adequate or even reasonable. Grappling with all these difficulties, I demanded the administration's unwavering support, but I was denied. That is when I began to butt heads with Gilbert Finn, then rector of the university. We always maintained a sense of mutual respect and collegiality, but we certainly clashed at times.

Despite all those obstacles, the school trained leaders for Canada's francophone community outside Quebec and made a significant contribution to the university's vitality. Access to justice was greatly improved, and that was a real accomplishment. The Law School proved its fiercest adversaries wrong, starting with the author of the report cited by those opposed to the undertaking.

"I met Professor Soberman in an elevator in Montréal one day, and he stopped the elevator to tell me, 'That was one of the biggest mistakes I ever made'," said Yvon Fontaine. Indeed, the Law School, which eventually became a faculty, is to this day a global leader. It has proven that it is possible to teach common law in French.

One thing the school's success enabled me to do was participate in an exchange program involving universities and the federal government, which was looking to recruit senior executives.

★★★

When I left the Law School, I had to find a career-advancing job, so I went to Ottawa to become the director general for the promotion of official languages at the Secretary of State of Canada, which has since become the Department of Canadian Heritage. There was a federal program at the time that gave academics a chance to do an internship with the government, after which they could apply for government jobs or go back to their university. I was certainly happy that the Law School had gotten off the ground, but I was somewhat dissatisfied with my own career progress. On the whole, I did not find teaching fulfilling, and I was hoping for a more intellectually vibrant environment and opportunities for multidisciplinary research. I think I had been carrying around a pretty romanticized view of academia and scholarly work itself my whole life because I had read biographies of some of the leading legal figures at Cambridge, Oxford, and Harvard, so I had these notions of what their lives were like. At that point in my life, I was still trying to figure out what kind of work would fulfill my ambitions, what kind of socially significant work I could do.

I had a two-year term at the Secretary of State, and I was tasked with overhauling the official language minority community support program and turning it into a more effective community development tool. The next step would be to land a high-level job at the Department of Justice.

Initially, my job was to focus on implementing institutional structures and federal-provincial government collaborations, things like community education centres. Enthusiasm was high going in, but a federal election brought the work to a halt before we achieved any positive outcomes. The new Mulroney government decided to freeze all budgets for a year and conduct a comprehensive evaluation of every single department. I was administering grants to minority communities and provincial governments, so I could not just sit around doing nothing.

One significant legal task I handled during my time at the Secretary of State was preparing a bill subjecting the Northwest Territories and, later on, Yukon, to the same linguistic requirements as the federal government. I travelled to the Far North several times to gain a better understanding of how the measures I intended to put forward would be implemented.

While I was in the position, a notorious incident occurred when the federal government got involved in a school management trial in the Ontario Court of Appeal. That court was the first to recognize that members of the province's linguistic minority had the right to meaningful participation in the management of French-language schools. Acting as an intervener, Canada's Minister of Justice submitted a factum expressing opposition to recognizing the minority's right to manage its schools. I read the factum and immediately notified the Deputy Minister, Huguette Labelle, and through her Canada's Secretary of State, Serge Joyal. Joyal challenged the Department of Justice's position and asked me to produce another factum. In the end, Joyal had to ask Prime Minister Trudeau to withdraw the Department of Justice's factum and submit mine instead. There has always been some tension between those two federal departments, and I am afraid nothing has changed in that regard.

In the months that followed, I went through the whole process to land the assistant deputy minister of public law job at the Department of Justice. I did the interviews, met all the requirements, and was told everything looked good. Then one day, I was informed that the government had decided to reserve all available senior executive positions for women. Still licking my wounds, I took a job at the University of Ottawa as associate dean of the Faculty of Law's Common Law Section. The faculty wanted me to set up a French common law program like the one in Moncton.

Some Acadians saw my move to the University of Ottawa as a betrayal of the Université de Moncton. I do not share that view. Ontario was in dire need of jurists to defend the seven-hundred-thousand-plus members of its francophone minority. Even though many of the students at the Université de Moncton were from Alberta, Manitoba, and Ontario, the university eventually realized it could never fulfill that mission on its own. I maintained close ties to the Faculty of Law in Moncton and occasionally taught courses there. I also contributed to the work of the International Observatory on Language Rights, and I was deeply touched when the Université de Moncton announced in 1998 that the faculty's library would be named after me.

I do not have much to say about my time at the University of Ottawa's Faculty of Law. It was not as memorable as my time in Moncton, though I did have the pleasure of working with Louise Charron, a consummate professional who joined me on the Supreme Court of Canada bench two decades later, and with many other talented young professors. There was a kind of rivalry between the English common law program and the French one; the latter was still finding its feet. The biggest issue was financial: the Anglophones were worried that funding allocated to Francophones could affect them in the long term even though the whole undertaking was very thoroughly arranged and special funding was obtained. The Faculty Council finally agreed to the proposal and presented it to the Academic Senate, which rejected it despite generous funding from the Government of Ontario. I gave a second presentation and requested an opportunity to explain the proposal to the Board of Governors, but that too was rejected. I no longer had any reason to remain with the faculty, so I resigned.

During my two years at the Faculty of Law, I also started a part-time legal practice. I focused on language rights and developed a particular fondness for pleading cases. I worked on Mahé in Alberta and Mercure in Saskatchewan, and I led the second phase of the *Reference re Manitoba Language Rights*. All those cases were heard by the Supreme Court of Canada. I became truly passionate about practising law in court. One day, another lawyer named Roger Tassé called me up. Children, the very memory of that call still fills me with joy. Tassé and I had known each other for years. We had worked together when I was at the SNA and during the constitutional negotiations. He was a deputy minister during my stint in the federal government. Together with Paul LaBarge and another guy named Eddie Goldenberg, who was Jean Chrétien's right-hand man, Tassé invited me to join the firm of Lang Michener Lash Johnson.

I spearheaded a number of important cases at Lang Michener, and I enjoyed pleading on a more regular basis. Unfortunately, I really did not like the whole business side of things, and I had a hard time bringing home a regular paycheque. That is a big problem for someone living month to month. Many of my clients were minority rights defence groups with limited financial resources. I had clients in six provinces and one territory, all of them dependent on the court challenges program. Practising law was gratifying. I loved pleading cases and drafting factums, but I was the only person in the office working in that particular field, so I felt quite isolated. Except for a few cases with Hackland and LaBarge and the time our firm represented Grand Chief Mike Mitchell of the Akwesasne reserve, there was not much in the way of diversity. The firm was totally obsessed with billing, and it did not take me long to realize I was not very popular. I worked on subsidized cases at reduced rates subject to maximums. The day it was announced that I had won a case at the Supreme Court of Canada, I got a message from head office in Toronto notifying me that I had not hit my monthly billing targets.

I also had to deal with the fact that my work forced me to be away from home a lot. We had lost you a few years earlier, Jean-François, and I hated leaving Yolande alone with you, Émilie. Around then, a crisis at Lang Michener resulted in about twenty of the twenty-six Ottawa-based lawyers resigning. A few months earlier, some Assumption Life executives had come to see me. Their proposal could not have been better timed.

12

Assumption

I WAS PERPLEXED. There I was in Ottawa, face to face with the President and CEO of Assumption Life. I actually knew Gilbert Doucet quite well and had enjoyed our time together at the Société des Acadiens du Nouveau-Brunswick. He was an upstanding man, somewhat more reserved than Gilbert Finn, but he knew the business inside out. He was trying to win me over. "You know the company, Michel. You know our values," he said. Gilbert had not come to offer me a job on a silver platter. He was not actually promising me anything, but he was on a mission. Another candidate, Rino Volpé, was currently the vice-president of subsidiaries and was aggressively pursuing the prestigious position.

"We hired a headhunter, but even before that, we had Michel in mind. We knew him well, and we knew what he could do. We wanted a visionary for the company. We also wanted someone who knew Assumption. Michel was a hard worker and a brilliant man, and the fact that he was well versed in the law gave him a clear advantage over the other contenders," explained Gilbert Doucet.

Émilie, our family situation forced me to make changes in my professional life. Jean-François, you had left us a few years before, and your mother was in a dark place. She would never admit it, but I was pretty sure she was depressed. Yolande was dead set against my taking the job. She reminded me that I was not a businessman, pointed out that I would hate the job because I was meant to be in the legal field, noted that I knew hardly anyone in Ottawa, and said I certainly would not get into notarial law. If I was going to continue practising law, it would be constitutional law, which, unfortunately, was not exactly an everyday thing in the national capital. There were not that many cases, and, for the most part, they took place all across the country. Your mother and I really did not see eye to eye on that.

"Going to work for Assumption in New Brunswick was not a good idea," she explained some thirty years later. "It wasn't even remotely his field. I watched him work on his cases and work with people, and it was good for him because he was fighting for causes that really mattered to Francophones. Winning cases was extremely important to us. I absolutely wanted it to work, and I knew he was good at it. It may have been one of the most prestigious jobs in New Brunswick, but I wasn't interested in the prestige or the job. What mattered to me was that he wouldn't be practising law."

The worst part was that I myself was not so sure it was a good idea. Would I like it? I did not know. I had left Assumption a decade earlier because I did not like the salesman's lifestyle. I was not thrilled about getting back into it. Insurance agents and I had zero in common. I had nothing to say to them, and the job description was off-putting. I said as much to Gilbert Doucet, and he said, "Listen Michel, Paul Arseneault will handle that stuff. You won't have to bother with it. All you need to do is look at the monthly report." Like it was no big deal, he was trying to convince me that I would not have anything to do with that aspect of the business. He had my number. What I was really interested in was running a big company, having that decision-making power, and making my mark by getting some significant projects up and running.

Law was still my priority though. I was happy practising. I liked defending my clients in court. I occasionally indulged in visions of myself as a judge someday, but what I really loved was spending time in courthouses and debating.

"We talked about it," said my old colleague, Paul LaBarge. "Whenever you see a good lawyer with an academic background handling cases that have to do with public policy, you have to wonder if he's interested. Well, he was. He had that mindset; he wanted to change things. And you have more scope for that when you're the one seated on the bench then when you're the one standing in front of it. He may not have talked about that ambition openly, but he was already behaving like a judge, even in the way he dealt with his clients."

My ambitions notwithstanding, there was a problem. I was an Acadian living in Ontario. Yes, I was surrounded by influential jurists, some of whom would get provincial judicial appointments, but nobody knew me or had even heard of me. Plus, I had spent more time in classrooms than in courtrooms. There was nothing special about me, especially in a province like Ontario, which had thousands of likely candidates.

I had to make a decision. Leaving law for the corporate world was not particularly appealing, but life is full of surprises. When a crisis arose at Lang Michener, lots of lawyers fled the ship. I was ready to go back home with you, Émilie, and your mother. I finally felt ready to provide you with some stability. I picked up the phone and called Doucet to let him know I would be applying. I became the president and CEO of Assumption Life in 1989. When they informed me I was hired, I told the board I would do it on one condition: I would do it for five years, max.

★★★

One of the reasons Gilbert Doucet came to see me and pressured me to apply was that the only other possible candidate was Rino Volpé, and there were mixed feelings about him. The Board of Directors was divided. Rino was an exuberant man full of big ideas. That appealed to some of the board members but worried others.

After I got the job, I asked Rino to meet with me. Rumour had it, I asked him to resign, but that is not true. I wanted to make sure we were still on good terms. I believe the feeling was mutual. I wanted to understand how he envisioned his contribution to the company. Right away, he said, "If I stay, I'll be handling my branch my way." Basically, he wanted to run his own company within the one I was now in charge of. The branch had a board of directors, and he went on to say, "The board will answer to me, not to you." That struck me as unrealistic. You see, a board of directors does not answer to an executive; it is actually the other way around. His plan was to appoint the board members himself. That was out of the question. I told him Assumption was going to have one president, not two. If he wanted to stay, he would have to do things my way. Getting the company's house in order was one of my top priorities. That is what the board expected, and I could not in good conscience run a company that did not uphold an acceptable standard of professionalism. Contrary to popular belief, Rino and I never fought. We disagreed on how to proceed, and he decided to leave Assumption.

On day one in my new job, I started reorganizing the management team. I asked Paul Arseneault to be my right-hand man. He was a man of integrity for whom I had enormous respect. I knew him from my first stint at Assumption, and I was sure he would be outstanding as our VP marketing. As I was scrutinizing the company's affairs, I realized we needed to change its actuaries. We were spending a fortune on contracts with consultants in Montréal. If I learned one thing at Assumption Life, it is that nobody bills more than an actuary. I wanted to scale back our dependence on them so that our Montréal contracts would be for actuarial examinations only.

That meant finding someone who could do product development and all the work internally. We had to come out on top in an extremely competitive market. I immediately started learning about actuarial science and product development. Most importantly, I learned how to make money. My assessment made it clear that we would not make money anytime soon if we did not change our products, keeping in mind that new products would take five to seven years to become profitable.

The company was very solid and stable, but it was making hardly any money—only one million dollars in annual profit. That was well beneath my expectations because it should have been generating at least six or seven million dollars given the value of its assets. At one meeting, I announced to the employees that our goal was to boost annual profits to five or six million dollars as soon as possible. Together with the new actuary I had just recruited, we focused on diversifying our product line and analyzing what was not working. We obviously needed two or three new money-making products, but we also needed to undertake a general analysis of best practices in the insurance world. What was hot? Were our products passé? Were our sales tactics too old-fashioned? Employees came up with ideas that were basically copy-pasting what the rest of the industry was doing. New products were largely made up of investments.

In the past, insurance companies sold "whole life" policies good for up to ninety-nine years. Clients paid their premiums, and when they died, that was it. Newer schemes included a savings component that transferred dividends or money paid in addition to the premium into a savings account. The advantage was that it was not taxed as ordinary income. Every company started developing that kind of product, so we created our own version, which we called "SecuriFlex," a pretty strange name in my opinion. We started selling it, and our revenue shot up exponentially, so instead of hiring new salespeople, we authorized brokers to sell these products for us.

At the time, we had maybe 150 employees at Assumption and another two hundred or so in our branches. We also had about one hundred full-time insurance agents and a few brokers. By the time I left, we had far more employees and far fewer insurance agents. An industry-wide shift was underway in the early 1990s.

★★★

I was determined to move the company forward, and I thought we could make more money by devoting our energy to group insurance. I set up a meeting with Premier Frank McKenna and his people and told him we wanted government contracts. My relationship with the Premier was strained. Neither our interests nor our temperaments were aligned. I harboured a deep dislike for politicians like him, for whom the end often justified the means. That kind of thing bothered me. We at Assumption wanted to administer pension funds and sell disability insurance, so I saw the provincial government as a potential client, but I knew that Blue Cross, which also had an office on Moncton's Main Street, had almost all the government's group insurance contracts. I put a lot of pressure on the government to be fair and give us our piece of the pie. My friend, Fernand Landry, was the premier's chief of staff at the time, and I called on him to make it happen. I was very impatient. He did end up helping us a little with assistance from Minister Raymond Frenette. McKenna and I were often at odds, but I finally won a few contracts, and we quintupled our group insurance sales.

About a year after I arrived, I could see that our new products were generating more cash. We were not making money on premiums though. We were making it on capital, the money we held on behalf of our policy holders. I got my team together, and I realized we were getting actuaries, who were not investment experts, to manage that capital. I wanted us to do the investing ourselves, professionally, for us and for a new client base. The board asked me to award a contract to Montréal's Bolton Tremblay to manage our investment fund. I strongly disagreed with the idea. Sure, it would be easy to delegate that task to an established firm, but then the firm would make money, not us. I argued that we should create our own investment firm. That would make us more independent and free to do as we wished. They did not all agree with me, that is for sure.

I went ahead anyway. I started looking for small investment firms we could take over and integrate into the Assumption Life fold. I made an offer to a Halifax firm, and it looked like the transaction would be approved, but the deal fell apart. I was getting impatient. Time was money, and we were losing a lot by not being in full control of our investments. I then met with six or seven big investment firms in Québec City and Ottawa, including Banque Nationale, Desjardins, Bolton Tremblay, Jarislowsky, and two others. I did not want them to manage our capital per se; I wanted them to work with us to create a company of which we would each own fifty percent. We would leverage their investment know-how and contribute our marketing expertise. Those negotiations ate up a lot of my time, and it was all for naught in the end. The company directors were getting frustrated; they thought I had spent way too much time on the whole thing.

While I was working on that, I discovered that two big insurance companies in Quebec were on the ropes. I went to see the senior executives at one of them, Les Coopérants, and we discussed various scenarios. I negotiated the purchase of an American portfolio that would have been a very good fit for us, but the company went bankrupt before we could finalize an agreement. I also met with Bolton Tremblay executives once, and they were on board with my original suggestion, going fifty-fifty on a new investment company. That is how Placements Louisbourg was born. I named it in honour of Acadia. Over time, Louisbourg became fully independent, though it has always been an Assumption subsidiary.

"Setting up a sort of independent entity was an excellent move," said former Assumption Life CEO, André Vincent, in May 2018. "Creating a spin-off was a great idea. Twenty-seven years on, Louisbourg is standing on its own two feet, managing $2.3 billion in assets and drawing less than twenty-five percent of its revenue from Assumption. Initially, Louisbourg was funded almost exclusively by Assumption, and its mandate was to grow. I'd say it succeeded."

That project was two years in the making. At the same time, Assumption's annual revenues hit five million dollars. I could easily have doubled that by making slight changes to reinsurance, which is what my successor did. Louisbourg's trajectory is now similar to Assumption's. No longer just a regional player, it is going national. Ever since the 2010s, Louisbourg has done business with clients in Ontario, Quebec, and even Western Canada. Early on, the firm specialized primarily in institutional management—managing assets for retirement funds and foundations. Now a significant slice of its revenue comes from private wealth management.

***

Founded in the United States, Assumption Life, in the 1990s, still had deep roots in New England and the states of New Hampshire, Connecticut, Massachusetts, and Rhode Island. I looked at the demographic situation in the Maritimes and what we were bringing in from Quebec and Ontario, and I concluded the U.S. market was particularly promising.

Once again, I convened my inner circle. I told them I wanted us to acquire Mountain States Life, which was based in New Mexico. My intention was to buy up small companies from the Cajuns in Louisiana and merge them with Mountain States to create a company as big as Assumption Life, but I did not have time to do it. The company directors at the time lacked an entrepreneurial spirit and were concerned about the company's geographical location. Also, the first Cajun companies I approached agreed to the deal, but their terms were very restrictive. The main issue was relocating employees at head offices in Louisiana who did not want to move to New Mexico. I was ready to compromise and set up a two-office system: one for sales and marketing in Louisiana and one for general administration in New Mexico. It would have been a good arrangement.

Unfortunately, both the U.S. companies and Assumption's Board of Directors started getting cold feet. The Louisianans did not think my proposal covered all the bases. That is the difference between success and failure. When I set out to create Louisbourg, I did my homework. My plan was unassailable. There was a lot of resistance, of course. The directors were very apprehensive, but the proposal was so airtight thanks to expert handling of every last detail that they had no choice but to approve it. It turned out to be a huge success; Louisbourg now makes more money than Assumption.

I have no doubt the American venture would have paid off in the long run, but my successor, Denis Losier, put an end to the expansion in the mid-2000s, and the U.S. operation is no more. Assumption Life appears to have disowned its American roots.

"Pulling out was the right decision because we were too small to diversify or expand," said André Vincent, who took over from Losier. "Things are probably better now that we've narrowed our focus to the Canadian market. Everyone was expanding left and right back then. Companies were trying to extend their reach, but we were a much more regional player in Acadia."

I disagree with Mr. Vincent. At the time, we were doing a lot of business in New England, but sales started to slide. The Board of Directors did not want to invest in developing that market, so we were steadily losing value and equity in the United States. Had we generated new business in New Mexico, we could have managed it together with our Boston affairs, adding value to the portfolio there, but we started selling insurance policies to reinsurers to drive profit, and volume was pointless. Either we invested in the United States or we pulled out; we could not have it both ways. The board was always indecisive, and, in the end, my successor opted to pull out.

★★★

In his memoirs, Gilbert Finn wrote, "As we all know, Assumption Life must remain the property of the Acadian people. Its institutional mission, role and image must always reflect that reality. It must not become consumed by the pursuit and accumulation of profit; that would undermine its very identity. The founders of the Société l'Assomption and their successors have always prioritized the well-being of the Société's members, the education of young people and the betterment of Acadia."

Throughout my tenure at Assumption Life, I always felt it was my duty to stand up for Acadians' interests and be visible in the community. That included having a media presence to comment on issues of the day. Our organization was unique. It was not just an insurance company; it was an institution with a social mission to advocate for the interests of minority Francophones.

The organization has changed so much that I hardly recognize it. Losier, who took over when I left in 1994, had been a minister under McKenna. He made a point of engaging in public debate and ensuring the organization played an active role in defending Acadians' interests and protecting the French language. He demonstrated outstanding leadership in that regard, but his successor seems to have abandoned that part of the job. Assumption's sole focus is now on business, and I believe its role as a member of society has taken a back seat. Before the City of Moncton dropped Assumption Life as its broker and handed its investment portfolio over to foreign entities, some of them American, I do not remember ever hearing Vincent say a single word about anything to do with the Acadian community or language issues.

Vincent explained it like this: "I saw this kind of thing in other organizations, such as Mouvement Desjardins, where I worked for five years around the time of the Quebec referendum. Desjardins's president spoke publicly about issues, and that really hurt the organization's growth prospects outside Quebec. It set them back at least five years. That was over twenty years ago, and at the time I was in an executive position with one of Mouvement Desjardins's subsidiaries. I was responsible for creating the organization's national platform for my sector, retirement funds and group insurance. I can tell you that Claude Béland's positions really messed things up for us for about three years. Based on my experience, I decided not to mix politics and business."

Vincent went on to say that he did champion Acadia by creating a corporate social responsibility program. We did not have that program back in my day, but our donations and sponsorship program had the same mission: to be a presence in the community and a good corporate citizen.

If not for the Université de Moncton, what institutional bastion would we have had in Acadia in the 2010s? I honestly have no idea. As CEO, Gilbert Finn used his platform to support Radio-Canada, education, economic development, and federal subsidies. When Vincent took the helm, Acadian-ness fell by the wayside. Under him, Assumption's sole purpose became to make money. Revenue generation was its vision, mission, and mandate. Community involvement was essentially a marketing campaign. The same thing happened with the Fédération des Caisses populaires acadiennes, which ditched its name to water down its identity and make a bid for broader appeal. It is now UNI Financial Cooperation. Sadly, the Université de Moncton is now the last holdout.

★★★

January 7, 2000, was a day like any other. It was a week after the new millennium dawned. The Y2K bug never caused the chaos people had feared. Beverley McLachlin took over from Antonio Lamer as chief justice of the Supreme Court, and all of us judges would go through a fairly orderly transition. But that day, I got a fax that instantly grabbed my attention. The Louisbourg Investments logo emerged from the machine. Instinctively, I wondered if there was some kind of problem with my investments. Laboriously, the machine went on printing. It was a letter from Martin Boudreau, the company's VP and general manager.

"Hello Michel," it read. "Happy new year! Just thought you'd like to know... Louisbourg Investments (Assets under management)—$1,004,763,533—Our first billion. Seven full-time employees and one million dollars+ in pre-tax profits. Quite the creation!"

I was speechless. It took a minute for that to sink in. A company's first billion was a pretty big deal. I replied that, despite the passage of time, I had never quite convinced myself that my tenure as head of Assumption was all that meaningful. Yes, we modernized our services, restructured, got our finances in order, and refinanced our real estate subsidiaries, but our attempts at repositioning in the United States and Quebec failed, as did our move to reorganize the agency system. I went on to say that I still believed greater solidarity within our sales force and a more engaged board would have made all that possible. I took comfort in the knowledge that we created Louisbourg, not only because of its success, but because we built it in spite of the board, the government, and our own financial services. We pulled together its first significant assets by dint of hard work, against all odds and with no support whatsoever.

I still believe that to this day. Louisbourg was my crowning achievement at Assumption Life. Even so, I think my decision to join the iconic Acadian enterprise was a bad one. Despite my intention, I never managed to distance myself from sales and product development. Opportunities to delegate in that regard were limited, and salespeople took up a lot of my time. Our actuarial resources could not get the job done without help from consultants. Had it been up to me, we would have grown through mergers and acquisitions, and I worked hard to make that happen, but the company was still too small.

I did not have the right temperament, and I was naive to think I could forsake my true vocation: the law. Once again, children, your mother was right.

Politics

CHILDREN, when I am home on the weekend and the phone rings, I know that is probably my cue to lace up my walking shoes right away. It is often a familiar voice on the other end of the line saying, "Michel, are you ready for our walk?" Once or twice a week, schedules permitting, off we go for a vigorous walk. We might spend hours every month wandering around Ottawa's Rockcliffe Park, talking about anything and everything: hockey, the weather, the Maritimes, vacations, business trips, American politics from Clinton and Bush to Obama and Trump, Europe, and, often, the Francophonie. Two old friends chatting away.

We must have gotten into the habit of meeting up sometime between 2008 and 2014 when we were both at Heenan Blaikie. His political career was behind him, and I had just retired from the Supreme Court of Canada. I had a lot more free time than when I was on the bench. As counsel, I did not have to stay on top of cases like associate lawyers. We were just there to support them, provide them with some perspective on the law, and offer advice.

The man who would become my walking mate was starting to get bored at work, and when nobody went to see him, he started coming to see me. We chitchatted. Then we started having breakfast together. Eventually we became friends. We lived near one another, and our wives also got along well.

My friend was honest and intelligent, and he had a fantastic sense of humour. In the fall of 2018 I stopped by his place, and he showed me a book about Francophones in the United States. The history of the French language in New Hampshire and around Boston, Massachusetts, with Jack Kerouac and his crowd, the beat generation, really made an impression on him.

He told me about a story he had read about George Washington's defeat in a conflict with what would become Canada and the important role that Francophones played in that battle. At that time, there was a debate going on in the United States about whether it would be worth trying to annex Canada and make North America into one single country. Apparently there were also discussions about what language people would speak if that happened. He was quite enthused about that chapter in history.

That was the backdrop to his appearance on Radio-Canada's popular TV variety show, *Tout le monde en parle*, to promote his latest book. Seated to his right was

When I went to work at Heenan Blaikie, I befriended the man whose government appointed me to the Supreme Court, Prime Minister Jean Chrétien. Every Sunday since 2017, we have gone for a weekly walk together. Yolande and Aline also developed a lovely friendship over the years.
Source: Collection of Michel Bastarache.

Denise Bombardier, who pelted him with compliments and criticism by turns throughout the interview. Ms. Bombardier, a journalist, had impeccable French. She also had a reputation for being intelligent and outspoken, and she was no doubt keen on some verbal sparring with my friend, yes, Jean Chrétien.

It was actually Serge Fiori, the lead vocalist for Harmonium, an iconic Quebec band from the 1970s, who got the ball rolling with a deeply heartfelt question: "Why not consider Quebec to be a country? Why can't you see Quebec's beauty as a country with its own language, culture, institutions, and resources? I just don't understand." "Precisely because you don't agree with me," replied

Jean Chrétien. "Canada is the reason you speak French today. Francophones in Louisiana are practically extinct. My father spent the first ten years of his life in Manchester, New Hampshire. Francophones in the northern U.S. have disappeared. The language has disappeared."

That is when things went off the rails. Denise Bombardier offered up a fine bit of sociological analysis, stating, "French no longer exists outside Quebec."

I expected Jean to bring up landmark moments in his political career: the adoption of the *Official Languages Act*, which he supported in the House of Commons in 1969, and the adoption of section 23 of the Charter, which was no doubt one of his greatest legacies. I figured he would talk about the success of French-language and immersion schools across the country. He would prove we were not dead. But he did not. He pointed to the Franco-American experience. He said French would have ceased to exist if not for Canada because the fact was that French was disappearing in the United States. His book was still top of mind, apparently, but that was not the best argument.

A few days later, we were out for a walk, and he knew very well he should not have played that card. "What would you have said to Fiori?" he asked me. I was pleased that he wanted my opinion. I would have said that what matters is for Quebec to have the opportunity to advance as a French-speaking society with a French culture. That is what matters most, and it is perfectly feasible within federalism. We have plenty of evidence. It is also important to remember that not all Francophones are in Quebec; more than a million of them live outside Quebec. Secession would be a death sentence for a million Canadian Francophones.

"And what would you have said to Bombardier?" he asked. I would have told her to check her facts and try to understand them. Children, when I argued Mahé in the 1980s, there was one French-language school in Alberta. Now there are about forty. A considerable number of francophone children attend French schools across Canada. As to Bombardier's suggestion that no Anglophones speak French, people need to know that has absolutely no basis in fact. That is another misconception. Now, there has not been as much progress on that front as we would like, and

> I would have said that what matters is for Quebec to have the opportunity to advance as a French-speaking society with a French culture. That is what matters most.

immersion schools have not produced the desired outcomes, but to conclude that it was a pointless exercise is unacceptable. Knowledge of the facts is crucial to an intelligent debate, but in Bombardier's case, even laying out all the facts in meticulous detail would not have convinced her we were not dead ducks.

***

In the late 1970s, I was deeply involved in fighting for minority Francophones. I was politically active only insofar as I worked with advocacy groups across Canada. I personally leaned Liberal, but I was open to working with governments formed by either major party. In 1978, Joe Daigle, my old boss from back when I was translating New Brunswick's laws, became the leader of the province's Liberal Party. Joe was in a tricky situation because the Progressive Conservative Premier could easily be mistaken for a Liberal. As a candidate, Richard Hatfield was more liberal than the Liberals in many ways, especially when it came to Acadians. As a francophone leader after the Robichaud years, Daigle felt obligated to seek the support of anglophone voters in the southern part of the province and around Fredericton.

One day, his campaign manager, my good friend Fernand Landry, came to see me for help developing a language rights policy. I was not a party member and I definitely was not involved in the campaign. I had been saying for years that I wanted to be a constitutionalist, which meant I had to remain independent. Like many scholars in all kinds of fields to this day, I agreed to advise the political party on one condition: my name could not show up anywhere. I never wanted to be associated with either the Liberals or the Conservatives. A few years later, I worked with the New Brunswick Conservatives on Bill 88, the linguistic duality bill, but that is when they were the governing party. I told Fernand I did not want anyone talking about my involvement with the party.

Fernand and I went to the Liberal Party war room in Fredericton. As always, I was well prepared and had five or six important francophone-focused action items that I strongly believed should be in the platform. The current premier had finally given us francophone school boards, and I thought the Liberals should keep going on that trajectory.

I do not remember the details of my demands, but I am sure they were similar to what was in the report I wrote four years later about linguistic duality in New Brunswick. I sensed resistance around the table right away. I was told the party would campaign for sound governance and good government. I pointed out that this was not why they had asked for my help. Fine by me if that was their approach, but I was there to make sure the minority got its piece of the pie. The Liberals wasted no time making it clear to me that the province's Anglophones, including those in the Liberal Party, would not appreciate my suggestions.

I told them I wanted to talk to Daigle right away because I wanted to know if I was wasting my time. I wanted to make sure the would-be premier, an Acadian to boot, was going to be decisive on this issue, which was the only reason I had driven two hours to be there.

Daigle came over to join us, and the discussion lasted five minutes. "No! There's no way we're campaigning as a nationalist party!" I turned to Landry and told him there was no point in my being there. Their minority issues agenda was more conservative than the Conservatives'! I told them I could not keep working with them. Before leaving, I took Landry aside and told him not to bother trying to win over the people of Woodstock, who would never vote Liberal anyway. It was a Conservative stronghold, and whether they were angry with the Liberals or not would make no difference on polling day.

"You know nothing about politics!" was his reply. I readily conceded my incompetence, but I made no bones about the fact that plenty of people would never vote for a party that was afraid. In the end, Joe Daigle lost the 1978 election by two seats. He even lost seats in francophone ridings.

The worst part is that the Liberals believed me, but they were not ready to stand up for their own ideas and convictions. In my view, what was the point of being in power if you promised to do nothing? That is when I knew for certain I would never get into politics.

"He told me he would be interested [in running]," insisted Daigle forty years later. "We talked about it, and he was very, very interested. He was ready to take the plunge, but then something happened career-wise, and he wasn't as open to the idea [...]. He definitely expressed an interest, and I was very much in favour of it. Michel was a real go-getter, so he would have been a major asset."

That is not quite how I remember it. I probably told him I would have liked a cabinet portfolio and that I was interested in getting into politics. That is true. The appeal of being a minister is that you can influence the government. Back then, I was naive and inexperienced, but I was never ready to take the plunge, largely because of our family situation. Plus, I am sure I would have found partisanship intensely irritating. Your mother was not very open to the idea either. I actually promised her I would not go there, not under Joe Daigle or Richard Hatfield, though both Jean-Maurice Simard and Hatfield asked me to run. Leading up to the 1982 election, Premier Hatfield insisted that I run in Dieppe. I was not interested, but my brother Marc, who was a Radio-Canada journalist at the time, heard rumours that I would be running in the riding of Caraquet, where Yolande was from. There was no truth to those rumours.

After I turned him down, Hatfield asked me if I wanted to be assistant deputy minister at the Department of Justice. Again I said no. When he asked me if I would work for the government in any capacity, I said sure, but as deputy minister, not assistant deputy minister. He balked at that and tried to sell me on the idea that being assistant deputy minister would prepare me to take on the deputy minister job. I told him matter-of-factly that I took promises like that with a grain of salt.

★★★

A few years after the Constitution was repatriated, Roger Tassé asked me to join Lang Michener's Ottawa office. That is where I met Jean Chrétien. "I knew who he was, but I didn't actually have a chance to sit down with him during the repatriation negotiations," recalled Chrétien thirty-five years later. "He was advising Hatfield, so he was with Hatfield's entourage. I didn't interact with him directly, but I knew who he was."

At Lang Michener, Roger Tassé was Prime Minister Brian Mulroney's adviser during the Meech Lake negotiations, Paul LaBarge handled a lot of the office management, Eddie Goldenberg took a few cases and Chrétien, well, he was not really a lawyer anymore. One of the first times I talked to him at the office, I asked him what case he was working on, and he said, "No, no, I do negotiations."

It was 1986, and Chrétien was taking a break from politics. He was not an MP then, but he would end up running for the Liberal Party of Canada leadership and defeating Paul Martin. Before that, though, he took on a few cases, often to help Indigenous groups. One day, a band council came to see him at the office. The leaders wanted to take the federal government to court. Chrétien asked me to handle the legal aspect of their action. I remember him inviting them to sit down and saying, "Okay, before you tell me what you want, I want to tell you this. I'm not a lawyer. I'm not going to go to court for you. I'm not going to write a legal opinion for you. If you want my help, I can offer contacts, I can set up meetings to convince people to do things for you. I'm prepared to do that. If you have a legal issue, talk to Michel." Chrétien never tried to hide anything. He never lied to clients, and he never misled people for his or the firm's benefit. During that meeting, he leaned toward me and whispered in my ear, "Michel, I've been in the House for thirty years, and I've forgotten how to be a lawyer."

★★★

Jean Chrétien's office at Lang Michener was more of a political office. It was at the end of the hall, and he was not there much. He did not really do lawyering; he did politics. He was preparing for a comeback. There were always people coming and going. Gordon Ritchie, a former ambassador at the United Nations, had a kind of sub-office in his office. Chrétien often had lunch with Ritchie and Saskatchewan's NDP leader, Roy Romanow, when he was in Ottawa. He had frequent conversations with Ontario Premier David Peterson and was also very close to the former Ontario premier, Progressive Conservative Bill Davis.

I personally had nothing to do with all that except for the Indigenous rights issues Eddie Goldenberg got me involved in. I crossed paths with him occasionally when I was not away on business. "We saw each other, we had coffee together in the building, things like that," explained Jean Chrétien. "Yes, we were friends; we knew each other well then. We didn't go out to eat together though. We didn't spend time together outside of work." I would not even have described us as friends.

"They weren't in cahoots; there was no intrigue there," said our former colleague, Paul LaBarge. "They respected each other. It was a friendly, collegial environment. I think both of them were very private men. They were both quite reserved and didn't necessarily show it, but there was a deep mutual respect there."

I was actually a little closer to Eddie Goldenberg at the time. He was Jean Chrétien's most faithful ally during his time in politics. One day, something happened that brought Chrétien and me closer together, not really on a personal level, but on a political one. That was right around the time of the Meech Lake debate. Roger Tassé was very much in favour. The morning the Accord was announced, Roger was in a celebratory mood at the office and asked Chrétien to throw his support behind the agreement to give it more heft. Chrétien later said that he had not really paid attention to the whole thing and that he just replied, "I have to think about it. I'll see." I felt disappointed that morning. I was disappointed that the Accord went through unamended. As I explained before, children, the main reason was that New Brunswick had just passed its *Act Recognizing the Equality of the Two Official Linguistic Communities*, so this was a step backward because we were once again being identified as a minority.

Jean Chrétien knew I had been involved with francophone advocacy groups on that file, so he asked me why I was against the Accord. I explained my position. The Accord was a significant setback for Francophones outside Quebec; it would benefit only Quebec. He said, "You know, Tassé sees it very differently." "Yes, and he's wrong," I shot back. He thought that was pretty funny and suggested organizing a little debate so he could make up his mind, so we got together with a few colleagues in the Lang Michener conference room. Tassé expressed his point of view, then it was my turn, and after that we debated. The whole thing took about forty-five minutes, and then Chrétien decided who won.

"I've always been concerned about what's to become of Francophones," said Jean Chrétien in November 2018. "I wasn't in a position to gauge the substance of their disagreement, but because I tend to root for the underdog, I sided with Michel against Tassé, whom everyone was congratulating when he got to the office that morning. Michel wasn't happy." Chrétien added that former Ontario Premier Bill Davis had also influenced his stance.

A few hours later, Chrétien spoke out publicly against the Meech Lake Accord. As reported in the papers back then, Chrétien made a statement on a Montréal radio show: "I'm very happy for Robert Bourassa and Prime Minister Mulroney, but the federal government's ability to redistribute wealth will be too restricted. What's going to happen is that the [rich provinces] will get their money, and the poor ones won't."

★★★

By the time I left Lang Michener, Chrétien was gearing up for a return to politics. He toured several parts of the country to meet with community leaders, local politicians, and so on. He had to develop his agenda, so he met with experts in various fields. I was CEO of Assumption Life when I got a message from Eddie Goldenberg. He wanted some pointers to help Chrétien with his meetings in New Brunswick.

In a confidential memo, I sent him a list of the issues Chrétien should keep in mind, including some important Acadian issues. Here is what I wrote:

> Francophones want to enshrine Bill 88, New Brunswick's Equality of Linguistic Communities legislation. Mr. McKenna says he's in favour, but he knows there's a problem with Ottawa. The Department of Justice sees that as conflicting with multiculturalism and with the very nature of the guarantees to be enshrined. He's stalling. He's going to want a PM who's prepared to help him with this. The best course of action is to let Mr. McKenna talk and then ask him, "How can I help you with the Acadian problem?"

I told Eddie Goldenberg that Premier McKenna was worried about two things in particular: possible changes to jurisdiction over fisheries and the lack of economic assistance for New Brunswick's infrastructure. The province's road system was what I had in mind. "He needs money!" I wrote, and I attached the text of Bill 88.

That remained Chrétien's MO after he became the leader of the official opposition in the House of Commons. As Goldenberg explained, "When Mr. Chrétien was the opposition leader, he sought advice from people knowledgeable in the areas of economic, fiscal and foreign policy, as well as constitutional law issues. Michel helped him with that."

I did so only because we had worked in the same office and had helped one another on occasion. I have never been a member of any political party, nor have I ever been paid by any party or donated money to any party's campaign fund. In fact, I only ever worked on the Liberals' federal campaign platform once, and that was leading up to the 1993 election. Goldenberg had asked Guy Pratte, a lawyer from BLG, to prepare something for the election campaign about constitutional reform vis-à-vis federal–provincial relations. Guy called and asked me for help, so I helped. I believe we spent about two days drafting documents, but I do not remember the details. Some time later, Chrétien asked me to run for the Liberal Party of Canada. I told him there was no point asking me because all the New Brunswick ridings already had their candidates. He suggested I run in Gaspé, and I burst out laughing. I had never lived in Gaspé! That was the end of that. I have no idea if he was actually serious.

"I don't remember," explained Chrétien. "Maybe you tell a guy, 'Hey, you should run,' but lots of people want to hear that kind of thing. 'You'd be a good candidate' doesn't mean you approached the guy, offered him a riding and talked to the riding association president." Anyway, I would never have run for office. I realized I just was not cut out for partisan politics. Plus, time had passed while I was at Assumption Life, and my future did not lie in insurance either. I was destined for court. As a judge.

***

My final few months at Assumption Life dragged on. I informed the Board of Directors that I would not be renewing my contract, which was about to end. It was clear to me that I would go back to practising law, and I had my eye on the prize: a Court of Queen's Bench appointment. Having spent hardly any time arguing cases in New Brunswick, though, I was not actually eligible for a judgeship. I did not talk about my intentions to anyone, not even your mother. Then, one day, I got a call from Justice Guy A. Richard. I knew Justice Richard well because his daughter Martine articled with me at Lang Michener and worked on Mahé with me.

Richard informed me that the chief justice position would be vacant in a year, and he strongly encouraged me to apply for a position on the New Brunswick Court of Queen's Bench, a trial court. "We absolutely have to make sure we get someone bilingual," he said. "We need someone who can do justice to Francophones in the system. When you're done at Assumption, apply for the position, and I'll back you. I'll make sure you have lots of support, so it should work out."

Justice Richard had a lot of influence in New Brunswick. He also had political connections. He knew Jean Chrétien and Roméo LeBlanc well. Justice Richard and I met two or three times, and I finally told him that my being appointed was a fantasy for three reasons: the government and the selection committee did not like appointing university professors to trial courts; most members of the selection committee were Anglophones who saw me as a nationalist; and, I had no experience practising law in New Brunswick. I had been involved in just two or three trials there. It is not that I was not interested—quite the contrary. When I left Assumption, I wanted to go back to law, but I definitely did not want to start crisscrossing the country again.

Richard persuaded me to apply anyway. To be eligible, I had to be affiliated with a firm. I talked to the Chair of the Board for Stewart McKelvey in Moncton. Justice Richard's son, André, was involved in the discussions because he really wanted me to join them. I ended up signing an agreement with the firm and became an associate.

Then one day, I got a call from the federal Attorney General and Minister of Justice, Allan Rock, who told me I had been selected for a position at New Brunswick's Court of Queen's Bench. That was the first time I talked to Rock. He said an announcement would be made in the coming days or weeks. I was pleased with that turn of events, of course. I would be able to do work I was passionate about, and I was especially glad I would be at the Court of Queen's Bench, where trials happened.

But then Rock called me back a few days later to tell me I would not be a judge after all. "The selection committee voted against it, and we promised we wouldn't appoint anyone the selection committee didn't support," he said on the other end of the line. Twenty years later, Rock still refused to comment on what happened.

I had a feeling Chrétien was aware of the situation. Contrary to what was reported in the newspapers, specifically *Le Devoir* in December 2010, I never called the Premier's office to ask for anything. In a December 4, 2010, article, a journalist wrote that I had talked about my ambitions with Roméo LeBlanc (who is from New Brunswick), who was about to become governor general of Canada and whom I knew well. There was zero truth to that. For one thing, I would not ever have talked to LeBlanc because I did not know him personally. For another, I would not have approached him, period. You see, I invited Canada's Justice Minister, Marc Lalonde, to give the opening address at the Université de Moncton's School of Law in 1978 instead of him, and he did not take that well. My cousin Bertin, who worked in his office, would tell you the same: "No connection at all. Not even remotely, I would say. LeBlanc was a political strategist, a political animal. He was in the same league as Marc Lalonde, Jean Chrétien, and Prime Minister Trudeau. I can't picture him wanting to share that spotlight with anyone else. Michel was closer to Joe Daigle."

The *Le Devoir* reporter went on to say that, according to a source, I had made some calls to Eddie Goldenberg, Chrétien's adviser. Also not true. "Never," said Goldenberg in 2018. "I don't know why people say he called me. Did he tell me at one point that he wanted to be a judge? Maybe; I don't remember. But he wasn't campaigning for an appointment at all. It would have been fine with me if he had called. I wouldn't have had a problem with that, but he didn't call." The truth is that I never talked to Goldenberg, Chrétien, or Chrétien's Chief of Staff, Jean Pelletier, with whom I was acquainted. I had always been of the opinion that, if I were to apply one day, the people in charge would look at my dossier and appoint me if, and only if, they thought I was the most qualified person. That said, I never doubted I had what it took to do the job.

Two months later, Rock called me back to let me know that Justice Jean-Claude Angers of the Court of Appeal wanted to go back to the Court of Queen's Bench, which meant that his position would be open. I decided to reapply.

"There was a problem with the Bar selection committee because Moncton is Francophone but Saint-Jean is Anglophone," explained Eddie Goldenberg. "They said Michel wasn't qualified for the superior court but was very qualified for the Court of Appeal because there was a francophone vacancy on the appeal bench and an anglophone vacancy on the other one. That was fantastic for him. As soon as he was appointed to the Court of Appeal, he started writing lots of decisions and became an ideal candidate for the Supreme Court."

A couple of months later, Minister Rock called me again to inform me that I was going to be a judge. Children, you must be wondering why the government was so intent on appointing me to the bench. "I knew of his reputation," explained Jean Chrétien. "I knew he'd been Assumption's CEO. That impressed me. I knew he'd been a university professor. And we needed a Francophone on the Court of Appeal. I talked to some people, his name came up, and I liked him, so I appointed him. I appointed him because I knew him."

★★★

I knew I would have a hard time convincing people that mine was not a partisan appointment. My Court of Appeal bench mates gave me a frosty reception. I was determined to do the best job I could, but navigating the relationship with my colleagues was quite difficult. One day, I met with Chief Justice William "Bill" Hoyt to tell him that people seemed fairly unhappy to be working with me. "They think you're like Michel Blanchard," he explained. Blanchard was one of the activists at the 1968 Université de Moncton student strike. They did not realize we were not the same person. They all thought I was some kind of revolutionary from the Université de Moncton. I told him they had the wrong guy. I was not even there in 1968!

Bill explained the mix-up, everyone relaxed, and then we all got along. I volunteered to write the decision for every case I heard. Several of my colleagues were happy about that because it would lighten their workload.

Children, I was at the New Brunswick Court of Appeal for two and a half years, and I worked like a dog the whole time. I loved everything about the job. I typed my decisions, I did my own research. Basically, I did everything. I rendered 160 decisions during my time in Fredericton. By comparison, I wrote 150 decisions in eleven years at the Supreme Court. Justice Hoyt and I wrote about forty percent of the court's decisions while I was there. We wrote so many decisions that the Department of Justice stopped publishing statistics because it made some of the other judges look bad.

When I started, I had a lot of anxiety around criminal law because I had never, ever practised it. I had never argued criminal cases. All I knew about it was what I had learned in school. I was instantly smitten though. I would not have wanted to do criminal law, but I found the jurisprudence and interpretation of the *Criminal Code* fascinating. In contrast to public law, which required knowledge of the body of law to solve a problem, criminal law could be addressed one section at a time. I am exaggerating, but my point is that criminal law is much less general. The vast majority of our cases were criminal in nature, so I learned fast. I also handled almost all the family law cases because my colleagues were not partial to them.

Initially, when they told me what they thought of that area of law, I was sure I would not like it. People in the field tend to have all kinds of prejudices about it. I myself used to tell colleagues that family law boiled down to five cases and two statutes and could be learned in a day. I was wrong about that. Nevertheless, the same issues tended to come up over and over, and the work was often easy because it involved parsing differences of opinion on the facts. The complexities of that area of law are not usually legal in nature.

The first decision I rendered in a complex case was cited with approval by the Supreme Court of Canada shortly thereafter and has been cited at least five thousand times across Canada. Maybe that is how I gained my bench mates' respect. I also rendered another decision to do with the scope of section 7 of the *Canadian Charter of Rights and Freedoms* when a person is in danger of losing their children or something fundamental in their lives. It involved a woman on social assistance who wanted to take her case to court but did not have any money. Section 7 states, "Everyone has the right to life, liberty and security of the person and the right not to be deprived thereof except in accordance with the principles of fundamental justice." My decision extended the principle of physical safety to mental safety. The Supreme Court also approved and cited that decision. I believe those two decisions had a lot to do with my being selected for a Supreme Court appointment.

***

It was one of the saddest times in our lives. I was a judge at the New Brunswick Court of Appeal. I had been CEO of an iconic Acadian company. I had won three Supreme Court cases. Yet there we were, Yolande and I, at Chalmers Hospital in Fredericton. Émilie, you were motionless in my arms. I wept and wept. I still get a lump in my throat just thinking about it. Your mother and I wanted to believe that your death was not a tragedy but a release for you. For months, you had battled one bout of pneumonia after another, and your condition was deteriorating rapidly. We still feel so much sorrow over your death and your brother's a decade earlier.

But life went on, even though our home felt so empty. As usual, I buried myself in my work. The grieving process changed me. I began to have a better understanding of the anguish of people going through life with a sick dependant and of those who had lost a loved one. It fosters compassion. I think I became more sensitive to the victim's situation in criminal and social cases. I kept up my work at the Court of Appeal as best I could, but life in Fredericton had become tedious and melancholic. Your mother and I were woebegone.

A few months later, Supreme Court Justice Gérard La Forest, who was from New Brunswick, announced his retirement. That meant a vacancy in the highest court in the land. I was sure the federal government would appoint a judge from Nova Scotia. Then the phone rang. "Mr. Bastarache, I'm pleased to inform you that you're the government's choice to sit on the Supreme Court of Canada."

> "Mr. Bastarache, I'm pleased to inform you that you're the government's choice to sit on the Supreme Court of Canada."

***

"Number one, I wanted someone competent," said Jean Chrétien. "Number two, there had never been an Acadian. That's what I had in mind when I made Roméo LeBlanc Governor General. I appointed Bastarache, and Arbour for Ontario, and both of them were the cream of the crop. Nobody ever said either of them was incompetent. Quite the opposite. They both had very good reputations. Yet they were both Francophones from outside Quebec." Even so, the opposition in the House of Commons went ballistic. Just like that, I became a prominent Liberal.

The Bloc Québécois leader, Gilles Duceppe, fired off the first shot during question period on October 1, 1997:

> Mr. Speaker, today the Prime Minister appointed a new justice to the Supreme Court of Canada, Mr. Justice Michel Bastarache. This is obviously a patronage appointment made under a system that allows the Prime Minister to appoint whomever he pleases depending on what he wants done. Does the Prime Minister not find it unacceptable, as much for the sake of the Supreme Court's credibility as for that of the judicial system, that the members of the highest court in the land are appointed by a single person without any sort of public consultation?

Then the Reform Party joined the fray, and I once again found myself caught up in a political storm. Twenty years later, Eddie Goldenberg explained that Prime Minister Chrétien was afraid there would be an outsized political and media backlash. He was even a bit hesitant to appoint me. "Chrétien didn't want to be criticized," said Goldenberg. "He didn't want Bastarache to face accusations of being a patronage appointment. Yet it was so obvious that there were no other candidates of his calibre." So how did they choose me, anyway? First, there was a vacancy. Second, a constitutional convention calls for regional representation, with one seat for the Atlantic region, three each for Quebec and Ontario, and two for Western Canada. Apparently, officials at the Department of Justice looked at people's dossiers. Supreme Court justices typically come from provincial appeal courts, and the officials examine their rulings. There is also the fact that Prime Minister Chrétien insisted on having a bilingual justice. Just the appearance of proximity to the Prime Minister could have disqualified me in the end.

Anyway, I did not apply to the Supreme Court of Canada. That is not how it was done at the time. I did not approach anyone in hopes of getting the appointment. To be honest, I was just fine at the Court of Appeal, so much so that when I got the call from the government, I asked for time to discuss it with Chief Justice Bill Hoyt, who advised me to think twice and not rush into anything. He himself was going to retire soon, and my name was being bandied about as his replacement. Still, you cannot say no to the Supreme Court.

Just one question remained unanswered, a question we need to ask ourselves as a society: should someone be excluded from the appointment process because of an acquaintanceship? Not even friendship; just acquaintanceship. It is a valid and important question, and it applies to everything from Supreme Court of Canada and other judicial appointments to positions in the public and private sector and even in sports.

Émilie and Jean-François, I will write more later. I need to think about things, about the scourge of excessive partisanship. Why are we willing to compromise people's prospects because of what they represent rather than who they are? Is political ideology more important than actual skill and experience? How did it come to this?

> Why are we willing to compromise people's prospects because of what they represent rather than who they are? Is political ideology more important than actual skill and experience?

★★★

"My advice to the Prime Minister," said Eddie Goldenberg, "was that if he wanted to appoint Bastarache because they were friends, it wouldn't be a good appointment. On the other hand, just having worked together in the past wasn't a good reason not to appoint someone highly qualified."

Jean Chrétien had made up his mind. He wanted to prove to the whole world, and especially to Quebec nationalists, that French Canadians were not martyrs and that they could succeed in Canada. "So I was prime minister, Roméo was Governor General, Lamer was Chief Justice, Jean Pelletier was my chief of staff, Jocelyne Bourgon was clerk of the Privy Council. At one point, five of the nine Supreme Court justices were Francophones. Add to that Canada's ambassador to Washington and the chief of the Defence Staff. I mean, for martyrs, we weren't doing too badly!" he quipped.

My own conscience was clear. I knew I was not an amateur getting into the big league. I had the skills required for the position. Even so, I was not impervious to the criticisms levelled against me. It still stings that people called me a political appointee, as if they had low expectations. I never thought I would be considered for the position when Justice La Forest announced his departure, though not because of my brief professional association with Chrétien. I thought they would want to appoint a woman and avoid having two people in a row from New Brunswick. There was talk in the papers about a female candidate from Newfoundland and another from Nova Scotia.

Children, a Supreme Court of Canada appointment is the ultimate honour for a jurist. Being unable to fully appreciate that honour because of disparaging remarks from elected members of Canada's Parliament hurt. A lot. Clearly, partisanship often goes well beyond the political.

The New Justice

ÉMILIE AND JEAN-FRANÇOIS, I was well aware of Francophones' expectations when I was appointed to the Supreme Court of Canada. I understood those expectations, but I was wholly committed to rigorous respect for the rule of law. I was certainly sensitive to language rights, but I was not one-dimensional, and I definitely had no intention of becoming an activist judge. The context surrounding my arrival at the Court in the fall of 1997 was rather unique. A year earlier, the Chrétien government had submitted the Quebec Secession reference to determine whether Quebec could unilaterally separate from Canada. Those were the post-referendum years, and the threat of another referendum was very real. I knew for sure that we would be busy; the papers called it "The Case of the Century."

I had a lot to take in when I arrived. I had to get acquainted with my new environment and understand how it worked because it was not at all like the Court of Appeal. The types of cases and the fact that I was always working with the same eight colleagues posed their share of challenges. Not to mention that there was no how-to manual laying out all the rules of the Court. I had to learn everything, and I asked a lot of questions.

Starting that job was one of the most overwhelming experiences of my career. It is hard to describe how it feels to take that seat in the courtroom. It is such a solemn space, and sharing it with eight of Canada's legal luminaries was certainly intimidating. Speaking in court for the first time as a lawyer did not faze me at all, but sitting at my desk with no idea what to do made me feel terribly insecure. I arrived five years after the previous retirement, so the rest of the judges knew each other very well, and each had their own way of doing things.

About a month after I started at the Court, tragedy struck. Our colleague, John Sopinka, died. John's trajectory was one of a kind. He started out in professional football, playing for the Canadian Football League's Toronto Argonauts and Montréal Alouettes from 1955 to 1958. As a lawyer, he rose to prominence in the case of Susan Nelles, a Toronto nurse charged with causing the death of several sick babies at the hospital where she worked. It was a historic case in the 1980s, and Ms. Nelles was acquitted thanks to John. Sopinka had never been a judge before Prime Minister Brian Mulroney appointed him to the Supreme Court of Canada in 1988. My colleagues knew he had been sick for some time. He had a

Yolande and Michel Bastarache with Jack Major. Jack Major and I were adversaries in court and colleagues at the Supreme Court. Over the years, we became great friends.
Source: Morris Fish; Collection of Michel Bastarache.

blood disease, but nobody knew much about it. Justice Sopinka's passing left a huge void, and all his long-time colleagues were deeply saddened.

Ian Binnie, a lawyer but not a judge, was appointed and joined us in the winter of 1998. This unconventional choice came about because the prime minister did not like the fact that two Ontario Court of Appeal judges had been lobbied during the appointment process.

I adjusted quickly, thanks in large part to my colleagues' warm welcome. In particular, Frank Iacobucci and John C. Major, both of whom had been at the Court for years, immediately invited me to breakfast with them. We became good friends and played a lot of golf and tennis together. As Frank put it, "When you're doing that, you know, because you're trying to get some relaxation and some activities outside the Court, then you form friendship. And if the personalities are compatible, then it's the normal development of a friendship. It's not that I didn't like other judges, it's just that they didn't have similar interests as we did with Michel and Jack. It wasn't a tennis club, don't get me wrong! It's just a connection with different people."

★★★

Children, I had not even been a justice for a day and already I was looking forward to the day the government would appoint new ones. Not that I did not like my colleagues; I like them a lot. You see, I wanted a new office, and I wanted it as soon as possible. Let me explain.

It all goes back to the adoption of the *Constitution Act, 1867*, which created the Dominion of Canada. At that time, the fathers of Confederation essentially laid the foundation for the justice system we have today. In accordance with the Act, the governor general, on the advice of Cabinet, appoints all superior court judges in Canada, and, of course, that includes the Supreme Court justices, who are appointed, cannot be terminated, operate independently of the executive branch, and may remain in office until they turn seventy-five. Before the *Constitution Act, 1867* came into force, provincial appeal court decisions could be appealed directly to the Judicial Committee of the Privy Council in London, over in the United Kingdom. Our new Constitution provided that the new federal Parliament could create a general court of appeal for Canada. In 1875, eight years after Canadian Confederation, Parliament created the Supreme Court of Canada, but it still was not the final authority in this country, and its decisions could still be appealed to the Judicial Committee of the Privy Council. That would not change until 1933 for criminal appeals and 1949 for civil appeals. Initially, the Supreme Court of Canada had six judges. In 1927, that rose to seven, and then to nine in 1949, which was also when the Court became completely independent. Over the years, it was housed in a number of different buildings in the capital, including a committee room in Parliament, before ending up where it is today, on Wellington Street in Ottawa, majestically sited atop a cliff overlooking the Ottawa River. The seven judges moved into the new building in January 1946, but three years later, there was a shortage of office space for the two new judges. As a result, smaller rooms were turned into offices for the Court's two junior judges. When a senior judge retires, the others move around to make sure the new judge gets the smallest office. Offices are essentially allocated based on seniority.

★★★

One of my first cases, if not the first, was a criminal case—not my favourite area of law. The case was R. *v. Caslake*, which turned on an RCMP search in Manitoba. I would hear many similar stories during my eleven years at court. A

Natural Resources officer observed a car by the side of a highway outside Gimli, Manitoba. The officer got out of his vehicle and saw a man in the tall grass thirty to forty feet off the roadway. The man said he was relieving himself in the bushes. After a short conversation, they returned to their respective vehicles, and the man drove away. The officer then went to the area where he first observed the man and found a yellow garbage bag containing approximately nine pounds of marijuana wrapped in cellophane. At that point, he contacted the RCMP to request backup. He pursued the man's vehicle and arrested him for possession of narcotics. A few minutes later, the RCMP officer arrived on the scene and took the man to the detachment. Approximately six hours after the arrest, the RCMP officer went to the garage, unlocked the man's vehicle and searched it. He had neither a search warrant nor the appellant's permission to do so. The officer found one thousand four hundred dollars in cash and two packages containing approximately 0.25 grams of cocaine each. According to his testimony, the search was conducted in accordance with RCMP standard procedure pursuant to a policy on searches. The man who was arrested was convicted of possession of marijuana for the purposes of trafficking, and possession of cocaine. He appealed the cocaine possession conviction on the grounds that the search of his car was, in his opinion, not reasonable and the cocaine should not have been admitted into evidence. We had to determine if the search violated the accused's rights.

I reviewed the factums thoroughly, and I was more than ready for the case. As the lawyers came forward, I was not nervous about asking them a few questions. The hearing ended, and we exited the room through the door just behind the chief justice's seat. We quickly made our way across the hall to the conference room, a huge space lined with bookshelves. It is like the Supreme Court's inner sanctum, a very private place exclusively for justices. It is off-limits to assistants, clerks, and other court employees while discussions are taking place. No minutes are kept, and no details of those discussions may leave the room. It is like the cabinet room in Parliament, but it is even more private.

The room has a certain majesty to it, and it is steeped in history. The books, though merely decorative, enhance its solemnity, and the huge solid wood table in the centre of the room contributes to the stately air of the place. There are nine seats at the table, each assigned to one of the judges in order of seniority. Armchairs are arranged more casually in a quiet corner nearby where we can have coffee and speak freely after handing our robes to our attendants for storage in lockers in the adjoining dressing room where we don our ceremonial garb. We all repair to that room after each hearing. The chief justice leads the discussion about what we heard during the hearing. That conversation typically lasts thirty or forty minutes, and it focuses solely on the ruling we have to make.

The meeting took an unexpected turn that time though. Chief Justice Antonio Lamer was not exactly feeling jovial. He scowled and shot me dirty looks.

Apparently, he did not appreciate my participation in the hearing, and he knew I disagreed with him about the case. That is when he went around the table asking each judge in turn for their opinion. Like all the rest of them, I shared mine, and he shared his. We all proceeded to discuss the case. I will not get into the details, but we were not unanimous, which is par for the course there. The dissenting judges were Charles Gonthier, Claire L'Heureux-Dubé, and me. It was four to three, and two of the three Quebec judges were on my side. The third Quebecker, Lamer, wrote the decision for the majority, and I wrote the dissenting opinion. Lamer was a criminal law expert who had taught for years at the Université de Montréal.

I was sure of myself, and I believed my dissenting opinion was valid. Lamer was furious though because I nearly won, and some of the newer judges hesitated to side with him. Lamer or Bastarache? The junior justice or the chief justice? They were not sure. During a subsequent conference, Lamer took me aside. I was not sure why. His jaw was set, and he clearly did not appreciate my position in R. v. Caslake. Right in front of everyone, he blurted out, "You shouldn't be writing for criminal cases. You don't know a thing about it, Bastarache! That's not why you're here!" I was taken aback, flabbergasted by what he said. So were my new colleagues. Very calmly, under the watchful eyes of the other judges, I went over to him and said, "Antonio, when I was appointed, my contract said nothing about being appointed only to hear non-criminal cases, so I think I'll do like all the other judges here and do my job. As for whether I'm competent to handle criminal law cases, if I'm not, it's your fault. It's your fault, Antonio, because you're the one who taught me criminal law at the Université de Montréal." Everyone had a good laugh.

★★★

Lamer was tough, but he had a wealth of experience. We did not always agree—far from it—but his approach to the law and his attention to detail really made an impression on me. I knew him quite well. He taught me, and I argued three or four cases before him in the Supreme Court. He was not happy about my appointment; I was not the candidate he wanted. I do not think it was personal. I later learned that Lamer had more or less lobbied for Nova Scotia's pick. I do not know what he said to Justice Constance Glube, but it is clear he had made her some kind of promise because, after I was appointed, she called to congratulate me and made a point of offering me an olive branch. "Listen Michel," she said, "I know you're going to hear that I was sure I'd be appointed, and I want to tell you I don't hold it against you. You didn't appoint yourself. We're still good friends."

I heard that Justice Lamer told Constance he had talked to Prime Minister Chrétien and received assurances she would be appointed. When I asked

Constance who promised her a seat on the highest court in the land, she said, "Tony Lamer."

Our relationship as colleagues got off on the wrong foot. Lamer was never easy to please. The week I started at court, I notified him that I was to be the keynote speaker at a major administrative law conference in Toronto. He said I was not authorized to go. I had not realized I needed authorization. "You don't need my authorization to go, but you need my authorization to get paid. I won't be covering your expenses," he said. I asked him why, and he said that judges could not give speeches during weeks the Court was sitting. But the Court was not sitting that day. "Doesn't matter. We're sitting that week," he insisted. I told him that was too bad, but I would be going anyway because it was too late to cancel. He protested a bit. When I came back, I sent him my bill, and he ended up approving the reimbursement.

Antonio treated me coolly for at least two years. Prior to his retirement in January 2000, he had started drinking. A lot. And often. At court, sometimes the phone would ring, and the owner of the restaurant where he was eating would let us know he was behaving erratically. The court registrar would call the RCMP, and the RCMP would send an officer to go pick him up and bring him back to us discreetly so as not to stoke downtown Ottawa's rumour mill. These sad events have already been written about, as in Philip Slayton's *Mighty Judgment*. From time to time, a small committee of three judges—Jack Major, Peter Cory, and Charles Gonthier—would go see him and ask him not to preside over a hearing because he was drunk. That was a hard time. They took turns trying to persuade him to leave the Court because of illness, to retire and focus on getting better. Lamer was tenacious, but he finally left before the mandatory retirement age of seventy-five. He sat for twenty years.

One evening, he invited your mother and me to his place for dinner. I truly believe he wanted to make things right between us. "His wife was so nice," said Yolande. "She invited me to breakfast with some friends so I could meet people. I had just arrived and didn't know anyone. She was really great. He was a boor. But he was boorish with everyone. Some of the women told me, 'Just ignore him if he says stupid things. He's always like that'."

A few months before Antonio retired, my brother Marc came to visit me at court. Antonio met with him in his office to talk for a few minutes. "Justice Lamer told me his office could well become my brother's," said Marc. "He showed me his office and seemed to think Michel would take his place." I will never forget that. Despite our differences of opinion, I spent three very full years at court with Antonio. He was one of the greatest jurists of his generation, particularly in the field of criminal law.

★★★

I have always believed the Supreme Court of Canada plays a role in society. The wealthy can influence government policy, government decisions, and how laws affect them. The poor cannot. Not only do they have no influence, but many of them do not understand the system and cannot present their case. Judges have to be sensitive to vulnerable people's realities because the fact is they do not have equal opportunities. That has always been top of mind for me. I believe we need social justice. We have to make sure we do not have one set of rules for the rich and another for the poor. As I see it, the justice system must serve everyone fairly. When it comes to trial fairness, it is important to remember that people have the right to a fair trial, not a perfect trial. After all, we do not live in a perfect world. We have to understand the victims' perspective and the needs of the system, and we also have to respect the rights of the accused. Most importantly, we must never convict an innocent person.

I approached every one of my cases the same way. They were all equally important from a preparation point of view, but the tougher ones, the ones that demanded a deep dive into the law, those were the ones I found most interesting. I did a lot of research, I read a lot, and it was not good enough to just cite precedents and go along with what others had said. I always had my own opinion on what was just. I wanted to interpret the facts before me my own way. That approach worked well with a three-judge appeal court panel, but it caused me problems at the Supreme Court.

When I arrived at the Supreme Court, I did not really follow trends or readily subscribe to big-picture analysis offered up by gimmicky ideologues. I was open to new ideas, and I wanted to understand what was behind each challenge, but I took the time to learn. I was not going to be a lemming. To be convinced of anything, I needed clear facts and rationale.

My colleague Rosalie Abella—I affectionately called her Rosie—often remarked that being a justice was like being married to eight people at the same time. Rosie could be a little off the wall with her examples, but that actually sums up the Supreme Court dynamic very well. We certainly had some heated discussions in conference and in private about certain cases. Sometimes we met in the Court's dining room. The number of judges who ate there depended on the year and who was on the bench, but it was a good opportunity to discuss things. We talked about long, high-profile trials and popular proposals for reform.

When Beverley McLachlin became chief justice, she started organizing lunch-and-learns at court to promote a more collegial atmosphere and keep us up to date on topical issues. We would get together for breakfast and hear from an expert. Many of the lectures were scientific in nature. A Nobel Prize winner came to tell us about his research. Another explained how nanocomputers worked. Former prime minister Brian Mulroney came to talk about free trade. All that information gave us a better understanding of the world we live in. I soon realized that those mini-lectures helped me ask better questions in court. Sometimes a case would come up a few months after a particular lecture, and I would feel much more comfortable with the case and ask more relevant questions.

Children, the workload at court was spectacular. From 1997 to 2008, we rendered an average of forty decisions per year, having first considered some five hundred applications for leave to appeal. A third of those applications are submitted by people who are not represented by a lawyer. Court lawyers draft a written recommendation to the judges requesting authorization to be heard. There are about ten of these lawyers, and they triage the applications, group them if they are about the same legal issue, and draw up a list of past cases on the same subject.

For a case to be heard by the judges, it must relate to legal issues of national interest. If the Court has heard a similar case recently, the application may be denied. A committee of three judges considers each application, and if they are not unanimous, the other judges join in to decide. In 2007, the Court received 550 applications for leave and rendered sixty-nine decisions. The following year, my last one there, we received 448 applications and rendered fifty-one decisions. As Roger Bilodeau, the Supreme Court of Canada Registrar in 2018, explained, "It's important to remember that the Court wasn't created to correct errors. Its purpose is to determine the state of the law on a given issue, develop the state of the law, or provide rulings to guide lower courts and the Canadian people. What the Court always does, therefore, is select cases based on what it determines to be relevant and the state of the law at a given point in time."

According to my back-of-the-envelope math, each judge delivered an average of five to seven decisions per year, but that is not really the best way to measure their work. Some decisions are rendered by the Court as a whole, and some are co-signed. Dissenting judges write their reasons for disagreeing. Every judge is involved in every case to some degree. During my years at court, some judges did not sign decisions but were nevertheless very involved even if they were in the majority because they wanted the author to convey their opinion. The task of writing the reasons for

Beverley McLachlin and I sat next to each other at court for a few years. Here I am during my final hours as a Supreme Court of Canada justice.
Source: Supreme Court of Canada; Collection of Michel Bastarache.

each case was assigned on the basis of the judges' areas of expertise. When Lamer was chief justice, seniority was an extremely important criterion. Back then, a senior judge who wanted to write the decision in a case assigned to a more junior judge could take over.

I had been quite prolific at the Court of Appeal, but I reluctantly had to slow my pace at the Supreme Court, where there were usually nine of us, and sometimes seven, sitting. The work was divvied up differently than at the Court of Appeal. Another major difference was the stress level when we came up against particularly thorny problems. I personally always tried to write my decisions in a month just because I did not want them piling up on my desk. It was very hard to catch up if you fell behind with drafting them. My short-term memory was not great, and I did not want to have to redo the work. Unfortunately, my approach put pressure on some of my colleagues who preferred to work when the mood struck.

Some judges had a hard time coping with the impact of being appointed on their social life. It all depended on each person's character and how they organized their life. The hardest part for me was being stuck in my office for pretty much two weeks a month just reading documents and not interacting with anyone for any real length of time. It was exhausting and, over time, it got tiresome. In contrast, I really enjoyed hearings, writing reasons for decisions, and working with my clerks.

★★★

"I remember that call from Justice Bastarache very clearly," said Caroline Magnan, laughing. "I was leaving my apartment near the University of Ottawa, and his assistant said, 'Would you please hold? Justice Bastarache would like to talk to you'." That had to be the spring of 2005. The young second-year U of O student really made an impression on me. Like all thirty of the clerks I hired during my nearly eleven years at the Court, she applied and came to an interview with me. Typically, the students I interviewed were twenty-two, twenty-three, or twenty-four years old, they were top of their class, and they were real dynamos with boundless ambition.

Every year, I followed a very clear selection process to choose three clerks. Unlike my colleague, Claire L'Heureux-Dubé, who interviewed some eighty young people a year, I preferred to interview twenty-five. I gave my list of twenty criteria to my three current clerks and asked them to identify the twenty-five best applicants based on those criteria. In the thirty-minute interviews, I asked the candidates to tell me about their take on the law. For example, I asked them if their outlook on certain principles of constitutional law was generally optimistic or pessimistic. I wanted to know about their philosophy and their approach to practising law rather than whether they were familiar with our current cases. I wanted to understand their research methods. I always liked having at least one clerk whose philosophy was not at all like mine. I wanted someone who would challenge me intellectually. I wanted these young people to have a chance to develop their analytical skills. After the interviews, I selected three young people to work with me the following year, though I had to choose nine so I could keep three because the other more senior judges had hiring priority.

At the Supreme Court, I had the pleasure of working with dozens of clerks and staff members. Pictured here are my executive assistant, Michelle Fournier, and my court attendant, Alain Maisonneuve. I am deeply grateful to them both.
Source: Collection of Michel Bastarache.

I always wanted to see at least one candidate on the list from the Maritimes, the region I represented, if possible. Nobody paid any attention to them during my first years at court. I also insisted on functional bilingualism. If the candidates could not write in French, they at least had to be able to speak it well enough to hold a conversation. I always made sure I had a clerk who could write well in French—proper French. I suspect my Franco-Ontarian colleague, Louise Charron, had similar criteria. Very often, she and I interviewed the same candidates, and, surprisingly, we were among the first to hire Indigenous candidates. And that was in the same year!

I always tried to hire a Francophone from Western Canada, and I usually succeeded. I almost always had one from Saskatchewan, Alberta, or Manitoba. Caroline Magnan was a Franco-Albertan from Edmonton who went to École Maurice-Lavallée after Mahé. I was impressed by her intelligence and quick-wittedness.

When she arrived in 2007, I had a feeling my time at the Supreme Court was coming to an end, and hiring a young woman who benefited from Mahé because it enabled her to study at a French-language school in Alberta from kindergarten through high school was important to me. That day, as she was leaving her apartment, I sincerely hoped she would accept the offer I was about to make.

"He needed a clerk, but it was for the following year, which meant I'd have a year between finishing my law degree and starting my articling," said Caroline. "He said, 'Well, you can do your master's!' So that's what I did. I went to Harvard on scholarship and did a master's in international taxation." In 2007, she came to work in my office at the Court.

I know each judge has their own way of working with their clerks. For example, some judges ask their clerks to write their speeches. On average, I gave fifteen speeches a year, and that was a lot of work because I always wrote mine myself.

Even judges give speeches! During my time at the Supreme Court of Canada, I delivered over ten speeches a year. Unlike some of my colleagues, I insisted on writing all my speeches myself.
Source: Collection of Michel Bastarache.

For day-to-day work, I gave specific instructions and delegated tasks. I did a lot of consulting along the way. Sometimes I did everything myself. Generally, though, I wrote the crucial part myself and assigned the description of facts and the jurisprudence to my assistants. My approach changed depending on my workload, the nature of the case, and the abilities of the clerk tasked with the work.

I tried not to be too demanding with them, and I avoided waking them up at two in the morning to do some job for me. Rumour had it that some of my fellow judges had no qualms about getting their employees to work on a case any time of the day or night. "Everyone says Justice Bastarache is a workaholic," said André Goldenberg, one of my clerks in 2005/2006. "He works constantly. But he didn't expect that of his assistants. He'd send me emails at 2 a.m. or 6:30 a.m. on a Saturday morning or at 3 p.m. on a sunny Sunday, but I never got the impression he expected an answer before 9 a.m. on Monday. I don't think he even expected me to read his messages before 9 a.m. on Monday. He definitely saw us as human beings and wanted us to have our social lives."

★★★

My clerks had to prepare each case before the hearing. I typically asked them to write a brief summarizing the facts of the case, the questions of law, decisions of lower courts, and the parties' arguments and claims. I always wanted them to share their opinion from the outset. I wanted to hear what they had to say and understand how they interpreted the case. I did not hire clerks just to write me summaries. I wanted their legal opinions. My fellow judges, Ian Binnie in particular, would tell you that I usually stuck to my guns and could rarely be swayed. That is true, but it is because I knew the case and was prepared. I did learn from Gilbert Finn, after all. Whenever I attended a meeting, I always expected to be better prepared than anyone else there.

I approached each hearing open to the possibility that the lawyers could persuade me with their arguments. Even so, I read and analyzed each party's factum carefully. Before each appeal hearing, I discussed the case with my clerks to ensure I had a solid grasp of the details. I asked them if they had any questions in mind that I could ask the parties. "Often, Justice Bastarache really wanted to know what I thought," said André Goldenberg. "He wasn't necessarily looking for an answer about who should win or lose. He wanted an analysis of the issue. In my briefs, I would suggest that the analysis should be approached in such-and-such a way, and then he would tell me the outcome." Sometimes the answers André and the others gave did not correspond to how I saw things, so I would make a different decision, but I would always explain why I disagreed.

I became known as a tough, even harsh, judge. Not harsh in my interpersonal relationships with my clerks and colleagues, but severe in the courtroom. Some lawyers told their friends that I was one of the toughest judges because I did not hesitate to ask difficult questions. I wanted to make sure I had a thorough understanding of the matter so I could render the best possible judgment. "I never found he had a specific agenda or perspective," explained André Goldenberg. "He wanted to take a good, hard look at all the issues and find the best possible answer in each case. I saw him as a classic judge. He was all about the law, about the legislation, about interpreting the law and applying precedents to guide him in his work, regardless of the outcome."

I would not say there were not ideological differences at court, because there were. That tended to come up mostly in criminal cases because each judge had deeply held values that guided their thinking. I have always had tremendous respect for my colleagues Major and Iacobucci even though we were rarely, if ever, in the same camp when it came to criminal law. A kind of alliance emerged in the 1990s among Lamer, Cory, Major, and Iacobucci. They almost always voted together on criminal cases; Morris Fish too. I completely disagreed with their approach and regularly sided with Justices McLachlin, Gonthier, Charron, and L'Heureux-Dubé. It was almost like in the United States! We did not attack each other like our neighbours to the south did, but the lines were drawn whenever we had a criminal case.

When my good friend Louise Arbour joined me on the bench in 1999, we decided to set aside our ideological differences. We agreed to disagree on quite a few things. The only time we really clashed was over prisoners' right to vote. The issue in the 2002 *Sauvé v. Canada* appeal was this: is Parliament able to temporarily suspend the exercise of the right to vote for criminals incarcerated for the commission of serious crimes for the duration of their incarceration? Gonthier, Major, L'Heureux-Dubé, and I said yes. Chief Justice McLachlin, Iacobucci, LeBel, Binnie, and Arbour said no. I found it unacceptable that Parliament could not adopt legislation to take away prisoners' right to vote during their incarceration. I did not see why people who had no respect for the law should be given the right to choose the lawmakers who would adopt laws the prisoners would refuse to obey. Louise and I had differences of opinion on the merits and constitutionality of the law. Our analysis often depended on where we stood on that.

***

In 2004, *Syndicat Northcrest v. Amselem* made its way to the Supreme Court of Canada. I had a feeling it would not end well. The case raised the difficult problem of reconciling the freedom of religion of certain individuals with the rights of others to private property, to security, and to having their contracts respected. Essentially, we had to decide whether the appellants had the right to erect private succahs on their balconies during the nine-day Jewish holiday of Succot, in violation of the declaration of co-ownership for Phases VI and VII of the Sanctuaire du Mont-Royal in Montréal, Quebec. The trial court judge wrote: "[...] practising Jews must, for a period of eight days beginning at sunset on the first day, dwell in a succah, that is, a rough structure made of wood or canvas with an open roof covered with only fir branches or bamboo, as the roof must for the most part remain open to the sky."

The biblical commandment is to dwell in succahs, but the climate is such that the mandatory religious practice is apparently to eat supper on the first day and all meals on the second day in a succah. The obligation is less strict for the days that follow. In October 1997, Mr. Amselem asked Syndicat Northcrest for permission to erect a succah for a period of eleven days, that is, from October 14 to 25, 1997. Permission was denied because it was prohibited under the declaration of co-ownership. However, the Syndicat offered to set up a large tent near one of the residential towers, which would serve as a communal succah for all Jewish co-owners wishing to celebrate Succot. Mr. Amselem and the Canadian Jewish Congress agreed to the offer.

Notwithstanding Mr. Amselem's acceptance, the four appellants decided the offer was unacceptable and proceeded to erect succahs on the balconies, porches, or patios adjoining their dwellings. The Syndicat took legal action to bar the appellants from erecting succahs on the common portions of the co-owned property that are reserved for exclusive use in the future and to have any such structures demolished or dismantled.

Justices Iacobucci, Arbour, McLachlin, Major, and Fish ruled that Mr. Amselem had the right to erect his succah. Frank Iacobucci wrote the decision, stating that: "a claimant need not show any objective religious obligation, requirement or precept to invoke freedom of religion. It is the religious or spiritual essence of an action, not any mandatory or perceived-as-mandatory nature of its observance, that attracts protection. The State is in no position to be, nor should it become, the arbiter of religious dogma."

Things got a bit heated as we conferred. Deschamps, LeBel, and I agreed that "since a religion is a system of beliefs and practices based on certain religious precepts, a nexus between the believer's personal beliefs and the precepts of his or her religion must be established." As I wrote in the decision on behalf of the three of us, "To rely on his or her conscientious objection a claimant must demonstrate (1) the existence of a religious precept, (2) a sincere belief that the practice dependent on the precept is mandatory, and (3) the existence of a conflict between the practice and the rule." Justice Binnie was dissenting as well, but he wrote his own decision.

In conference, I singled out Major and Iacobucci. I felt they were setting a dangerous precedent. I was not surprised at Arbour's stance, but I could not believe that was where those two stood. I thought the case was full of holes that prevented us from ruling in Amselem's favour. The claimants stated they were required to erect their religious structures on their balconies. The year before, they had it in the yard. The Canadian Jewish Congress had accepted the Syndicat's offer. In addition, officials responsible for security and fire safety said it posed a risk to the safety of all occupants of the residential tower.

"We have different opinions," said Frank Iacobucci in 2018. "This is an example of two reasonable people who respect one another but reach two different conclusions. That's all I have to say about it. I haven't changed my opinion since that case, and neither has Michel."

Not only have I not changed my mind, I stand by my assertion that the majority decision was absurd. An individual cannot change a religion himself, nor can he create his own religion because religion is, by definition, a collective endeavour. Frank did not see any evidence that it was collective. "I think you can have reasonable accommodations," said Frank. "It's a constitutional obligation, and I think it was appropriate to have a reasonable accommodation for Orthodox Jews who wanted to celebrate Succot. Where things get touchy, and I don't think what they've done since has helped, is the definition of religion."

In conference, none of us were willing to budge because there were two or three similar cases making their way to court. One was a zoning dispute. Can freedom of religion force a municipality to change its zoning bylaws? Iacobucci's precedent alone would give claimants all they needed for an open-and-shut case. I could not believe it.

15
Globetrotter

WE WERE ALL DISMAYED. Air Canada had lost Jack Major's suitcase. The poor judge called every day to see if his bag had been found. A small Supreme Court delegation—Jack, Beverley McLachlin, Nancy Brooks, and I, plus our spouses—were on a trip to China. Jack was usually pretty laid back, but suddenly he lost patience. Every day, the airline assured him he would get his suitcase the next day. In the meantime, he had to buy new clothes. The thing is, Jack was very tall, and the Chinese tended to be shorter. Finding clothes that fit was quite a challenge. He never actually found shoes in the right size and ended up having to get track shoes. His suitcase never did show up while we were there. Once he was back in Ottawa, he got a call from a guy in Vancouver. Apparently, his suitcase had been found in the Port of Vancouver near the cruise terminal. He finally got the thing back about ten days later.

That was not the end of Justice Major's problems during our trip. We were staying at a government hotel for foreign dignitaries. Jack's wife had decided to put her jewelry in the room safe. In the morning, she had a hard time opening it and asked an employee to fix it. Thinking nothing of it, she put her jewelry back in the safe the following evening. The next day, it was gone. What a disaster! We could not accuse the Chinese valet of stealing them, obviously. Who knew what kind of punishment he would get? It was all we talked about at the breakfast table. Jack explained that he had taken the little safe out of its spot, examined it and shaken it. Then the hotel employees came to have a look. Everyone tried to figure out what might have happened next. Yolande suggested they had probably replaced that safe with another one without checking the contents. The empty safe might just have been a different one. You had to be tactful with the Chinese. Our main concern was avoiding a diplomatic crisis. Well, maybe that was not the Majors' main concern. With Jack walking around in track shoes, let us just say it was not the trip of a lifetime for them. A small group of us went over to the hotel employees to explain our theory. They immediately opened the old safe. Eureka! There was Mrs. Major's jewelry! The trip was saved. We all heaved a sigh of relief. We were in the middle of a business trip that included meetings with influential members of the Chinese judiciary, but, honestly, I think the whole jewelry debacle was the most stressful part of the whole thing.

Business trips with the Supreme Court of Canada took Yolande and me to destinations like India. Here we are taking a break in front of the Taj Mahal.
Source: Collection of Michel Bastarache.

Children, not a lot of people know that the Supreme Court engages in diplomatic relations. While I was there, we travelled quite a few times to maintain ties with other courts around the world. I myself visited places such as Romania, India, China, and Russia. Every court in the world deals with similar legal issues, so they like learning about how those issues are dealt with elsewhere and what decisions have been made on issues of interest to them. Parliamentarians also participate in lots of exchanges with many different countries. We do similar work on the legal and political fronts, respectively, but judges do not travel as much.

Some countries deal with a lot of the same problems as Canada. For example, after the September 11, 2001, attacks in the United States, every country wanted to update its anti-terrorism laws, so the big issue was striking a balance between privacy and national security. Every government on the planet was figuring out how to handle the situation, and there were lots of diplomatic exchanges.

Governments, parliamentarians, and courts all worked on it. The Supreme Court's focus was on how to modernize our approach to the administration of justice.

The Supreme Court of Canada also belonged to international networks, including two associations of supreme courts from francophone countries, and participated in their activities regularly in Europe, Africa, and Canada. There were also bilateral exchanges from time to time with supreme courts in the United States, England, and India. We took turns hosting our counterparts so we could discuss matters of mutual interest and compare notes on similar cases.

At one point, Romania hosted courts from members of the Organisation internationale de la Francophonie. We were at the Ceausescu Palace right in downtown Bucharest. The entire Romanian court was in the room. The meeting was chaired by my colleague, Canada's Chief Justice, Beverley McLachlin. Suddenly, the doors opened wide and guards came in. They announced that the Parliament, gathered in a neighbouring room, had just relieved all the judges of their duties. The Chief Justice stood up and called on the assembly to condemn this illegal action. The meeting adjourned just like that. We talked among ourselves and decided it would be best not to get involved and to find a way out. We realized the European Union had mechanisms in place and could arbitrate. We resumed our meeting and proposed that solution to the Romanian judges. At dinner that evening, I was seated near the Minister of Justice, a former lawyer who worked on human rights cases. I asked her to explain the attack on judicial independence. She said, "They're all corrupt. We will respect judicial independence, but we have to start fresh." We sure learned a lot during our travels.

The frequency of our international meetings varied. We generally met with our U.S. counterparts every four years, at least while I was sitting. There was a more or less regular cycle. The Court's participation gave me a chance to meet jurists from every province and territory, as well as quite a few from other countries. It was truly an education and definitely a privilege. It was pretty easy to establish a dialogue with other judges and discuss matters of mutual interest even though we were from very different parts of the world and operated in different legal systems.

Children, it was the first time I ever visited Russia. It was the 1990s, and Boris Yeltsin was the leader of the new Russia after the break-up of the Union of Soviet Socialist Republics (USSR). Russians wanted their new democracy to have a more efficient justice system.

I was invited to give seminars for the judges of the Constitutional Court of the Russian Federation and participate in a small symposium. Right at the start of the whole event, I was informed that the Chair of the Court, Marat Baglai, wanted to meet me. He invited me to his Moscow office for a brief meeting. Moments before walking into his office, I was told he had had a bad experience with the Americans

Yolande and me in Moscow's Red Square. She and I travelled just about all over the world together!
Source: Collection of Michel Bastarache.

and concluded he had nothing to learn from them. Plus, he saw Canada and the United States as one and the same. I was with my wife and Suzanne Labbé, who was representing the Commissioner for Federal Judicial Affairs. An interpreter was in the office with us.

I sat across from Chair Baglai, the Court's chief justice. The other two stayed in the background. Our discussion took place through the interpreter. I introduced myself and briefly explained my mandate as I saw it. He was frosty and impassive. He listened, but he seemed detached. I tried to spark his interest in why I was there by talking about how I wanted us to get to know each other, exchange ideas, compare notes, and learn from one another while explaining our own system's strengths and weaknesses. I told him that our delegation's goal was to move our relationship to the next level, beyond the kinds of meetings we already had with several other courts. I just said that we knew Russia was in transition, that its democracy was brand-new and that the courts would play a much more important role than they had in the past. I made it quite clear that I was very interested in how he planned to achieve that and how he envisioned the transition. I also explained how Canada's system works, without holding it up as a standard to aspire to. I told him that my goal was not to tell them what to do, but to work with them and compare our two systems. Perhaps we could learn from one another. I think I reeled him in by saying that Canada's approach was not at all like that of the Americans, who, according to the Russians, tend to be arrogant in such situations.

He started to thaw. He asked me a question, and I answered tactfully. I wanted to know which areas of law interested him most so I could draw comparisons between our approaches to problem-solving. As I was asking my question, a secretary came into the office and whispered in his ear. It was obviously a prearranged signal to get him out of the meeting. I could see it in the officials' eyes. To everyone's surprise, he waved the secretary away and called the interpreter back. He wanted to talk.

"He was a real Russian bear, gruff and firmly planted in his chair," recalled your mother. "We could tell he wasn't very happy [...]. He had just been with the Americans and the Germans. Michel talked to him, and he listened, and then suddenly, his mood seemed to lift. His secretary came in after fifteen minutes and whispered in his ear, but he sent her away. Then he looked at me and held out some Russian chocolates. Michel kept talking to him, and he kept edging closer along the table. He got closer and closer. After half an hour, he was in the middle of the table, practically on top of Michel, listening to him talk. It was like day and night. He was in a good mood. He was happy. He was talking to us. Michel had found the right way to talk to them, and the judge realized Michel was interested in them. That's how he won people over. He took an interest in them. Truly. That's how he got through to them."

We talked for quite some time and went on to hold several meetings in both Russia and Canada. We discussed seven or eight very different subjects ranging from human rights, federalism and tax policy to the right to judicial review, the Quebec secession reference and policing terrorism. Afterward, the Russians published a book containing each of our texts. They changed how they drafted judicial decisions to provide litigants with clear reasons. Later, the Court invalidated several decisions by the Duma, Russia's federal assembly. During our visits, we enjoyed dinners together, we danced, and we talked about our families as well as everyday problems.

★★★

During my years at court, I worked with the Russians more often than any of the other judges. Antonio Lamer delegated me in the 1990s, and Beverley McLachlin just continued to let me represent our institution. "People were very interested in learning about Canada then, and I think they still are," explained McLachlin. "As a nation, we have done good work from a legal standpoint since the *Canadian Charter of Rights and Freedoms* was adopted in 1982, and by the 2000s, the Supreme Court of Canada was seen as a global leader. We were invited to participate in all kinds of exchanges and trips. I believe that an international understanding of the rule of law is very important. We learned a lot too. People thought of us as a model. Once we gained respect on the international stage, being more open and travelling more was crucial."

After I left the Court in 2008, that relationship with Russia petered out. Beverley asked Ian Binnie to do it, and then she asked my successor, Thomas Cromwell. I do not know what happened, but the bilateral meetings dried up. "Those types of projects tend to be limited to a particular period of time," said Roger Bilodeau, the Registrar of the Supreme Court of Canada.

Children, I often hear people say that our relationships with Russia and China are artificial and pointless. I totally disagree. Our judges need to set aside their prejudices and foster dialogue with judges in other countries. In Russia, for example, we tried to convince judges to embrace all the democratic standards underpinning our judicial system. We did not discuss specific political cases; we focused on principles. Their principles were certainly not always the same as ours. Russia does not have a good human rights reputation, sometimes for good reason, sometimes not. They have repressive legislation and repressive enforcement. However, I think the media went too far when it portrayed the controversy around Pussy Riot, which violated Russian law by organizing illegal assemblies, as par for the course in the Russian justice system. We know Russian dissidents do not have the same rights as Canadians, but it is dangerous to judge what goes on in a foreign state by Canadian standards.

I worked with the Russians several times, and they made considerable progress after my first meeting with Justice Baglai. Previously, there was no police power oversight whatsoever. Once they brought in police commissions, that really had an impact. During that time, the number of civil proceedings quintupled, a sure sign that people had gained confidence in the courts. That kind of progress was good for ordinary people, not those involved in policy and human rights. In that respect, they obviously have not made the progress they should have made.

The Constitutional Court was created in the 1990s, and corruption was much worse at that time than it was after Vladimir Putin came to power. According to the judges I met, Putin went after the oligarchs and did some major housecleaning, but he did not always play by the rules.

When Vladimir Putin was elected, many Russians were afraid of him. To this day, the former KGB officer has a reputation for being a tough, heavy-handed, arrogant man. When he took office, he passed a clearly unconstitutional law. The press said he manipulated and threatened members of the assembly to push his law through. Someone submitted an application to the Constitutional Court, and a few weeks before the case was heard, I met the judges who were preparing to rule on the constitutional issue.

One evening, after three or four glasses of wine, I was conversing with one of the judges who spoke pretty good English. "Some of my colleagues are really afraid of deciding against Putin," he said. I asked him if they would do it anyway. He said he was pushing for the Court to do it and establish its legitimacy. I commented that there were risks to doing so. The judge whispered that some of his colleagues were speculating they might be shipped off to courts in Siberia or other far-flung places. I asked him if he and his colleagues were so scared that they would not be able to carry out their duties freely. In the end, he convinced a majority, and they overturned the legislation.

A few months later, after their offices were moved to Saint Petersburg, Vladimir Putin, who had studied law at the University of Leningrad, paid them a visit. The judge I had spoken to told me that Putin went to see them and said he was very unhappy with the decision, which he felt sure was a bad one. He felt that the judges had not taken the nation's best interests into account. However, he also said he respected their decision and would not retaliate. From my point of view, that is noteworthy progress.

Canada plays such an important role vis-à-vis countries like Russia. We can have a positive influence, but we have to be patient. I do not think boycotting and cold-shouldering them sets a good example. When Chief Justice McLachlin declined the Russians' invitation to participate in the grand opening of the Constitutional Court in Saint Petersburg, which was attended by all the European chief justices, my Russian colleagues certainly did not react positively. Apparently, she told them she had other engagements. I thought the event was extremely important to bilateral relations. Her absence was conspicuous, and the Russian judges made their displeasure clear to me.

★★★

Children, the only totally pointless relationship I witnessed was what I saw in Cuba. Judges there are mere bureaucrats with no independence. Vietnam was the same; I was told judicial decisions were subject to the approval of military authorities. What we have here in Canada is fundamentally different. India is a democratic country, but the courts there operate differently. We visited the court in New Delhi. The courtroom was jam-packed. Every seat was taken, and lots of people were standing in the aisles. Lots of lawyers were lined up in the middle of the room, facing the bench. It was chaotic, people jostling for what little space there was. The presiding judge called a name and asked if the lawyer was present, then told him to come to the front of the group and asked him a few questions. The judge listened to arguments for a few minutes, then asked what the defendant thought. The matter was considered, and it was on to the next case. We were told there could be as many as ten thousand cases pending and that most decisions would not be handed down for five or ten years. Decisions were often grouped by subject. It obviously was not an acceptable system, especially given that judges told us many of their decisions were ignored. In fact, if the government did not agree with a decision in the realm of public law, it would often make a constitutional amendment to overturn it. Naturally, the amendment formula was in no way comparable to ours. That way of doing business was appalling.

As I said earlier, my only negative experience personally came on a visit to Cuba. One day the Canadian embassy invited me to Havana to meet with professors in the faculty of law and deliver a speech to mark the anniversary of the *Canadian Charter of Rights and Freedoms*. The audience was professors and students. I was the vice-president of the Canadian Institute for the Administration of Justice, so I was also asked to meet with the judges and public servants responsible for training judges. At the end of the event, I was supposed to meet the Minister of Justice. As

I got off the airplane, two embassy officials intercepted me and told me the Cuban authorities wanted a copy of my speech. I was quite surprised. I did not ask a lot of questions and just handed over my speech. A few hours later, the same two people returned. They wanted me to go talk with them in the middle of the garden. We were worried about wiretapping, so we turned off our phones and put them down under a tree some distance away. Children, it felt like a secret mission, but it was just a speech. They told me my speech was not approved. I asked how that was possible; I was only going to talk about Canada. I was told that saying something was acceptable in Canada because it was "justified in a free and democratic society," as set out in section 1 of the *Canadian Charter of Rights and Freedoms*, amounted to saying that Cuba was not a free and democratic society if it banned such a thing. I was not to talk about section 1 of the Charter. Other passages also raised objections. I was told, "If you want to speak tomorrow, you have to write another speech and submit it for approval." I was stunned. I obviously did not want the whole trip to be a write-off. I wrote a new speech late that night and submitted it for approval. The Cuban authorities okayed it, and the Canadian government took some precautions in order not to compromise diplomatic relations.

Despite these constraints, some seventy-five people attended the speech. Officials took down their names. The students did not learn anything useful, but a question-and-answer period yielded a somewhat richer exchange. We steered clear of controversial topics. The regime did not appreciate that part because it could not vet the questions and answers in advance, so all my appointments were cancelled. That was the Cuban regime for you! There was no room for cooperation on judicial matters.

★★★

Émilie and Jean-François, I developed a taste for diplomatic relations during my time at the Supreme Court of Canada. I always thought that influencing other nations in favour of the Canadian approach could best be achieved by visiting them and talking to their representatives. I really thought Richard Nixon did the right thing by going to China even though the Chinese were considered so foreign and people were worried about their support for the Viet Cong.

That is why, when I left the Court, I was delighted to accept a position as a member of Kenya's Interim Constitutional Court. That was in 2010, a few years after the post-election violence in 2007 and 2008 in the west African country. Some 1,200 people were killed in the conflict, which led to the former UN Secretary General, Kofi Annan, intervening as a mediator in diplomatic talks between the African Union and the parties involved. Annan developed a plan for a return to social and political stability, beginning with the adoption of a brand-new constitution. The constitution included judicial reform, starting with the country's highest court. That is why I was invited to be an interim member of the court along with six Kenyan colleagues, one from Botswana and one from Britain. Our mandate was to serve as an interim constitutional court to hear complaints concerning the adoption of the new constitution and the election to follow.

I ended up working with Kenya for a little over a year, and I went there twice. It was a very enriching experience for me, but I soon realized that our approaches to justice clashed. The first thing I did when I got there was meet the six Kenyan judges. It was immediately obvious that they were not motivated by the public interest. The only thing they talked about was the benefits that came with the position: the pay, the chauffeur, the expense account, and so on. That is all they talked about. When it was time to consider actual court cases, only the Brit, John Alistair Cameron, and I talked about them. Nobody else made any real contribution. In the end, the Kenyan judges told us it did not really matter anyway because they were going to hire a university professor to write the decisions and all we had to do was rule on the outcome. That is exactly what they did. It was deeply discouraging.

Children, I do not regret my work in Kenya. I believe that my colleague and I did everything we could to change the culture and the approach to justice. We just did not have the power. I learned a lot even though the outcome of the whole experience was not positive. Ultimately, what was the point? I had the opportunity to gain more international experience, and I am sure that is one reason I was appointed vice-president and then president of the Administrative Tribunal of the Organization of American States. We were six judges responsible for hearing disputes arising between members of the General Secretariat of the OAS because of administrative decisions.

On the ground though, my Kenyan engagement did not produce much in the way of results. The 2013 and 2017 elections led to further conflict, and dozens of people died. The Kenyan interlude left me with a profound sense of hopelessness with respect to the possibility of institutional reform in that country.

16

A Historic Case

ÉMILIE AND JEAN-FRANÇOIS, the failure of the Meech Lake Constitutional Accord was a win in my view. I was fiercely opposed to the Accord because it penalized Francophones outside Quebec and Acadians. At the time, I had no inkling the failure of the Accord would come back to haunt me eight years later.

During the Meech Lake talks, our goal was to strengthen minority francophone rights. The Bourassa government's lead minister, Gil Rémillard, had expressed his support for that at a symposium at Mont-Gabriel. "In short, our stipulations for supporting the *Constitution Act of 1982* are based on three main objectives: making the Act acceptable to Quebec, improving it to the benefit of the entire Canadian federation and improving the situation of Francophones living outside the province of Quebec. This last point is especially important to us. In fact, the situation of Francophones outside of Quebec will be one of our major concerns during the upcoming constitutional talks." That top priority was conspicuously absent from the final version of the Accord, in which we were called "French-speaking Canadians." Minorities, basically. We were not particularly happy, and Frank McKenna's government appreciated the Acadian community's grievances. He asked the federal government to include a new provision in the *Canadian Charter of Rights and Freedoms* about the equality of New Brunswick's two official language communities. Bill 88, which I talked about before, would need protection from any future constitutional amendment.

In May 1990, a House of Commons committee chaired by Jean Charest submitted a report to Prime Minister Mulroney recommending that the McKenna government's proposal about two official language communities be integrated into the Meech Lake Accord. After Charest's report was submitted, Canada's Minister of the Environment, Lucien Bouchard, resigned and went on to found the Bloc Québécois, a sovereignist party in the House of Commons. As Bouchard related in his book, *À visage découvert*, which was translated into English as *On the Record*, he said he could not accept "the levelling of Quebec society's distinctive character by inserting in the same clause the equality of New Brunswick's anglophone and francophone communities." New Brunswick's Liberal premier, Frank McKenna, was the first to express serious reservations, and a few weeks later, Manitoba and Newfoundland and Labrador got on the bandwagon and rejected the Accord. People often forget that the failure of Meech Lake had something to do with the fact that, during the negotiations, the Government of Quebec passed new legislation governing language requirements for public signage that severely restricted the use of English. In many provinces, including New Brunswick, support for the Accord evaporated. After all, why do anything to please Quebec when it obviously could not care less about Anglophones?

Provincial Liberals, starting with Quebec Premier Robert Bourassa, became increasingly uncompromising toward the other Canadian provinces. Speaking in the National Assembly on June 22, 1990, Premier Bourassa said, "English Canada must understand in no uncertain terms that, no matter what is said or done, Quebec is and will always be a distinct society, a free society capable of taking control of its destiny and development." That speech marked a turning point in Quebec history. The popularity of the sovereignist option leaped in the polls, and Mr. Bourassa instantly became a driving force in Quebec's nationalist movement. He even threatened Canada with the prospect of a sovereignty referendum during those early weeks.

Canadian Prime Minister Brian Mulroney was nervous and felt the need to reconcile Canada and Quebec yet again. After Quebec refused to sign the new Canadian Constitution in 1982, Mulroney made that rapprochement his personal mission. The failure of Meech Lake hurt him, but he was not ready to throw in the towel.

In 1991, he decided to reopen talks with all the provinces and both territories in hopes of reaching a new constitutional agreement. All the provinces, including Quebec, agreed to the pact. There was just one thing: Canadians would have to give their approval by way of a referendum. The referendum on the Charlottetown Accord was held on October 26, 1992.

What was actually in the Accord? It gave Quebec special status by recognizing the province as a distinct society. It entrenched the requirement that three Supreme Court of Canada justices be from Quebec. Quebec was guaranteed twenty-five percent of the seats in the House of Commons. The Senate would become "triple-E": elected, effective, and with an equal number of senators from each province. New Brunswick continued pushing to entrench the principle of linguistic duality in the Constitution.

At the time, I was president of Assumption and not politically active at all. My involvement was limited to lobbying the government on the company's behalf, and I kept close tabs on language cases across the country. One day, I got a call from Canada's employment and immigration minister, Bernard Valcourt, who was also the minister responsible for New Brunswick. He wanted to talk about the Charlottetown Accord, and he asked me to meet with Joe Clark, the federal government's lead on the referendum, because he was looking for a national co-chair.

I did not know why he wanted me on his team. I suppose he wanted a Francophone from outside Quebec. The other co-chair was a Francophone from Quebec and a close friend of Brian Mulroney, Yves Fortier, the former Canadian ambassador to the United Nations, and a world-renowned lawyer in the field of arbitration and international law.

I still do not know why I agreed to get involved. I was not particularly excited about the whole thing. I was actually quite indifferent, in contrast to how I felt about the Meech Lake Accord, when I was driven to engage with francophone organizations in minority communities. I saw it as a second attempt after the failure of Meech and I thought the fact that all the provinces had agreed to the deal this time would finally enable us to bring Quebec into the constitutional fold.

From day one, though, I sensed that I would regret getting involved. The "Yes" side organizers' brilliant idea was English-only messaging when the campaign launched in Ottawa. I remember showing up at the event and seeing nothing but "Yes" all over the place. I could not believe it. The organizers, who thought shouting "Yes" was their ticket to victory, were utterly tone deaf. "Yes" was everywhere: on posters, in press kits. Things were off to a terrible start.

Even so, I thought we would come out on top. Some aspects of the undertaking seemed more significant to me because they would transform Canada in fundamental ways, starting with Senate reform, and I believed I could have a hand in it all. I soon realized that it would not work because of lobby groups hogging the spotlight. Everyone was looking out for their own interests, and nobody cared how that would affect anyone else. They did not see it as an all-encompassing undertaking in which everything was interconnected. Indigenous groups and feminist associations made the whole thing practically impossible. Westerners nursed an anti-Ontario sentiment that was hard to explain. They were also not keen on strengthening bilingualism.

I devoted half of my own efforts to New Brunswick. Together with my friend Fernand Landry, who was in government, I campaigned vigorously in the province. In the end, New Brunswick, Ontario, Prince Edward Island, Newfoundland, and the Northwest Territories were the only provinces and territory that affirmed the Accord. Just over seventy percent of Canadians voted, and fifty-five percent of them rejected it.

So we lost, but I did not lose sleep over it. I did my job, and then it was over. I hardly ever heard anyone say anything about my role. It was such an important matter, and so costly. It was a national referendum after all, but it seemed as though Canadians just got bored with it. The results were made public and analyzed, and then, just like that, everyone stopped talking about it. Oddly, hardly anyone even mentioned the Charlottetown Accord during the constitutional debates that followed. I do not know why. It just suddenly lost its significance. Or maybe it never mattered as much as expected in the first place.

Winning sixty-two percent of the votes cast, the "Yes" side did so well in New Brunswick that the provincial government was able to reopen bilateral talks with Ottawa to enshrine the two linguistic communities act in the Charter. On March 12, 1993, section 16.1 received royal assent at Rideau Hall.

★★★

In 1994, Quebec's independence movement was stronger than ever. Mario Dumont, a twenty-five-year-old Liberal, founded the Action démocratique du Québec, the ADQ, a centre-right nationalist party, and represented it in the National Assembly. Jacques Parizeau's Parti Québécois was elected. During the election campaign, sovereignty was the word on everyone's lips, and the PQ leader seized every opportunity to sell the idea. Once elected, he forged ahead and, in June 1995, announced that he had signed a partnership with the Bloc Québécois and the ADQ. That partnership laid the foundation for the Yes committee gearing up for a Quebec sovereignty referendum to be held on October 30, 1995. As a Canadian, a Francophone outside Quebec, and an Acadian, I was obviously against Quebec declaring independence. I did not campaign during the referendum, and I did not participate in the downtown Montréal love-in, where tens of thousands of Canadians displayed their affection for Quebecois. For one thing, that really was not my style. For another, in July 1995, Canada's Minister of Justice, Allan Rock, called me to announce that I had been appointed to the New Brunswick Court of Appeal.

The referendum exacerbated the already acrimonious federalist-sovereignist debate. Before people went to the polls, Guy Bertrand, a lawyer who had run for the PQ leadership in 1984 but had since become a federalist, launched a long series of legal proceedings to cancel the referendum, overturn a Yes victory, and then attempt to prevent the Government of Quebec from holding a third referendum. The Chrétien government weighed the pros and cons of participating in Bertrand's legal action, but any signal it sent in support was fiercely criticized and attacked by the Government of Quebec.

On October 30, 93.5 percent of Quebeckers went to the polls to vote *yes* or *no* to this question: "Do you agree that Quebec should become sovereign after having made a formal offer to Canada for a new economic and political partnership within the scope of the bill respecting the future of Quebec and of the agreement signed on June 12, 1995?"

Prime Minister Jean Chrétien and members of his government told anyone and everyone that the question was not clear and discredited the Yes option. I agree that the question could have been clearer. Despite its meteoric rise in the polls once Lucien Bouchard took the helm, the Yes side lost the referendum. In the final tally, the No side garnered 50.58 percent of the vote to the Yes side's

49.42 percent. The defeat left a bitter taste in the sovereignists' mouths because they had believed their dream of independence would come true. Despite the defeat, Bouchard's personality inspired a sense of optimism. He was a brilliant lawyer and an extraordinary orator, a charismatic man skilled at holding the crowd in the palm of his hand.

In Ottawa, the victory was bittersweet. The Liberals were keenly aware that defeat could be snatched from the jaws of victory if another referendum were to be held in the future. In the lead-up to the referendum, one person rose to prominence among Ottawa federalists. A Université de Montréal political science professor made multiple national television appearances, vigorously defending the federalist option. A few weeks after the referendum, Prime Minister Jean Chrétien called this professor and asked him to make the leap into politics. Mr. Chrétien seemed keen to revitalize his Quebec team in particular. The general election was two years away, and there were murmurings in the sovereignist camp about a third referendum.

On January 25, 1996, Stéphane Dion was named Canada's minister of Intergovernmental Affairs. He was elected to the House of Commons in March of that year. Two days after Dion entered politics, Lucien Bouchard announced that he was leaving the Bloc Québécois to become leader of the Parti Québécois. A few days later, he became premier of Quebec. The spectre of a third referendum loomed, and the difficult task of thwarting Bouchard's attempts to sway public opinion fell to Stéphane Dion.

★★★

For Jean Chrétien, it was all about clarity. The referendum question had to be clear. But he also wanted to know if Quebec could make a unilateral decision about its future within Canada. He was sure it could not, but he needed a definitive answer. In Ottawa, the rumour mill was in overdrive. Would he join Guy Bertrand's legal action? In December 1995, Bertrand had argued that politicians had lost all credibility and that a "neutral" arbitration process was the only way for the public to get the facts from a legal perspective.

Ottawa kept trying to come up with a strategy to better lay the ground rules for a potential referendum. In Ottawa, rumours abounded on all sides, and on September 26, 1996, Justice Minister Allan Rock announced his intention to request a Supreme Court of Canada reference on unilateral Quebec secession. He wanted the Court to answer three questions. "We must continue to work to avoid ever having to deal with an attempt at secession. The world would never understand the failure of a country like Canada which embodies in so many ways that which is best in the human spirit. Indeed, Canadians would never forgive themselves," said Rock on the floor of the House of Commons.

***

"As premier of Quebec and leader of the Parti Québécois, I think this ruling will be political and therefore null and void. We will ignore it," Lucien Bouchard announced to a sovereignist crowd in May 1997. In the weeks that followed, Justice Gérard La Forest, who represented the Maritimes, announced his retirement from the Supreme Court of Canada. The case was already behind schedule, but the surprise announcement by a twelve-year veteran of the bench caused further delays. The Chrétien government announced my appointment to the Supreme Court of Canada on October 1, 1997. "Well, there was a vacancy," said Eddie Goldenberg in 2018. "It's not like we created a vacancy so we could appoint him. I think Justice La Forest was either at retirement age or done with the whole thing. The reference was on the docket. Who was the most qualified judge? Besides, you never know what a judge is going to do. Lots of judges disappoint those who selected them."

In both the House of Commons and society at large, my appointment was seen as yet another example of how the deck was stacked in favour of the federalists for the Supreme Court reference. "It wasn't like in the United States," said Jean Chrétien some twenty years after I was appointed. "I looked at their careers, at whether they had been good judges. Their job wasn't to advocate for causes. Their job was to uphold and apply the law. He applied the law as he saw it. Some judges think they're above members of Parliament. He wasn't like that."

I took up my post at court during interesting times indeed. Hearings were postponed yet again. We heard the case in February 1998. Ian Binnie joined us in January. We spent a week hearing arguments.

The Government of Quebec refused to participate in the reference. The Supreme Court therefore appointed André Joli-Cœur as *amicus curiae*, a friend of the court, to defend Quebec's position. Yves Fortier, who co-chaired the Yes campaign for the Charlottetown Accord referendum with me, was the federal government's lead counsel for the case. The three questions submitted to the Court were as follows:

1) Under the Constitution of Canada, can the National Assembly, legislature or government of Quebec effect the secession of Quebec from Canada unilaterally?
2) Does international law give the National Assembly, legislature or government of Quebec the right to effect the secession of Quebec from Canada unilaterally? In this regard, is there a right to self-determination under international law that would give the National Assembly, legislature or government of Quebec the right to effect the secession of Quebec from Canada unilaterally?

3) In the event of a conflict between domestic and international law on the right of the National Assembly, legislature or government of Quebec to effect the secession of Quebec from Canada unilaterally, which would take precedence in Canada?

I felt the Quebec case should be treated like any other regardless of its historic significance. Politics could not be allowed to factor in. We could be absolutely fair because we were not judging the choice made by Quebeckers. My hope was that we could accommodate Quebec and persuade Quebeckers to build a stronger Canada, but that was not going to influence my judgment in this case. The task before us was monumental, and I fully intended to play a decisive role.

★★★

I spent eleven years at the Supreme Court, working with some of the biggest names in Canadian law. They were extraordinarily rigorous, analytical, and meticulous. Charles Gonthier was a true gentleman. Appointed in 1989, he had already spent considerable time on the bench. Charles grew up in an affluent part of Montréal with a self-taught father who dedicated his life to encouraging French Canadians to take an interest in business. Gonthier used to talk about how his father was instrumental in founding the École des hautes études commerciales in 1907 and, in 1923, became the first French Canadian auditor general of Canada, a position he held until 1939. He was also very fond of his mother, Kathleen Doherty, who was of Irish descent. During his working life in Montréal and Ottawa, he seemed to take after the anglophone side of the family. A friend once said that Charles was always a little more Doherty than Gonthier, but his primary personality traits were integrity and kindness.

We were always close at court. I always liked him because he was an excellent jurist, particularly in civil law. He did not write much in other fields, but he never lacked for common sense. He was a kind of legal philosopher. He was always searching for new solutions to legal problems, but he never lost sight of the importance of contributing to the evolution of a long-term social justice framework. He never lost his cool. Gonthier exemplified poise, fellowship, and professionalism.

His deeply held Christian values always informed his work; he was a man of principle. His religious faith shaped many of his judgments, especially as the dissident voice in cases such as *M. v. H.* on the right of same-sex couples to spousal support.

Every time a civil law case landed on our desks, we automatically turned to Charles. In court, lawyers often addressed him directly in their arguments and ignored almost all the other judges. That was no doubt part of their strategy.

Convincing Gonthier could be the key to winning over all the other Supreme Court judges.

One day, we were in the courtroom for a case I do not remember the name of. It was a case from Quebec, and the young lawyer in front of us calmly addressed me as though I were the only other person there. He was passionate, and I let him talk. I did not really know why he was so focused on me. I figured he thought I could influence the others. As the minutes passed, the lawyer did not waver from his plan. Then he cited one of my previous decisions. We all looked at one another, incredulous. He had mistaken me for Charles. The party was over. I interrupted him and said, "Sir, you're talking about me, you know." The poor man's physical reaction was instantaneous. He turned beet red and completely lost his composure. Out of the corner of my eye, I could see Charles barely containing his laughter.

★★★

My fellow judges and I were conscious of the historic weight of our decision in the Secession Reference. For years, decades even, public confidence in the Court had been dwindling. The political context was explosive. The federal government was contemplating legislation to block a potential referendum, and the Government of Quebec was refusing to participate in the reference. Politicians in Quebec and Ottawa were quick to label us as judge and party. Virtually everyone expected us to give the federal government what it wanted.

We wanted our decision to be unanimous. We were all on the same page from the start. Ordinarily, Chief Justice Lamer would have asked all the judges their opinion in conference and would have offered to draft the decision; the others would have offered comments. "If the comments were agreeable to others, it led to the judgment and something would come out," recalled Jack Major. "To try to satisfy nine people, you know, there were nuances some liked and some didn't like, but it was really a collective effort."

But that is not what happened. Our first meetings were spent on very general discussions. Everyone commented, but no answers to the three questions were put forward at that time. Rather, we talked about whether to focus solely on international law, whether it was a constitutional question rather than an international law question, and whether it could be both at once. That was the substance of our debate, of which there was plenty over the course of our four or five meetings.

Children, to reveal what was said during our exchanges would be to violate confidentiality. I cannot tell you who said what or which position a particular judge defended. However, I can tell you that the reason the decision was not signed by any one of us is that we all truly helped formulate it in one way or another. Some judges contributed texts relating to aspects of the case. Others proposed changes.

We all discussed the proposals. A typical conference lasted half an hour or so. That first meeting, when I checked my watch, well over an hour had gone by. The debate was intense, respectful but definitely lively. I remember Frank Iacobucci quickly assuming a leadership role in our discussions. "There was a group of us that did a lot of work, and I strongly recommended a smaller group do this and that we would have to drive it down to a decision by the Court to be unified," he recalled.

Suddenly, he began to take on the role of Chief Justice Lamer, who became more distant and detached during the debates. In public, Lamer was the only one who asked questions during the hearings in order to preserve the appearance of a united bench in this important case, but he was very worried about the impact this reference would have in Quebec. For one thing, he represented Quebec at court and was intimately acquainted with its idiosyncrasies. In conference, some judges said, "To hell with politics. We're not here to do politics. Parliament can figure that part out." Some were certainly of that school of thought, and Antonio may have felt isolated. Who am I to judge? That was the impression I got. People said the Quebec judges were uncomfortable about the reference, but I doubt that was the case. Maybe for Antonio, but definitely not for Charles, who was deeply engaged from the get-go.

I put forward a series of suggestions early on. Everyone had to offer their opinion because the decision was not going to have a designated author. The discussion was dominated by those who wanted to air more sophisticated interpretations. Justice Lamer insisted that everyone agree to the final decision being by the Court, with everyone contributing. There was to be no author. It would be unanimous and anonymous.

As the weeks went by, a number of drafts made their way around our offices. Not all the judges wrote them, but everyone read and commented on them. Charles Gonthier, newcomer Ian Binnie, and I took on the task of drafting. Gonthier worked on the substance of the case, Binnie on the international law aspect, and I on minority rights and general principles. "I was in favour of him being in the group that worked on it," said Iacobucci, who kept close tabs on our work. "We needed Quebec's point of view as well as the minority point of view. We needed to consider francophone issues and the two legal systems. I wanted his perspective, and he gave it."

Binnie also had his work cut out for him on the international law aspect, which I was very interested in. I wanted it to be much clearer than just "International law does not apply in this type of case." Like several others, I offered him my comments. Gonthier went about his work quietly but industriously. His clerks scurried up and down the courthouse hallways fetching him opinions and research findings. The first draft of his text was very broad in scope.

My three clerks, like their colleagues, were very keen to take part in this historic case. International law was a huge factor, and we all knew we would be writing the rules of the political game. We had to dig up every relevant piece of jurisprudence. Anything in any way related. In one of our meetings, I told them it was all hands on deck and the coming months would be very demanding. I am sure the other judges said more or less the same to their clerks. "We worked on that in ways that we never worked on any case before," said Iacobucci. "We had more meetings on that case than any other cases I was on in my close to fourteen years. We had many meetings. We all did our own drafts of what the major points should be so that we had input. And then we would take those inputs and fashion them into a bigger judgment. The whole approach was much more participatory than any other judgment I had participated in."

When I read Gonthier's draft, I thought it lacked substance. In some ways, he had missed the target. Sitting down with him, I said, "Charles, there's nothing about minorities in your draft. If you want to lay down principles, you need one about that." He nodded. That was about what he would expect from me, the "minority francophone vigilante."

Gonthier was not particularly aggressive. He spoke slowly, but when he spoke, all the judges listened. He was thoughtful, credible, and eminently sensible. There were times when we did not agree, of course, but we were always rational and respectful. Charles told me early on in the process that he wanted to participate in the case because he considered himself to be both an Anglophone and a Francophone. The spirit of compromise was very important to him, and I think that is why he was so engaged from the start.

Anyway, our discussions led to an agreement that minority rights should be front and centre in the text. We knew that approach would bring colleagues who wanted to include Indigenous rights on board. We were making headway.

★★★

One thing every single judge agreed on was that Quebec could not separate unilaterally. The challenge, a monumental one, was coming up with a formula that both Quebec and the rest of Canada would accept. That is when we turned to the fundamental constitutional principles, which led us to conclude that, if Quebec held a referendum and the outcome was crystal clear, there would be an obligation to negotiate with Canada. That is something we invented; it did not exist prior to our debate.

In conference, Gonthier and I discussed the minority angle with our colleagues. In our text, we emphasized the likelihood that Quebec secession would have a dramatic impact on minorities from one end of the country to the other and made it clear we could not ignore that aspect of the problem. My colleagues readily agreed to address the issue in the final document. As expected, others stressed the impact of secession on Indigenous Peoples. Things proceeded from there, and most of the judges shared their views on other aspects of the decision.

So there we were in uncharted legal territory. We were essentially all in agreement on the principles, but the issues remained unresolved. How were we going to approach it? What legislation would guide us? What would our decision be based on? The Constitution was absolutely silent on this matter.

The only thing we had any clarity about was the international law element. That was crystal clear. The right to unilaterally separate from a federation hinged on being a victim of discrimination or political domination and being subjected to appalling treatment. Let us be clear: Canada was not occupying Quebec. And although the October crisis was a dark chapter in the province's history, it did not meet the definition of military or political occupation. It was a tragic and deplorable event, but it was contained. Quebec would never be considered a victim of oppression under international law. After all, Quebec was culturally rich and independent, and there was nothing at all preventing it from growing and thriving. In fact, federalism was actually a pretty good deal for Quebec because it got about thirty-seven percent of federal funding for culture even though Quebeckers made up a quarter of the Canadian population. Every five or six years, Quebec's demographic weight in the federation slipped by about a percentage point because of immigration and a low birth rate.

We also had to look at the percentage required to legitimize sovereignty. I do not remember exactly how we decided on the notion of a "clear majority" without mentioning a percentage. Memory fails me, children. I cannot really remember if we voted on that. Not every judge commented on every element during our discussions. Typically, four or five judges weighed in on a given subject, and the active participants changed when we moved on to another subject. Some issues required a vote, if I remember correctly.

"It's confidential," insisted Beverley McLachlin when I asked her to refresh my memory. "Other judges may tell you things, but I cannot talk about this."

***

On August 20, 1998, after a long and arduous process, we handed down the eighty-page decision in which we answered the questions the federal government had referred to us. Children, we combed through thousands of pages of documents and, in the end, we cited about forty decisions from many different areas of law and dozens of pieces of legislation, regulation, and doctrine. That was how we answered the three questions before us.

1) *Under the Constitution of Canada, can the National Assembly, legislature or government of Quebec secede from Canada unilaterally?*

No. Even with a clear majority, Quebec cannot secede from Canada without first negotiating an exit agreement. "Negotiations would need to address the interests of the other provinces, the federal government and Quebec and indeed the rights of all Canadians both within and outside Quebec, and specifically the rights of minorities," says the decision. This conclusion is based on the unwritten principles of democracy and federalism, principles that are invested with a normative force under the circumstances.

2) *Does international law give the National Assembly, legislature or government of Quebec the right to effect the secession of Quebec from Canada unilaterally? In this regard, is there a right to self-determination under international law that would give the National Assembly, legislature or government of Quebec the right to effect the secession of Quebec from Canada unilaterally?*

No. All peoples have the right of self-determination. By virtue of that right they freely determine their political status and freely pursue their economic, social, and cultural development. As we said in the decision, this principle is enshrined in the *Charter of the United Nations*. However, this right arises in the case of colonial peoples to enable them to break away from what can be described as an "imperial" power or in the exceptional situation of an oppressed people. We decided that this principle was irrelevant to the reference. We wrote: "Quebec does not meet the threshold of a colonial people or an oppressed people, nor can it be suggested that Quebecers have been denied meaningful access to government to pursue their political, economic, cultural and social development. In the circumstances, the 'National Assembly, the legislature or the government of Quebec' do not enjoy a right at international law to effect the secession of Quebec from Canada unilaterally."

3) *In the event of a conflict between domestic and international law on the right of the National Assembly, legislature or government of Quebec to effect the secession of Quebec from Canada unilaterally, which would take precedence in Canada?*

There is no conflict to be addressed.

★★★

"It's a strange thing when you reach a judgment. From the time the judges sign, it's like three weeks before the judgment goes out because the editors really go through the grammar. So you move on to other things. If you're a judge long enough, you know that, if you're lucky, it's going to be fifty-fifty who agrees with you. Once you sign you don't spend much time celebrating. Was there champagne? No!" Jack added with a wry smile during a long conversation in a big Calgary office tower in October 2017. He was right. There was no champagne. "I just think it was a very important case and it was a great achievement. I've always said it's one of the most important cases I've ever had the privilege to participate in. I think it showed the system working well."

When we finalized our decision, we did not think it would get much attention outside of political circles in Quebec and Ottawa. Never did it occur to us that it would spark a big national debate. We did not think our answer would come as a surprise because it should have been obvious to everyone that we would say Quebec could not separate unilaterally. Well, we were wrong about that.

The day after our decision, I was feeling a little curious. I wanted to see how journalists, columnists, and editorialists would respond to the decision, and I was particularly interested in how the federalist and sovereignist camps would interpret it. When I read, "Bouchard applauds decision" in *Le Soleil de Québec*, I was kind of relieved. When I read the first sentence of the article, I smiled: "Premier Lucien Bouchard and Prime Minister Jean Chrétien are both pleased with Thursday's Supreme Court ruling on Quebec secession."

When the decision was released, I was not sure our solution would satisfy many politicians and jurists. I expected quite a few jurists to say we had made up things that were not in the Constitution. I was anticipating "government of judges" accusations from civil society. I worried that might limit the impact of the decision from a legal perspective. I was actually somewhat surprised that Quebec did not have a strong reaction to the fact that we said it had no right to unilateral secession under either international or constitutional law. I had expected them to challenge that.

In his August 22, 1998, editorial entitled "The calm after the storm," *La Presse* journalist Alain Dubuc wrote, "The decision was so balanced and its authors so politically astute that all the politicians had no choice but to adopt the same strategy: focus in abundant moderation on those parts of the decision that bolstered their own beliefs and ignore any inconvenient or uncomfortable passages. Yesterday afternoon, it was almost comical to see Lucien Bouchard and Jean Chrétien offer such diametrically opposed interpretations of the reference that it was hard to believe they were talking about the same document."

★★★

Children, I am so very proud to have contributed to such a significant decision. The reference was one of my first cases at the Supreme Court, and it helped define who I was as a judge until I retired in 2008. More than twenty years have passed since the decision, and I believe it dramatically improved the Court's reputation both in Canada and internationally because it was seen as very creative, very practical, and very much in keeping with the fundamental principles of constitutional law. It was new, it was imaginative, and it worked. Politicians did not cry foul either, not even in Quebec, where the decision was seen as reasonable. In that respect, virtually everyone considered it to be a huge success. It was very satisfying to see the legal community, the political sphere, and the population in general conclude that the court can play a very positive role in the evolution of our country and our democracy. When our country faces big problems, we have institutions that can come up with creative solutions.

The decision dealt a devastating blow to the sovereignist movement, of course. No PQ government has held a sovereignty referendum since. In response to some of the criticism, the Parliament of Canada passed the *Clarity Act*, which was drafted by Stéphane Dion. Those seeking to attack the Act did not emerge victorious. As soon as the reference case was launched, sovereignists condemned it. They said the panel of federalist judges would hand down a decision consistent with the Supreme Court of Canada's "Tower of Pisa" reputation: always leaning in one direction, as former Quebec premier, Maurice Duplessis, used to say.

The reference also enhanced cohesiveness within the Court. More frequent discussions and meetings resulted in better dialogue among us all. Our debate was frank and open, and we were all free to say whatever we wanted. I think the judges' solidarity, collegiality, and camaraderie were greatly improved.

Here is one thing that has really stuck with me about the decision: integrating the fundamental constitutional principle of minority protection had a major impact. It is one more way to protect our rights, and this principle is now used to assist in interpreting laws. Children, this decision helped pave the way to linguistic minority equality across the country. It was just one step forward. But it was a big step. And it did not end there.

Not in My Back Yard

AT 8 A.M. ON FEBRUARY 18, 1981, the lifeless body of Mary Anne Costin was found in a Lynn Creek tributary in North Vancouver. Costin had serious injuries consistent with having been violently beaten, but the cause of death was drowning in the tributary. Her blood alcohol level was 282 mg per 100 mL, which means that, when she was placed in the water, she was drunk. Traces of sperm were found in her vagina.

According to court documents, on the evening of February 17, 1981, the young woman went to a local bar and met a young man. They drank together, and the man also consumed cocaine. Before returning home with the young woman, the twenty-one-year-old man remembered that he did not have any more alcohol at home and had to stop for some at the store. All the stores were closed. He decided to break into a liquor board store on Robson Street near Stanley Park in Vancouver. Mission accomplished, he left with a few bottles. He was with Costin and another man named John Eldon Norris. The three of them went to his East Vancouver apartment.

At his apartment, the man engaged in intimate relations with Costin. Norris expressed his intention to do likewise, but the young woman refused and slapped his face. Tension mounted in the apartment. Norris responded by punching her in the face several times. Then he stopped and went to hide out in the bathroom. Meanwhile, the young woman was beaten by the other man, who then asked Norris to help him transport the young woman in the trunk of his car. They drove several kilometres to an isolated location where Costin was hit numerous times with a rock. Norris was there, but he did not participate in the act. However, he did help his friend throw the victim's body into the water.

The police investigated, but no charges were laid against anyone until the day in 1988 when a man provided evidence relating to the murder to the police service in Sherbrooke, Quebec. The man knew the suspect. It was his brother.

★★★

On October 26, 1988, seven years after the fact, Jean-Victor Beaulac was arrested and charged with first-degree murder. His first trial at the British Columbia Supreme Court ended in a mistrial because of a conversation between a juror and his wife, who had overheard prejudicial information. The second trial resulted in the conviction of the appellant, but this conviction was overturned by the Court of Appeal on the basis of errors in the jury charge concerning the issue of self-induced intoxication.

The third trial also ended in a conviction, but, like many litigants, Beaulac was tenacious, claiming that he was not tried in his mother tongue, which was French. He felt his language rights had been violated.

So who was Jean-Victor Beaulac, anyway? Born in Quebec on June 24, 1959, he moved to British Columbia when he was seventeen. At the time, he did not speak a single word of English. He went back to Quebec for a while but returned to British Columbia to stay in 1977. Having spent so much time in the West, he felt he was bilingual but first and foremost a Francophone. During one of his trials, he said, "in French I can express myself and I can get to the point without having to go around for an hour." He said that speaking English involved translating from French in his head.

Beaulac was no choirboy. In 1978, he was convicted in Vancouver of theft under two hundred dollars and sentenced to a fifty-dollar fine. In 1979, this time in Toronto, he was convicted of possession of two hundred dollars' worth of stolen goods. The following year, in Vancouver, he was convicted of failing to appear in court. In 1981, still in Vancouver, he was convicted of obstructing a peace officer. Later that year and in the years that followed, he was convicted of more minor crimes. In 1986, he was found guilty of aggravated assault and sentenced to nine months in jail.

The point is, Beaulac had a lot of experience with the justice system. In all his encounters with the law, he defended himself in English without the help of an interpreter. Not for his first-degree murder charge though. On October 30, 1990, five days into the trial, he applied for a trial before a judge and jury in both official languages. The application was made during a *voir dire*, a step in the judicial process that enables the judge to determine whether an issue pertaining to the case is admissible by questioning a witness to an event, but the application was denied by Judge Skipp.

He claimed that he had never been properly informed of his rights and had been unable to find a francophone lawyer within a reasonable time for the first trial. He therefore hired Mike Rhodes, one of the best criminal lawyers in Vancouver, to defend him. As Beaulac told the court later, in English, "I figured that, even if I couldn't have a trial in French, at least I would have a very good lawyer, which would help me. I was between a rock and a hard place." His first trial resulted in a mistrial, and he applied for a new trial before a judge and jury who spoke both official languages of Canada.

Beaulac told Justice Macdonell that he had been given the option of pleading in French with the help of a translator but was not comfortable with that because he wanted to be sure his defence was addressed directly to members of the jury. He was worried that the interpreter's filter might hurt his case. "I didn't have a choice," he told Justice Macdonell, referring to his first trial. "I mean, I had to testify, and it was out of the question for me to testify and have someone else translate what I was saying. I was forced to testify. I didn't have a choice, and I chose to testify in English because I wanted to address the jury directly."

In his February 11, 1991, decision, Justice Macdonell rejected Beaulac's application based on the transcript of his testimony at the first trial, which was held in English. He found that, while Beaulac's English was not the most refined, he could make himself understood. Macdonell concluded that no injustice would result from a new trial in English. He also commented on the logistical difficulties connected with mounting a trial in French in British Columbia.

When the application was renewed, Beaulac's lawyer argued that the judge did not consider whether Beaulac was entitled to a bilingual or French trial under section 530 (1) of the *Criminal Code*. Section 530 (1) stipulates that "On application by an accused whose language is one of the official languages of Canada [...] a judge [...] shall grant an order directing that the accused be tried before a [...] judge [...] who speak[s] the official language of Canada that is the language of the accused or, if the circumstances warrant, who speak[s] both official languages of Canada." Justice Rowles determined that no new element had been presented in court since the defence's previous application with respect to language of trial and that there were no grounds to grant Beaulac's application.

The second trial was heard by Justice Murray who dismissed a fourth application. He asked the Beaulac legal team what had changed since the previous application. The defence replied that two trials in French, with a French-speaking judge and jury, had taken place since their previous appearance in court. The defence also said that an interpreter was available during the second trial. Justice Murray did not consider this sufficient grounds for overturning the decision of the two previous judges.

The defence tried again in the third trial. Beaulac's new lawyer, Mr. Leask, argued that his client had been able to use an interpreter during the second trial and that there did not seem to be any further logistical issues preventing a bilingual trial in British Columbia. Prior to the third trial before Justice Boyd, Justice Owen-Flood dismissed the defence's application on the grounds that it was insufficient. "I am satisfied that in light of the fact that the accused is bilingual and fluent in English I cannot say that the best interests of justice require that he be tried before a bilingual judge and jury," declared Justice Owen-Flood. The defence did not ask Justice Boyd to review Justice Owen-Flood's decision. The judge convicted Beaulac of first-degree murder at the end of the third trial.

The British Columbia Court of Appeal considered all these elements in its decision to reject the mistrial of the third trial. In a unanimous decision, Justice

Southin upheld the previous decisions, concluding that, "Mere inconvenience is not serious disruption."

***

This case was mine, and my colleagues knew it. On February 24, 1999, we heard what was shaping up to be a historic case. The Attorney General of Canada, the Attorney General of Quebec, the Commissioner of Official Languages, the Association des juristes d'expression française de l'Ontario, and the Association des juristes d'expression française du Manitoba all had intervener status in the case. I watched Lamer like a hawk because I knew he did not really like cases that were linguistic in nature. Although a murder had been committed, murder had absolutely nothing to do with the case before us, nothing at all.

In conference, my colleagues were undecided. All but Lamer, who did not want us to talk about the *Canadian Charter of Rights and Freedoms* in this context. He agreed on the substance, the fact that the accused was not given an opportunity to plead his case in his own language in accordance with a *Criminal Code* provision. "It's not about the charter," Lamer said to me. I shook my head and replied that I had to talk about the language rights interpretation rule and its restrictive interpretation to decide the scope of the law. That way, I would be interpreting a law, but not the Charter. It was a language law, after all. He wanted me to leave the Charter and principles of interpretation out of it, but he himself had supported a disastrous decision in 1986 stipulating that language rights are political rights and are to be interpreted restrictively. I looked at him and said we had to fix that to make a decision in Beaulac. He disagreed, but he did not seem inclined to debate it further, so I was the only one who talked about the Charter, and my colleagues willingly supported my position. The discussion lasted about ten minutes. My colleague Binnie did not say a word.

Then we started discussing the possibility of a fourth trial, which the judges found very disturbing. "Are we seriously going to order a fourth trial?" said one of them. Everyone around the table was uncomfortable with that, including me, but I stood firm. My colleagues conceded that on any less serious matter, they would drop the case, but this was murder. You cannot just decide to drop a murder case; you have to order a new trial.

At that point, we all knew the Court had not respected the accused's language rights. There was absolutely no doubt about it. The law was very clear on that point. The courts had even said the accused spoke English and it was all fine! My colleagues all acknowledged that there was a distinction to be made and that the rights of the accused had been violated. The real question we asked ourselves, however, was whether we could really quash the conviction of a man found guilty of first-degree murder. If we did not want to order a new trial, what was the alternative? There was none. We kept talking about it, and eventually the judges accepted my interpretation. All but two of them: Antonio Lamer and Ian Binnie, who said nothing but sided with the Chief Justice.

It was important to me that the decision be unanimous though. I wanted to send a clear message to the whole country that minority rights are not second-class rights. On May 10, 1999, I wrote to Lamer and Binnie with a proposal to change my decision slightly to accommodate them. I offered to temper my interpretation of *Société des Acadiens*, 1986. I added that I did not have any major concerns about concurrence. "I wonder if it is really worth the trouble given that our opinions differ only slightly [...]." I wrote. "I am just trying to be useful."

I suspected they did not really understand the majority's position. On May 13, 1999, I met with the Chief Justice and Justice Binnie to discuss their concurring reasons and convince them to join the majority. I even floated the idea of wording the majority's reasons in a way they would be comfortable with. In a May 14, 1999, memo to the Supreme Court justices, I wrote that our colleagues, Lamer and Binnie, "will no doubt inform us whether they will maintain their concurring reasons on the issue of the rules of interpretation applicable to language rights in due course." The ball was in their court.

They would not budge. In a nutshell, their concurring judgment said, "We agree with [Bastarache's] conclusion and [...] analysis. However, with respect, we do not consider this to be an appropriate case to revisit the Court's constitutional interpretation of the language guarantees contained in s. 16 of the Canadian Charter of Rights and Freedoms. It is a well-established rule of prudence that courts ought not to pronounce on constitutional issues unless they are squarely raised for decision. This is not a constitutional case. It is a case of statutory construction."

A week after that meeting in the Chief Justice's office, my decision, backed by six of my colleagues, was handed down. A new trial was ordered. I felt it was pretty much mission accomplished. In my decision, I wrote:

> I wish to emphasize that mere administrative inconvenience is not a relevant factor. The availability of court stenographers and court reporters, the workload of bilingual prosecutors or judges, the additional financial costs of rescheduling are not to be considered because the existence of language rights requires that the government comply with the provisions of the Act by maintaining a proper institutional infrastructure and providing services in both official languages on an equal basis. As mentioned earlier, in the context of institutional bilingualism, an application for service in the language of the official minority language group must not be treated as though there was one primary official language and a duty to accommodate with regard to the use of

the other official language. The governing principle is that of the equality of both official languages.

That was one of the most important judgments of my life.

★★★

Children, when I reflect on the fact that our society still needs judicial recourse to ensure the application of language rights that are supposedly recognized by all governments, it is obvious to me that this problem has not yet been resolved. Twenty years after Beaulac and Arsenault-Cameron, many governments still do not really believe in collective rights. They see language-related demands as political demands, as calls for greater autonomy that would obligate them to modify their institutional structures and functions. Especially disturbing is the fact that the Government of New Brunswick had to be taken to court to ensure respect for Acadians' right to health care in 2013 and that three more actions had to be brought in 2014.

Before Beaulac, the government interpreted the right to a trial in one's language as an accommodation. In places like Vancouver, the accused, be it Jean-Victor Beaulac or anyone else, must navigate an intrinsically anglophone system. The accused has the right to ask for a trial in French, but the system is not at all proactive. Courts will seek solutions to accommodate the accused. They try to find bilingual judges, good translators, and clerks. That is the wrong approach though. It does not honour the principle of linguistic equality, which is supposed to be a fundamental concept. In Beaulac, I said it was not about accommodating a Francophone; it was about ensuring equal access to justice for both Francophones and Anglophones.

I witnessed the injustices inherent in New Brunswick's system before the law was reformed. Imagine being a Francophone charged with murder and appearing in court to answer one very simple question: "How do you plead?" Guilty or not guilty. You would be standing there in front of a unilingual Anglophone judge who has to ask if you want a trial in French. Right from the get-go, you are walking on eggshells, wondering if the court and the prosecutor will think you are a nuisance if you request a trial in French. Could it hurt your case? You can see why a person might think that, and it would have a major psychological impact. Starting a trial with one strike against you does not exactly scream equality.

In the past, some sixty-five percent of New Brunswick Francophones who appeared in court asked for an English trial because they did not want to cause an inconvenience. After the law changed and the system was reformed, defendants started appearing before bilingual judges. In New Brunswick, more often than not, those judges are Francophones, so defendants feel more comfortable asking for a trial in French. The number of requests for French trials has gone up.

Nevertheless, Mary Moreau, now chief justice of the Court of Queen's Bench of Alberta, believes the battle is far from won.

"Institutional openness to language rights is not yet up to the level of the constitutional requirements laid out by Michel in Beaulac. Beaulac is like our reference point, our marching orders to go to the other branch of government and say, 'This is an invitation to the public.' I firmly believe that. That's what's missing. That initial contact in French, letting people know the court will uphold their rights in criminal matters. Unfortunately, that's harder to do with civil cases."

For Mark Power, a lawyer who practises all over the country, the main benefit of the decision is that it offers clients hope that they can have their trial in French whether they are in Charlottetown or Whitehorse, Windsor or Prince Albert. "For clients who are wondering if they'll even have a chance to challenge, Beaulac makes that a realistic possibility," he explained. "Before Beaulac, it wasn't, really [...]. Beaulac gave the Canadian Francophonie fresh hope and the confidence to believe they could use the courts to stabilize and improve the status of French in Canada."

***

Reaction to Beaulac was swift and outraged. After all, we had just declared the mistrial of a man convicted of murder. Provincial governments had to adjust, and the federal government had to take steps to support the courts. That negative response was not going away anytime soon. One day, I was at Ottawa's Rideau Club, a private club attended by ministers, ambassadors, judges, and other business people in the national capital, and I crossed paths with Irwin Cotler. This was after he became Canada's justice minister in 2003. I had never met Cotler before, and I greeted him politely. Irwin Cotler had a well-earned international reputation as a champion of cultural and religious minorities, particularly in the Jewish community.

Cotler stopped and introduced himself. It was totally informal. He said, "You really made our lives difficult with Beaulac. It cost us a bundle." I was taken aback. It was the first time a minister had approached me to comment on one of my decisions. I definitely did not get the sense that he had sought me out. We just happened to cross paths, and he took the opportunity to share that with me. I saw fit to reply politely, "No, I didn't make your lives difficult; you made your own lives difficult." After all, it was the Liberals who adopted the *Canadian Charter of Rights and Freedoms* and had been patting themselves on the back ad nauseam ever since.

Of course provincial governments were furious because they saw it as the Supreme Court of Canada giving people the option to demand yet another layer of services. I thought that was excellent news. If they were that upset about it, clearly they realized they had a long way to go to create a functional system that strives to uphold the principle of equality.

"Maybe for some politicians it was hard to digest," said Cotler in a December 2018 interview. "But it wasn't something hard to digest for myself because I knew where it was coming from and I saw it in terms of minority rights sensibility and how that was germane to what a constitutional democracy was all about. Now, there may be some who would look at that in terms of do we have the resources, etc., but I think it had a vision of what this country is all about." He thought he had expressed his appreciation for the decision when he spoke to me that day and said that, although some people would find difficulty with it, he was not one of them.

What is really surprising is that Cotler was an ardent defender of the *Canadian Charter or Rights and Freedoms*. He claims to have spent his life fighting for the equality clause. That is why his reaction puzzled me. I was not going to lose sleep over which level of government footed the bill. If the political arm of government accepted the principle of equality, it had to accept the consequences of that too.

"There is a long list of things to do," says Mary T. Moreau, a fully bilingual judge. "I think that, from time to time, authorities with the ability to change things can go that extra mile so as to signal that francophone rights are just as important in criminal law. It's not the right to an interpreter. It's more than that in terms of the *Criminal Code*. If a government recognizes dualism, that opens the door to all other cultures. I did an eight-week civil case in French in the Northwest Territories. It was all about government services. In the territories, people are guaranteed an offer of service in French at the hospital, the records office. That was an important case for the Franco-Ténois, Francophones in the Northwest Territories. I would like governments to approach language rights with more openness. There are also the practical, everyday life things like signage in French and bilingual websites."

The fact remains that there are not enough bilingual judges in the country. As Mark Power sees it, having bilingual Supreme Court justices is key. According to him, the fact that it still is not possible for all members of the Court to fully comprehend proceedings in both official languages and to rule in favour of or against a case is outrageous. I agree with him. Simultaneous interpretation is not perfect, and my unilingual anglophone colleagues had a very hard time participating in French-language cases. Power noted that the Université de Moncton, the University of Ottawa, and McGill University offer common law programs in French and that Canada's institutions are more bilingual than ever before. "The fact that functional bilingualism is not required for all Supreme Court of Canada justices is indicative of the disconnect between the law and what happens in practice," he said. "People talk about how the law shapes what happens in reality. Here it's literally the opposite. The law doesn't even reflect the degree to which Canada has changed."

18

The Battle Rages On

BLUE WATER, RED SOIL. Children, I do not have a photo, but here we are on Prince Edward Island (PEI). Canada's smallest province may also be its most interesting one, sociopolitically speaking. On PEI, everything is political, especially education and language rights. When Noëlla Arsenault-Cameron answered a knock on her door one beautiful August day in 1989, little did she suspect she was about to engage in one of the most intense legal battles in the province's history. Ms. Arsenault-Cameron was a Francophone from PEI's Evangeline region who was living in Summerside with her anglophone husband and their four children, Mitch, Jeremy, Kyle, and Candace. In August 1989, Mitch was attending a French immersion school and Jeremy was at an English school. Kyle was about to start kindergarten. The woman on Ms. Arsenault-Cameron's porch, Nicole Richard, an active member of the Fédération des parents de l'Île, got straight to the point: "If there were a French school fifty feet away from your house, would you send your kids there?"

"What are you talking about?" exclaimed Ms. Arsenault-Cameron. What Ms. Richard was about to tell her would change her life: "Did you know that if you don't put your kids in French school, your grandkids will never have the right to go to French school?"

"That really struck a chord with me," explained Noëlla Arsenault (she dropped the "Cameron" after her divorce). "It was very clear. I couldn't make a decision for future generations."

And so the group of parents embarked on an incredible adventure. They convinced the francophone school board to set up a school in an old English school board building, which also served as a community centre. Ten or so students attended the school. After the first year, the parents asked the school board to open a permanent French school in time for the 1995/1996 school year.

French school board officials met with Department of Education representatives and told them that, as of January 1995, thirty-four students were preregistered: twenty-nine from Summerside, four from Miscouche, and one from Kensington. Most parents did not want to send their children outside their community. École Évangéline in Abram's Village was twenty-eight kilometres from Summerside, twenty kilometres from Miscouche, forty kilometres from

Kensington and Bedeque, and forty-six kilometres from Kinkora. Parents really were not happy with the bus system that had been available for two decades, so the school board did not offer student transportation. Of the thirty-four preregistered students and thirteen others prepared to attend a French school in Summerside, fifteen enrolled in French immersion in English schools in the area for the 1995/1996 school year because their parents felt the bus ride was too long for young children.

In February 1995, the Department of Education turned down the school board's request and instead offered to maintain transportation services to École Évangéline. The school board then suggested offering French-language instruction in Summerside through École Évangéline, but the Minister rejected that idea too. In November 1995, Noëlla Arsenault-Cameron, Madeleine Costa-Petitpas, and the Fédération des parents de l'Île-du-Prince-Édouard Inc. initiated proceedings against the Government of Prince Edward Island seeking a declaration to the effect that they have the right to have their children receive French first language instruction at the primary level in a facility situated in Summerside. In 1997, Prince Edward Island Supreme Court Justice Armand DesRoches, an Acadian, found that the number of children from grades 1 to 6 that could be assembled for instruction in Summerside was sufficient to warrant the provision of French-language instruction out of public funds in Summerside and that the parents of these children had the right to receive that service in the Summerside area. Round 1: Francophones.

The provincial government was not about to let the matter go. It appealed to the Appeal Division of the Supreme Court of Prince Edward Island, where Justice MacQuaid held that the advantages that may result from the establishment of a French-language school in Summerside could not supersede the disadvantages of receiving instruction that would, in the opinion of the Minister, be inferior in pedagogical terms to that offered to the children of the official language majority. The Court added that bus transportation could be considered an educational facility and did not constitute an impediment to the exercise of the parents' rights given that the average time of travel did not exceed the provincial average. Round 2: the Province.

In 1999, the matter came before the Supreme Court of Canada. It was good timing; there I was.

***

The Supreme Court of Canada's main courtroom was packed, as it usually was for high-profile cases. In the hallways behind the courtroom, my eight colleagues eyed me skeptically. I had been awaiting this case impatiently for weeks, months even. A good week before the hearing, I was already thinking about what kind of decision I might render. "Maybe he wasn't sure the Court would fully understand it as well as he did, but I think we all did," said Jack Major.

My interest in language rights was not exactly a closely guarded secret. This case bore a strong resemblance to Mahé, which I had worked on as a lawyer, going up against the very same Jack Major. Before the *Arsenault-Cameron v. Prince Edward Island* case, I did my homework, as always. One of my clerks combed through the files and sent me his analysis and notes. But I could never have predicted what was about to happen. Before the hearing, Roger Langille, the Government of PEI's lawyer, made a political move in court. Langille was essentially defenceless. He really did not have a leg to stand on, but he attempted to silence me by applying for my recusal. Why? Apprehension of bias. It was one of the first times in the history of the Court that a lawyer had asked a judge to recuse himself from a hearing. Beverley McLachlin and I talked for a bit after the motion was submitted. "No one understood really, but judges have their own views on whether they can serve neutrally on a particular case," said Beverly many years later.

I did not know the appellant in the case, and other than an intellectual interest in language rights, I had no interest in the matter. Had I worked with the parent group fifteen or twenty years earlier? Perhaps, but that had no bearing. It was nonsensical. My blood began to boil and I turned beet-red. I was thunderstruck. I was sure my colleagues had all kinds of questions, but I did not really know what to tell them. I said I would take some time to consider the motion for recusal right away. "He consulted me, and we handled it step by step," said Beverley McLachlin. "You know, the whole court was involved. I guess he was furious, but it had to be dealt with in a very proper manner. You have to take these things seriously, and it was."

I immediately informed Chief Justice Lamer that I would take half an hour or so to deal with the application. He knew I would reject it. Such motions were very rare at the Supreme Court. According to Jack Major, "Most of the time, a judge will just say, 'I don't need to waste my time on this,' and move on. But Bastarache was very stubborn on certain subjects."

> Langille was essentially defenceless. He really did not have a leg to stand on, but he attempted to silence me by applying for my recusal. Why? Apprehension of bias.

When this happens, the judge named in the application can recuse himself—I certainly was not about to do that—or render a decision. If the solicitor is not happy with the decision, he can appeal to the other eight judges, who decide whether to hear the appeal. At the time, Justice McLachlin and others had already been thinking it might be time to change the rules, not because I had made a bad decision, but just to boost confidence in the Court. "I would never question his integrity or his decision," explained Iacobucci. "He is a man of integrity, and that's what he wrote. He didn't think he needed to recuse himself. In another case involving a colleague, the Court made the decision without the person who had been asked to recuse himself. You learn by what you do; you learn to improve things. I think the second process was better than our initial process."

I called in my clerks and asked them to dig up whatever they could about applications for recusal. Meanwhile, Chief Justice Lamer assembled all the parties to the case in his big second-floor corner office. There were almost ten of them packed in there.

"We found out the morning of the hearing that the province's lawyer was going to argue that Justice Bastarache was in conflict of interest. It was absolutely crazy," said Christian Michaud, the lawyer for the Société Saint-Thomas-d'Aquin. Roger B. Langille was there too. "I figured he would stay," said Pierre Foucher, the lawyer for one of the interveners, the Commission scolaire de langue Française de l'Île-du-Prince-Édouard. "That application was a last-ditch attempt, a Hail Mary. If you ask me, it made no sense. Seriously, imagine someone not being able to serve as a judge because they had argued this, that, or the other case as a lawyer."

I let Justice Lamer know I was ready to deliver my decision. The lawyer had gotten under my skin. "I have considered the notice of motion of the applicant as if it was addressed to me in the form of an application for recusal on the basis of apprehension of bias. I deny the motion," I wrote in my four-page decision. When I re-entered the courtroom, I felt the tension in the air. Speaking directly to Langille, I read my decision. His argument did not hold water. I rejected it. I was ready to hear the case.

In an article by *The Globe and Mail* reporter Kirk Makin, Langille is quoted as saying, "It may have been the convention to do it that way, but it is nonetheless troubling that a judge who is the subject of concern would take it upon himself to endeavour to determine how a reasonable person would perceive it." Poor Langille could have appealed to the other eight judges, but he did not. That is his problem.

To this day, I cannot figure out what prompted him to apply for my recusal. I suppose he thought the Court's expert in language rights should not participate in the hearing. I have tried to understand his motivation, his logic. After all, if my prior participation in language-related cases was grounds for disqualification, the same standard should have applied to my former adversary, Jack Major! I wanted to know what his reasoning was and get a sense of what kind of pressure he might have been under from the Province, so I called him up. It took him a week to decide whether to comment on the matter, and after giving the matter much thought, he opted not to. "I'd rather not comment because I don't think you really want to hear what I have to say. It's not very nice, and anything I say could end up in print," he said before saying he was sorry, but he had to go. Interesting...

★★★

The case itself was simple enough, but I wanted the Court to establish a clear roadmap for language rights in education by delivering a decision that would put an end to all the section 23 cases that kept popping up. Major and the others were well aware that I wanted my name on the decision. As McLachlin put it, "Judges are human beings first and foremost. You cannot divorce your sentiments and what you care about from being a human being and from the fact you're a judge. At the same time, it's a mistake to think a judge, no matter how passionate he may be about a particular issue, doesn't have the ability to look at it, on the record and on the law in an impartial way." She was right, but she also knew that if I delivered the decision solo, controversy would ensue. Children, ask any chief justice of the Supreme Court if they want to court controversy, and you will get an unequivocal no for an answer. Naturally, the Supreme Court wants to hand down as many unanimous decisions as possible. Dissenting opinions happen, and they are important, but in landmark cases such as the Quebec secession reference, unanimity was the goal. Arsenault-Cameron was not up there with the reference, but it was in a class of its own, partly because of the application for recusal. It was the kind of case that called for a strong message. In conference, we discussed the possibility of delivering a decision "By the Court." Some colleagues said that would give too much weight to the decision. Someone came up with the idea of Jack Major and me signing the decision. I liked the idea,

> Children, ask any chief justice of the Supreme Court if they want to court controversy, and you will get an unequivocal no for an answer.

and so did Jack. He felt that if he signed his name next to mine on the decision, that would solve the problem once and for all.

"Why have him on a hotseat?" asked Major. "He would've written it. I knew no matter what the others did, he would write it. I thought if we did it together, the others would agree, it would be a judgment that wouldn't cause a lot of controversy because it was a pretty clear case. You know, Prince Edward Island, you could say they didn't really read the judgment from the Supreme Court because the case affirmed what the Supreme Court said." After the conference, it was still up in the air. Who would write the decision? The only thing we all agreed on was that I would write the substance of the decision. I worked on it with Jack, who more or less gave me free rein. "He wrote most of it," said Jack in the fall of 2017. Ultimately, all the judges agreed to our decision and we were able to co-sign it.

In the decision, Jack and I wrote that the Appeal Division "erred in accepting that the Minister could unilaterally decide what level of service was appropriate. The priorities of the minority community had to be given precedence because they lie at the core of the management and control conferred on the minority language rights holders and their legitimate representatives by s. 23." Noëlla Arsenault-Cameron and her group won a major victory on January 13, 2000.

You know, symbolism is very important to me. The fact that Jack and I co-signed the decision still makes me smile. A decade after slugging it out in court over Mahé, there we were, hand in hand, delivering a historic decision for PEI Francophones. "Sometimes I think it would be attractive to me that Michel and Jack could write," said Frank. "The idea of someone from Alberta and someone from New Brunswick, with an Acadian background, making joint reasons, I think it was an advantage."

For many jurists, what stands out about the decision is who signed it. Pierre Foucher put it this way: "Who signed the decision? Counsel for opposite sides in Mahé. That was the Court's way of sending a strong message to all solicitors: stop hassling us with your accusations of bias because these people used to be lawyers."

Children, I wrote hundreds of decisions during my time on the bench. Arsenault-Cameron still stands out as one of the most important ones for me along with the Quebec secession reference and Beaulac. To this day it means a lot to me for a number of reasons. It was from the Maritimes; it revolved around education; it reminded me of the big victory in Mahé; and it was the first time anyone asked me to recuse myself on the grounds that I might be biased.

Twenty years later, I wanted to know more about the impact of the historic decision I co-signed with Jack. So much has happened since January 2000. I wanted to know how Francophones and Anglophones in Canada's smallest province were getting along. How had the decision affected young Prince Edward Islanders? To gain a better understanding, I had to go to PEI to see why this was such a significant case. Émilie and Jean-François, I have to say that what happened after Arsenault-Cameron is absolutely surreal.

★★★

I really wish you could experience what it feels like coming up to the Confederation Bridge. If you stop to think about it, the fact that this architectural masterpiece links Prince Edward Island, Canada's smallest province, to the North American continent is pretty amazing. The last few kilometres on the New Brunswick side are straight as an arrow, and at dawn, a thick fog engulfs your car. You roll down the windows to feel the salty sea air on your face. You cannot help but smile. Up you go, and there you are on the longest bridge in Canada. And then you drive and drive across a twelve-kilometre-wide strait. And then you are in paradise, or as close as it gets to paradise. The island is so soothing. You drive through little valleys of red earth, the rusty red you find only in the birthplace of Confederation. You cross potato fields stretching as far as the eye can see, and then you veer left onto Route 11.

Summerside is lovely. As PEI's second-largest city, it has that typical Maritime feel. Old nineteenth-century buildings stand as reminders of the province's history. A seaside drive leads to the wharves where fishers unload their tonnes of ocean-caught lobster. Nearby processing plants do a roaring trade, especially in the summer. Then it is inland through residential neighbourhoods to a little avenue called Maris Stella for a first-hand look at the outcome of the Arsenault-Cameron decision.

École-sur-Mer is a K-12 school attached to a francophone community centre and populated by nearly two hundred students (and counting) and about fifteen teachers. In 2018, Summerside's francophone daycare spaces were chock-full. According to the principal, Justine Roy, "We can't keep up with demand. We don't have the capacity to serve all the children who want to enroll in our daycare. There's not enough space." When children go to French daycare, it's practically guaranteed they'll go to École-sur-Mer. The student body has grown so much that the school has expanded four times since it was built in the early 2000s.

Justine gave us the grand tour. The building is modern, with a circular layout. The school's mission is student-centred. Every single detail was carefully considered, right down to the floor tiles, which are designed to stimulate students' mathematical thinking. Culturally, the school is mindful of its roots and reflects its community. "We don't necessarily talk about Arsenault-Cameron in class," explained the principal, "but we do talk about language law and francophone culture and current events. It's important to understand those things and be open to those learning opportunities."

The same building houses a daycare that feeds into École-sur-Mer year after year, and the school itself boosts attendance at the Belle-Alliance community centre. It is a virtuous circle by design. The community centre supports the school by organizing activities in French to foster francophone identity, and the school returns the favour. Fear of assimilation is ever-present, but the school and the community centre carry the torch for the Francophonie in Summerside. I needed to meet the person who pulled out all the stops to keep that flame alive.

★★★

Hervé Poirier is a typical "come from away," a person from somewhere else who decides to settle on Prince Edward Island. They are not from there, and neither are their parents. They are total strangers, and they will always be strangers. Poirier first set foot on the island in 1979, went back to his home province of Quebec briefly, and then returned to the island for good in the 1980s. He studied to be a teacher and worked first in an immersion school and then the French school. Naturally authoritative, he worked his way up to school principal and became École-sur-Mer's first principal.

In May 2018, Poirier welcomed us to his magnificent Oyster Bed Bridge home on a gorgeous eighty-four-acre estate not far from North Rustico and Cavendish. We sat in his living room, and, sipping tea, he told us how, in 2000, he applied for the position of principal at the new school. Once he got the job, he became a man on a mission, throwing himself into the adventure of a lifetime: building a new school. He was hired three months after our decision and one month after the Department of Education and the French-language school board announced plans to provide instruction in French to students in and around Summerside. In October of that same year, the federal and provincial governments both committed funding for the city's new francophone school and community centre.

Arsenault-Cameron snowballed. The Summerside School is a direct result of the decision, but Summerside was not the only community entitled to a French-language school under section 23. West Prince had been fighting for one for years; so had Rustico. Like some kind of missionary, Poirier took it upon himself to head up all three schools for a period of time. He was still looking for a site for École-sur-Mer. The provincial government had promised $6.1 million to build the new school. When the Anglophones found out about that, it nearly touched off a rebellion. Many people in the community condemned what they considered to be an astronomical amount of money for "just four students." There was much more to it than that though. In addition to building a school, programs had to be created and staff hired.

The building was constructed in 2001. The school was designed for 150 students in grades 1 through 6. At that time, nobody thought the school would one day have to accommodate students from kindergarten through grade 12. The thinking was that highschoolers would go to Évangéline. It was a community agreement. After Arsenault-Cameron, the people of Abram's Village were furious that a school in Summerside would take away their students. École-sur-Mer opened in 2002, two years after the Supreme Court ruling. That first year, the magnificent red-brick building, whose roof represented a blue wave, welcomed about twenty young Francophones. Water crashing against the island's red soil; the blue waves of the Francophonie breaking against the Anglophones' red earth, eroding it bit by bit, year after year. This French school, like every other French school in the province, bothered people. A lot.

★★★

At the Charlottetown Courthouse, it took eight or nine registry employees to carry all the documents. We wanted to review the evidence presented during the 1997 trial. The woman at the counter was startled when we said the case name: Arsenault-Cameron v. Prince Edward Island. She hustled off to see her colleagues. Everyone was surprised. "Oh!" said a couple of them. "Are you familiar with the case?" we asked. "Everyone on the island is familiar with it whether they were for or against it," the woman replied with a sigh. "There's a brand-new school in Rustico now that has thirty students. That doesn't seem viable to me," she added.

All over the island, people looked askance whenever the case was mentioned. Twenty years after the decision, the tension between Anglophones and Francophones over education was still palpable. Anglophones said they were being reasonable; they were open to and tolerant of the French-speaking segment of society. They thought Francophones should appreciate what they had been given. Francophones argued that they were being treated like second-class citizens and were entitled to quality instruction in French. Politicians chimed in too, talking up the bilingual signage they had installed in various parts of the province and their support for Acadian culture.

"Think of them as wolves in sheep's clothing," warned Émile Gallant, Chair of the French school board. "Sure, people here can speak French, but just wait until it's time to make real decisions." He was taking aim at politicians who did not have the courage to take a stand in support of Francophones. "Saying nice things every now and then is one thing, but championing their rights is another," he declared.

In 2018, the school board announced its intention to take legal action against Wade MacLauchlan's Liberal government on the grounds that it had used federal money from the Official Languages in Education Program to pay teachers' salaries. In a notice to the government, the school board and their lawyer, Mark Power, stated that the Department of Education was violating section 23 of the *Canadian Charter of Rights and Freedoms* and interfering with its full implementation. The school board claimed that the Department did not engage in adequate consultation to ascertain the community's needs with respect to education and that federal funds intended to support French-language instruction were being used to reduce regular operating costs and pay more than thirteen teachers, resulting in an annual million-dollar shortfall in funding meant for programs to promote French language learning and identity construction.

In an April 2018 interview on Radio-Canada, PEI's Minister of Education, Jordan Brown, said that five of the province's six French-language schools had been built in the last fifteen years. "Students in the French school board make up five percent of PEI's student body. Over the past fifteen years, we've invested twenty percent of our capital budget in French-language schools," he said. The fact is it was not funding for infrastructure; it was for instruction. And what about the cost of bringing French-language instruction up to par?

Arsenault-Cameron seems to have produced one specific outcome. According to Émile Gallant, "It gave us infrastructure. At least we can threaten them and say, 'Here's what we want,' and then eventually, after years and years of asking, we get our schools. That's the extent of it though." In any case, section 23 of the Charter enabled Francophones to keep their school board when the government decided to abolish PEI's school boards.

The school board's demands started making some members of the francophone community uncomfortable, especially francophone public servants in Charlottetown. Francophones in the Evangeline region were negatively impacted by the development of the French-language school network. Rising enrollment at École-sur-Mer meant declining enrollment at École Évangéline. The rural exodus in action. Keeping French alive in the island province is a day-to-day battle.

Children, I wanted to know what my friend, Wade MacLauchlan, PEI's premier in 2018, had to say about his relationship with Francophones. I wanted to know how he saw them, how he viewed their status in his province. Wade is a respected jurist. He taught law at the University of New Brunswick and was president of the University of Prince Edward Island. He is an upstanding guy, and I have always liked him. I was curious about what Arsenault-Cameron meant to him. Why was it so hard for Francophones to convince the province to provide them with adequate educational services? How would he describe the relationship between the two founding peoples on the island? I was keen to ask him these questions, but his office did not respond to my meeting requests. As he was leaving a Liberal Party event in Charlottetown in May 2018, he said these were sensitive topics because the French school board was about to launch legal proceedings. He said he would get back to me, but he never did. In the end, it was not his problem because the Liberal Party was decimated in the April 2019 election. Wade even lost his own seat in the Legislative Assembly, and he is no longer the leader of PEI's Liberal Party.

★★★

Noëlla Arsenault is a unique woman. She is expressive, funny, and determined. In the kitchen of her semi-detached home in Charlottetown, she reminisced about the trials and tribulations that made her national news. The former hairdresser, now with Veterans Affairs, cradled her coffee cup in both hands as she recalled what happened after the decision, after her big Supreme Court of Canada win.

"They'll hold this against me forever," she said of the province's Anglophones as well as the Francophones in Evangeline. Her 1990s activism did not sit well with them, and her Supreme Court victory ruffled a lot of feathers. It really annoyed everyone from total strangers to her husband and children.

This battle cost her her marriage. Her husband just could not withstand pressure from his clients or make a genuine effort to support her. Her children were victims of discrimination on the school bus and at school. Some of them even got beaten up. The two who were in grades 9 and 10 at the time decided to leave French school, moved in with their father and went to English school. "They'd had it up to here with French and decided they wanted nothing more to do with it," said Ms. Arsenault.

The fifteen years following the decision were emotional ones. She got into the habit of grocery shopping late at night to avoid angry anglophone outbursts. She lived in Summerside for five years after the decision, then moved to Charlottetown and met the love of her life, an Anglophone from Montréal who ended up in PEI during the case and was attracted to the woman who was fighting for a school. They made a life together in PEI's capital for eleven years until he died in 2014. "He was my everything," she said, wiping away a tear, then collecting herself and resuming her narrative.

She was fired up. She wanted Francophones to set aside their turf wars and stop fighting over which community should be first in line for a new school. "Are you trying to improve things for your own little corner of the province or for the francophone community as a whole?" she said. She urged Francophones to come together. "To get community development funding from Canadian Heritage, Francophones have to make up five percent of the population. If we go below five percent, that money could dry up at a moment's notice," she explained.

She talked about how proud she felt at the grand opening of École-sur-Mer, but that pride did not dispel the grey cloud hanging over her. "I've never been able to show that pride in public!" she exclaimed, and sighed. If she did, she would be opening herself up to attacks not only from Anglophones but also from Francophones in her hometown, never mind the fact that it was twenty years after the case. Anglophones had given her a hard time over the years. While in office, a former premier had discreetly warned her against ever applying for a provincial government job. Whatever—she got a federal government job.

She had some pretty terrible encounters with Anglophones, but none so bad as with Francophones. "Our very own Acadians were the worst," she said accusingly. That's so hard to understand. Acadians who did not want to rock the boat and make waves and held a grudge against the person who did. She revealed that her parents never, ever congratulated her, and neither did her brothers and sisters. Just because she dared to ask the government for something. Apparently that is just not something island Acadians do.

"I know people don't understand what this cost me personally. My children really suffered. I can't ever give them back those parts of their childhood that we lost because of what we did. Two of my kids didn't finish French school because of it," she said, choking back tears. She had a heart attack, suffered from depression, and developed diabetes. The stress had a profound impact on her.

Twenty years after Jack's and my decision, Noëlla Arsenault now has six grandchildren. They are all in French immersion. Not one attends French school. "It's because of everything that happened," she lamented. "My kids were so sick of French, but they knew their kids had to be able to speak French, so they put them in immersion. They don't want them in French school." The subject is still far too touchy for her to even talk to them about it. Her goal was to ensure her children, and especially her grandchildren, had access to education in French on the island. It was the fight of her life. Sadly, she lost that fight. Her victory only ever benefited others.

Farewell to the Court

OH, ÉMILIE AND JEAN-FRANÇOIS, how I wish I could have shown you what Canada was like in the 2000s. I wish I could have shown you one people's resistance in the face of assimilation, the vibrant francophone communities shaping our country. Thirty years after our victory in Mahé, thousands of francophone children can receive instruction in their language and grow into their own cultural identity. I wish I could have shown you the myriad realities making up what had become the country's most conservative province, introduced you to tenacious Franco-Albertans in Peace River and Edmonton, and the immigrants breathing new life into the French presence in Calgary. The role of French schools has changed quite a bit since Mahé. Today, young people get the support they need to claim their space. They are bilingual, they preserve their language, and after graduation, they will go on to become doctors, entrepreneurs, engineers, nurses, and even lawyers. Some will leave their communities and relocate to Ottawa, Montréal, or Toronto, bringing with them all their regional and community pride. Others will go in the opposite direction and put down roots in these Western communities. One such person is Dominique Jean, who, while Mahé was still before the courts, left his native Saguenay-Lac-Saint-Jean to settle in Alberta. He travelled for hours by plane and then by Greyhound bus across the prairies, finally making his way to the small community of St. Isidore, where he helped reinvigorate northern Alberta's francophone community. Over the years, he forged close ties not only with the locals, but also with people in the wood industry whose ancestors all hailed from Quebec. They still speak the language. They maintain it. They are proud of it. At his École des Quatre-Vents office in Peace River, Dominique Jean recalled, "In those days, for a guy from the Saguenay, French communities outside Quebec weren't on my radar at all; we simply didn't know they existed. Then, you get here and you meet some very welcoming folks, true-blue Francophones, entrepreneurs. There's Boucher Brothers Lumber, but also some major agricultural operations in St. Isidore, such as Lavoie farms and Bergeron beekeepers. These are all thriving businesses." You guessed it: Mr. Jean still lives in Alberta. A journey that was meant to last three months ended up spanning more than thirty years. His mission as a teacher and school principal is to share his love and passion for the French language with young people, but it goes way beyond that. As he explains it, "Education here in Alberta is about more than just French. The education system here is very different from the one in Quebec. If you walked into a school over the weekend, on a Sunday, it wouldn't be unusual to find teachers at work. They come in to do prep and collaborate with their colleagues." French education in the area is community-centred, local. Schools are the brain, the heart, and the lungs of the French-speaking community.

A few dozen kilometres south of Peace River, in Falher, Nicole Couillard Wallisser strides briskly along the halls of École Héritage, where she is the principal, and says, "Let me introduce you to the newest Sanchez." The newest Sanchez? Mr. and Mrs. Sanchez left their native Peru to settle in Falher, known as the honey capital of Canada, where they became beekeepers themselves and enrolled all their four children in French school. The entire family is trilingual, but their connection to the French-speaking community is very strong.

Ms. Couillard Wallisser puts it like this: "You hear a stranger speaking French, and you're instantly drawn to them. The number of families with one parent who speaks French and one who speaks another language is on the rise, but French is still their everyday language. It comes naturally. I'd say that École Héritage is doing a lot to preserve the language in town and in the surrounding area. We organize community events. We try to include our French immersion counterparts, but culture isn't always a part of their mission, or of their identity." You cannot miss the French presence at the neighbourhood co-op. As I walk up to the counter, I am greeted with a "Bonjour, monsieur." To converse in one's own language, that to me is cultural pride, cultural affirmation.

The kids are attached to their communities, too. Although many of them are leaving the region, that is just part of the larger rural exodus happening everywhere in Canada. For the most part, these young Francophones who went to French schools pursue post-secondary education. Those who do not tend to go to trade school instead. Very few drop out of school for good. The drop-out rate among Francophones is extremely low in this part of the country.

Couillard Wallisser goes on to explain that, "The more educated they are, the more likely they are to come back. For example, take the really big farms around here. The dads won't hand the place over to their kids just because they graduated high school. It's business, after all. They'll say, 'You there, you're taking business admin, and you, you're going to agricultural school to learn about crop rotation, and you'll do something else.' Because we're talking about really big operations."

The feeling of pride is palpable. Just because they happen to be far from the big city does not mean they cannot live their lives entirely in French. Sports are another way for them to shape their culture. Seeing the smile on kids' faces when they learn that they will be able to participate in the Jeux de la Francophonie more than makes up for whatever the naysayers have to say about dead ducks. This sporting event is hugely important to these kids. Before we leave her office at

École Héritage, Couillard Wallisser shows me a picture of her daughter, a member of the Université de Moncton's volleyball team. "The Université de Moncton, can you believe it? She's halfway across the country, in a reputable French-language university," she beams. Will her daughter ever come back home? "I hope so. She has a boyfriend over there now. An Acadian."

★★★

More than five thousand kilometres away, Emmanuelle LeBlanc sips coffee in a Summerside, Prince Edward Island, café. Her band, Vishtèn, is between tours. Outside, the sky is grey and the seas rough, waves slamming into the docks. The downtown strip has restaurants, coffee shops, and the library. Off in the distance, you can just about see the old railway station on Water Street. Ms. LeBlanc talks about her childhood growing up in a strictly French-speaking household where even a single word of English was out of the question. It was much the same in daycare, since all Emmanuelle's and her twin sister Pastelle's friends spoke French. The sisters attended École Évangéline in Abram's Village from kindergarten all the way to grade 12. This was sometime in the 1990s. In grade 1, they were some fifty students split up in two classes, but by the time they graduated grade 12, they were down to twenty-four. Half of them were gone. Some left the town or the province entirely, while others transferred to the English school in Summerside.

LeBlanc recalls, "The Jeux de l'Acadie and the first Congrès mondial Acadian were turning points for me. At the congress in 1994, we felt as though we really belonged to the greater Acadian family."

Her Acadian identity was becoming an important part of her life. Those were formative years, when she came to know and understand the unique character of the Island's francophone and Acadian communities. As a child, she certainly did not feel any different from the anglophone girls. As an adult, however, she can see a world of difference. "Being a minority isn't always easy," she says, "because you end up with a smaller group of friends and wonder why." Part of it has to do with the need to belong, to feel safe. The depth of Acadian cultural pride is unmatched in the English world. Putting her coffee cup down, she adds, "I've seen assimilation in action, and I still see it."

Although they speak French at home, some kids like to speak English at school because it is cooler. When the time came to organize their twenty-year high school reunion, she soon realized that her old school chums all communicated in English in a private group on social media. Are they all unilingual Anglophones, now? Have they lost their mother tongue? Now that they are parents themselves, a great many of them are having a hard time deciding whether to send their children to English school or French school. Many of them will end up choosing English school, just because it is easier that way. Ironically, at the other end of the spectrum, anglophone families are sending their kids to French immersion to give them a chance to speak both languages. "I sometimes wonder if the Francophones I went to school with still have that pride," muses Emmanuelle. The consequences are far-reaching. Gradually, the community erodes. The schools empty out, and the next thing you know, the credit union shuts down. Before long, the co-op store that serves customers in French is gone too. And no one says a peep; that is the world we live in.

Emmanuelle and her sister held on to their pride. When their band, Vishtèn, goes on tour, they share their Acadian musical heritage with the world. Their style is heavily inspired by traditional music, rock, and indie-folk, with some Celtic melodies thrown in. Their fans are mostly Acadian, but they are also American, Irish, and British. And yet, Vishtèn sings exclusively in French. A music producer from Alberta once suggested that they consider singing in English in order to make it on the world stage. Otherwise, he claimed, the audience would not understand their message. The band refused. The French language is an instrument. The Americans understand that, and so do the Brits, so why not an Albertan? Of course, she still addresses the crowd in English between songs to explain the meaning and the message behind the melodies she sings. She will never change her identity.

My whole life I have fought for the French language and for the equal status of both linguistic communities. It brings me great joy to see athletes like Geneviève Lalonde make it all the way to the Olympic Games in Rio proudly wearing both Acadian and Canadian flags. It brings me comfort when artists like Emmanuelle LeBlanc as well as entrepreneurs, doctors, and others are loud and proud about their Acadian or French-Canadian heritage. Perhaps the war I waged my entire life will not have been for naught, even if the defeats keep piling up.

★★★

When I first started working at the Supreme Court of Canada, it was especially important to me to reverse the harmful effects of what was known in the legal community as the 1986 trilogy. Allow me to explain, children. In May 1986, the Supreme Court of Canada handed down three rulings that were devastating for minority francophone communities. "If you'd been at the law faculty on May 1, 1986, you would've seen a sea of long faces," recalled my one-time colleague, Michel Doucet.

All three rulings were handed down around noon. All across Canada, lawyers, legal practitioners, and law professors wondered why they ever chose to specialize in language rights. The Supreme Court's message in these three rulings could not have been any clearer: do not count on the judiciary's help to advance language rights; seek political support instead. Right up until 1986, things had been moving and shaking in the world of language rights. The *Canadian Charter of Rights and Freedoms* became law in 1982, and in the ensuing years, the courts essentially sided with minorities in Canada. What happened in 1986, however, threw everyone for a loop.

Relying on a very narrow interpretation of language rights, the Supreme Court of Canada found that, although an accused does indeed have the right to use the language of their choice in court, the *Canadian Charter of Rights and Freedoms* does not give them the right to be heard by a judge who can understand them directly. It is up to individual judges to assess their own language proficiency and decide whether to use an interpreter. Rights apply to all parties equally; consequently, the Crown has the right to draft its documents in the language of its choice without considering the language of the accused.

The first case, *MacDonald v. City of Montréal*, involved an English-speaking inhabitant of Montréal who appeared before Montréal's municipal court to answer a charge of violating a municipal by-law. The entire case was tried in French. The accused challenged the jurisdiction of the Court on the ground that the Court violated his fundamental rights as an English speaker. In the end, the Court ruled that the gentleman's rights had not, in fact, been violated. Justice Beetz wrote the decision, with Estey, McIntyre, Lamer, and Le Dain concurring.

The second case, *Bilodeau v. A.G. (Man.)*, is special because the accused, Roger Bilodeau, was a student of mine at the Université de Moncton's Faculty of Law at the time. This is the same Roger Bilodeau who went on to be appointed registrar of the Supreme Court of Canada in 2009. Back in 1980, in his home province of Manitoba, Bilodeau was pulled over for speeding and subsequently challenged the fact that the summons he received was written in English only. The case made its way to the Supreme Court, where a majority of judges ruled:

> Although the appellant's conviction will stand, it must be acknowledged that he was successful in challenging the constitutional validity of the unilingual statutes. He was also successful in asserting that the requirements of s. 23 were mandatory. The appellant's conviction only stands because of the application by this Court of the rule of law principle to avoid legal chaos in Manitoba, which would have otherwise resulted from the appellant's successful challenge to the legislation of Manitoba enacted since 1890. In the very special circumstances of this case, it is appropriate that the appellant be awarded his costs in this Court and in the Court of Appeal.

The third, *Société des Acadiens v. Association of Parents for Fairness in Education*, is about whether a party pleading in a New Brunswick court is entitled to be heard by a court, the member or members of which are capable of understanding the proceedings, regardless of the official language used by the parties. The ruling states that "the courts should pause before they decide to act as instruments of change with respect to language rights. This is not to say that language rights provisions are cast in stone and should remain immune altogether from judicial interpretation. But, in my opinion, the courts should approach them with more restraint than they would in construing legal rights."

Michel Doucet believes, and I happen to agree, that the three rulings are closely linked to the whole debate around the Meech Lake Accord. Everyone was afraid of alienating Quebec at the time, and no one wanted to give the nationalist movement an excuse to accuse the Supreme Court of giving additional powers to Quebec's anglophone minority community.

"This is really significant," he said. "It's a new vision of the Supreme Court as abdicating its role with regard to minority language communities. We see this as an affront, a slap in the face that's hard to swallow."

I saw those rulings as mistakes that absolutely needed fixing. That is why, as soon as I was appointed to the Supreme Court, I wanted to find a way to establish that linguistic equality goes deeper than people's ability to express themselves in their language. It is so much more than that. We need an institutional structure that is designed not to accommodate individuals' extraordinary demands but to acknowledge that everyone has the right to be heard on the same level and to have equal access to equal service. The individual right implies a collective right.

The *Reference re Secession of Quebec* had the most impact because it declared the protection of minorities to be a basic constitutional principle and was signed by the entire Court, not an individual judge. In addition to being important case law in several respects, Beaulac also set the tone for future interpretation of linguistic rights. I am still disappointed in my failure to rally the support of Justices Binnie and Lamer. And then there is Arsenault-Cameron, which sent a strong message to governments that they have a duty to offer service of equal quality to both official language communities in matters of education. Significantly, the decision was unanimous, co-signed by my friend Jack Major.

I have always been passionate about minority rights, which occasionally ruffled feathers among my colleagues on the bench. Am I an activist? No. Passion and activism do not necessarily go hand in hand. Maybe it is just about doing the right thing and respecting everyone's rights. The battle for equality is never-ending in Canada.

★★★

I was sitting at my desk, carefully considering the shortlist of twenty-five names my clerks put together for the 2006/2007 hiring process. One name stood out: Naiomi Metallic, a young Indigenous woman from the Listuguj Mi'gmaq First Nation, in

Gaspésie, right on the border with New Brunswick, studying at Dalhousie University in Halifax. There was something remarkable about her. Justices Binnie and Charron must have felt the same way since they interviewed her as well. The morning of our meeting, she flew in from Halifax, arriving in Ottawa with only a few short hours to spare. She had not had much sleep since she was attending a major conference in the capital over the next few days. So here was this brilliant young woman sitting across from me showing absolutely no sign of nervousness. And yet, deep down, she did not really believe she would land the clerkship. Naiomi was one of the first members of her community to graduate law and was hoping to be the first to work at the Supreme Court of Canada. That same year, Madeleine Redfern, the first Inuk woman to work at the Supreme Court, was hired first by Louise Arbour, just prior to her retirement, and subsequently by Justice Louise Charron. Louise and I both realized at the same time how important it was for the institution to hire a First Nations woman. Naiomi may not have been head of her class, but her attitude made her a much better candidate than the more book-smart students.

> I have always been passionate about minority rights, which occasionally ruffled feathers among my colleagues on the bench. Am I an activist? No.

Ten years after her clerkship ended, Naiomi said, with a laugh, "There are those who focus on the students with the best grades, but as Bastarache once told me, 'I don't want somebody who has so many degrees that he is as old as I am!' or something like that." You guessed it, kids, I hired her.

I assigned Naiomi many different tasks that year. She did not get special treatment. Her performance was flawless, and she made it look easy. She would have been roughly the same age as you, Émilie. The more time we spent together, the better I got to know her. Where she came from, how she lost her father shortly after her stint at the Court. We had a connection. As she put it, "I lost my father in 2008, and I think Bastarache started giving me advice as a father would, especially as my legal and academic career progressed, which I appreciated."

During my time on the bench, I tried to organize an annual reunion, and I invited every clerk who had ever worked with me. Sometimes, I brought in some Acadian musicians to put on a show. I wanted to get everyone together to celebrate and thank them all for what they had done for me. I wanted them to know just how much their presence and support had served as an antidote to the kind of cynicism that can begin to take hold when you get older and maybe a bit disillusioned. I wanted to tell them what a privilege it was to know them, these passionate young people who would change the world. I always gave a toast, and as I gathered my thoughts before speaking, I could not help but reflect that they, in some small way, made up for losing you, my darlings.

Naiomi Metallic recalled, "He said that, when he went to give speeches at graduation ceremonies, he would be sitting next to a parent, and that parent would turn around and exclaim, 'That's my kid!' when their child was called up to the podium. That emotion that parent felt, he said, 'I feel that way for each and every one of you.' It was beautiful, so touching."

I did my utmost to make sure the clerks used their time working at the Court to learn how to properly analyze legislation, how to identify the underlying issues in a case, how to complement their research by consulting foreign case law. I always wanted the year they spent with me to be a learning experience, and I wanted them to feel valued and respected. More than a decade after I retired from the Court, I am still in touch with a great many of them. In fact, I once accepted a senior counsel position at a law firm where two of my previous clerks happened to be employed.

I never wanted to influence their career choices, and I was certain that each of them would accomplish great things. I could not help thinking that some of them would one day become judges like me. And in Naiomi's case, why not go all the way to the Supreme Court of Canada? After her year in Ottawa, she completed her master's in Toronto and then spent nearly ten years practising law at a major firm in Halifax before becoming a professor at Dalhousie University. You might think her trajectory bears a striking resemblance to mine. That may be, but what I know for sure is that she is an incredibly intelligent and meticulous woman with an exceptional work ethic. She is an unstoppable force. Nobody could slow her down but she herself. She is a woman on a mission, and just like her mentor before her, she chose her mission very early in her career. For me, it was language rights; for her, Indigenous law.

"He and I talked about it," she said. "It makes me feel proud, but also very humble. It's wonderful to know that he trusts in my abilities and sees me occupying such a position one day. It's something I'm interested in, and I'll certainly consider it, but not right now. I love my job teaching at the university."

★★★

Children, I will never forget my last day at the Supreme Court of Canada. That morning, it was with a heavy heart that I took my seat just to the right of the Chief

My last day at the Court. *From left to right*: my brothers Jean and Marc, my mother, and my sister Monique. They have always been there for my greatest triumphs and in my darkest moments.
Source: Collection of Michel Bastarache.

Justice. The courtroom before me was packed with former colleagues, members of the Canadian Bar Association and the Law Society of New Brunswick, Justice Minister Rob Nicholson, and, way at the back, Yolande, sitting with my mother, who was ninety years old at the time. It occurred to me that she probably never stopped believing I might one day find stable employment. At that very moment, the job I was leaving behind was probably the one that had come closest to achieving her objective.

Working at the Supreme Court is not like working anywhere else. I worked there for eleven years, but every single time I went to the office, I drove up to the garage door feeling like I was a guest—a transient, fleeting presence in this storied establishment. You are no ordinary employee when you work in an institution like that. Even when I looked at my fellow judges sitting at their desks, I did not see them in the same way I did my colleagues at the Court of Appeal or elsewhere. Every morning for eleven years, I walked into my office feeling like an outsider. My fellow judges appeared to me as characters acting out a play. The legendary quality of this august institution is only enhanced by the court protocol, its majesty and mystery. My colleague Claire L'Heureux-Dubé once likened the Court's enigmatic air to that of a great monastery, a comparison that served to remind us that our presence within it was ephemeral indeed. We all have an expiry date, and it is set at seventy-five years.

Still, I very much enjoyed the hearings and drafting reasons for decisions. During my final two years at the Court, our conferences became shorter and less frequent. I found that difficult. In my opinion, when you are trying to develop a clear and sophisticated interpretation of the law, you need to talk, not just send memos back and forth. Perhaps it had something to do with my friends and colleagues Louise Arbour, Frank Iacobucci, Charles Gonthier, and Jack Major leaving? I cannot rightly say. I enjoyed working with the sixteen judges whose paths I crossed at the Court, but I have a particular fondness for Jack and Frank, with whom I spent many hours outside of work. That might seem unlikely in Jack's case, given what a formidable opponent he had been back in Alberta, but I found him to be a good man with a great sense of humour who helped me become a better judge. In our line of work, talking things through is important. You need to meet in person. Nurturing that sense of collegiality is vital, and it happens not only within the institution's hallowed halls but also in less formal settings.

In the years after Lamer's retirement, we spent less and less time talking. I was not happy about that, nor did I like the fact that we made some very significant rulings without ever discussing the issues in depth.

Beverley McLachlin disagrees. As she sees it, "We had some difficult conversations when Lamer was chief justice, and we also had difficult conversations when I was chief justice. It's a tough job! I did what I could to unite the Court, to foster collegiality and consensus. There was more [when I was chief justice]. The way it was done traditionally, everyone left the courtroom, said what they thought about the case and then went on their way. When I got there, we had more discussions. [Anyone who says otherwise] is simply wrong; they must not have had reliable information. Anyone in the know, however, would say that we held long meetings and that I often called everyone back into conference for further discussion." She insisted that there were more discussions during her tenure as chief justice than Lamer's. I know many judges who, like me, would say the opposite. Everyone remembers things their own way. I do not want to offend the Chief Justice, whom I like. To be perfectly candid, even on legal matters we always got along quite well. More often than not, my votes aligned with those of Justices McLachlin and Binnie, but not necessarily with those of the other judges.

Cases began dragging on, especially the landmark cases. You know, maybe I should have done things differently. Had I become too emotionally involved? Maybe under the circumstances I should have taken a step back. As Paul LaBarge, my old colleague from Lang Michener, would say, "Michel is a passionate guy." I should have tempered my reactions. I became much too emotionally involved during my final years at court. That is when the weariness set in, and when I am tired, I sometimes react poorly.

I started thinking about resigning sometime in 2007. The very thought vexed me to no end. I could not fathom feeling compelled to leave the Court because of my working conditions, and not because of the work itself. The two often intersect, you know; they are very closely linked. It took me six months to come to terms with my decision. At court, I became increasingly frustrated and irritable. One day, I picked up the phone and called some of my judge friends—people like Joe Robertson and Charles Hackland, long-time friends who know who I am and where I have been. Neither of them encouraged me to resign, nor did they try to talk me out of it. They listened, which was exactly what I needed at that point. Did it make any sense to even consider quitting a job like that? It made my head spin.

"No one suspected it would be his last year," remarked my clerk, Caroline Magnan. "It seemed like a normal year. There was a handful of major rulings. I believe Justice Bastarache wrote the decisions in Dunsmuir, Société des Acadiens, and *Honda Canada v. Keays*, if I remember correctly. Everything seemed normal until the last two months, I'd say. People were concerned about his health. He had always had so much energy. He never let on anything was amiss. I remember a meeting with him and the other two law clerks in his office on his last day. It was all very moving. What were we supposed to call him now? He would always be Justice Bastarache to me. I really couldn't believe he wasn't a Supreme Court justice anymore."

But I had made up my mind. On April 9, 2008, I announced that I was resigning my seat on the Supreme Court of Canada. It felt completely unreal. June 30 was to be my last day. And just like that, I would be free.

After my retirement from the Supreme Court, I asked painter Christan Nicholson to paint my portrait. My mother was quite pleased with the result.
Source: Collection of Michel Bastarache.

It did not take long for the phone to start ringing. On the other end of the line was Roy Heenan, a founding partner of the prominent law firm Heenan Blaikie. He wanted to bring me on as senior counsel. Naturally, the rules of the Supreme Court prevent sitting judges from negotiating new employment, but Roy just wanted to let me know that he would like us to meet and chat about it sometime. I agreed. The very day I retired, the phone rang once again, and a few days later, the week of July 1, he came to meet me in Ottawa. Funnily enough, Ronald Caza, my research assistant when I taught at the University of Ottawa, just happened to be the firm's office manager. So I had a meeting with Caza and Heenan in the nation's capital. We had dinner and laid out the terms of employment on the back of a napkin. Teaming up with Heenan Blaikie would mean joining a roster of renowned lawyers, including former justice minister, Martin Cauchon, former premier of Quebec and one-time classmate of mine at the Université de Montréal, Pierre Marc Johnson, and, last but not least, Jean Chrétien.

A few weeks prior to my meeting with Roy Heenan and Ronald Caza, the University of Ottawa also came knocking. They were recruiting someone to replace Gilles Patry, who had been serving as president since 2001. Canadian universities were thriving back then, but cuts to government funding for research chairs and post-secondary education grants meant the private sector had become a key player. The university was looking for someone who would first and foremost be able to raise the necessary funds to ensure growth. That is why Marc Jolicœur, Chair of the Board of Governors, reached out to me. I met with him and he did his best to convince me to throw my hat in the ring.

The thing is, I was not looking for a full-time job, and I just knew that it would be a very demanding position. I was also very candid with Jolicœur right from the start that I had no interest in fundraising. Even chasing down money from various governments is a chore. At the time, the University of Ottawa was gearing up for a massive fundraising campaign. I had no interest in any of that, but I did give it some thought. Children, I had given the Supreme Court almost everything I had, and my health was starting to suffer. A forty-hour work week was not ideal for me at that point in time. I was more interested in working part-time and travelling a bit.

A few weeks later, in early June, the university announced the appointment of Allan Rock, the very man who had appointed me to the Court of Appeal of New Brunswick thirteen years prior. Rock would go on to do great work at the University of Ottawa. He weathered the economic storm and brought the institution's finances back on track, all while presiding over significant growth in enrollment. Unsurprisingly, there was a marked increase in construction projects during his eight-year tenure at the university.

Nevertheless, circling back to the University of Ottawa would have been nice. I studied there in the 1970s and taught there a few years later, plus I helped set up the French-language common law program. Had I been offered the presidency sooner, or even on terms that suited me, and if the position were more research- and teaching-oriented, I probably would have wound up there again and then retired for real.

One Hellish Commission

CHILDREN, 2010 WAS OFF TO SUCH A NICE START. Yolande and I returned from a glorious trip to Kenya, and work was low-key, just what I wanted after my years at court. I set my own schedule, worked on a few interesting cases at Heenan Blaikie. Then the phone rang. Maybe I should not have answered, but I did. The caller was Jacques Dupuis, Quebec's public security minister. We had spoken a few months earlier during the study of Bill 74, which authorized consecutive sentences for financial fraud and other situations, so I knew him a little, but that had been our only contact. I had a feeling the purpose of his call was not the bill, but something far more serious.

A day or two before, Quebec's former justice minister, Marc Bellemare, had made a surprising revelation during an interview on Radio-Canada's popular investigative television show, *Enquête*. He claimed to have been at the centre of influence peddling involving major Quebec Liberal Party donors, specifically in connection with the judicial appointment process. What is more, he said, Premier Jean Charest was aware of the situation. In the interview with host Alain Gravel on April 12, 2010, Mr. Bellemare said, "People who were seen as important and influential party fundraisers wanted their say on several appointments and had no qualms about asking me for appointments at the time, in 2003 and 2004, with the understanding that favours were expected in return because we had to position our own people, as they said." He said he appointed three judges "because that's what top party fundraisers wanted, and the Premier agreed." It was revealed that the three judges in question were Marc Bisson, son of Guy Bisson, an influential Quebec Liberal Party organizer; Michel Simard, a former Liberal supporter; and Line Gosselin-Després, who was related to former Liberal minister Michel Després. The first two appointments, from 2003, were allegedly made at the behest of construction contractor Franco Fava and accountant Charles Rondeau, both of them top Quebec Liberal Party fundraisers.

I could not believe my ears. These were extremely serious allegations. Instinctively, I thought of the judges he claimed to have appointed illegally. The former minister's assertions would have a profound impact on their lives. They would no doubt face tremendous pressure in court, including applications for recusal. If they had done nothing wrong, why should they pay that price? Mr. Bellemare was discrediting the Ministry of Justice, the judicial appointment process, and the reputation of the judges in question. I was also very surprised that he was making these statements so long after the fact.

These public accusations really struck a chord with me because I am a firm believer in the integrity of the justice system. Nevertheless, I did not think there was anything I could do about it. Until I got the call from Jacques Dupuis.

In essence, what Minister Dupuis told me was that his government was concerned about the judicial appointment process after Bellemare's very public statements. He needed someone perceived as perfectly neutral to lead an inquiry commission on the process. He figured his best bet was a Francophone from outside Quebec with the Supreme Court seal of approval. I usually take the time to really think things through before accepting a contract. I talk to your mother; we discuss it. Sometimes I seek advice. In this case, Minister Dupuis wanted an answer right away because the government wanted to launch the inquiry commission as soon as possible. I do not know exactly why they were in such a hurry, but I am guessing they did not want to give Bellemare a chance to keep telling tales in public. I had also read in the papers that things were a bit rocky for Charest's government just then.

I think it made perfect sense for the government to choose someone from the Supreme Court of Canada. The situation was explosive, and it behooved the government to choose someone objective who was removed from it all. I think they liked the fact that I was not a Quebecker and did not live in Quebec because I could not be connected to a political party or anything else. Charest repeatedly made that argument to anyone willing to listen—and many who were not—adding that I had never served as a judge in a Quebec superior court. I thought it was a pretty strong argument.

Partly because I did not have much work just then, but mostly because I felt a sense of solidarity with the judges in question, I quickly agreed to lead the legal and administrative commission. Officially, the commission's mandate was to inquire into the allegations made by Marc Bellemare respecting the process for appointing judges to the Court of Québec, municipal courts, and the Administrative Tribunal of Québec and to "make recommendations to the Government with respect to potential changes to the process for appointing such judges and members."

Reaction was swift and really never let up. In a Radio-Canada report broadcast on April 14, 2010, the opposition parties criticized "the troublingly narrow mandate and the fact that the Premier was aware of the influence peddling, according to Marc Bellemare." PQ member Stéphane Bédard, parliamentary leader for the official opposition, said, "You can't be judge and jury. The accused can't choose his judge and his charges." Action démocratique leader Gérard Deltell said, "This inquiry commission was created not by the Premier, but by the Liberal Party leader, and that is disappointing to Quebeckers."

Children, it was regularly suggested that Jean Charest and I were friends, but I did not know him at all. I had never seen him or spoken to him. We had never crossed paths at an event. Zero contact. Nevertheless, the Quebec media would not let it go. In her April 15, 2010, editorial, Le Devoir's editor-in-chief, Josée Boileau, wrote,

> It must be said that Premier Jean Charest is as bold as brass. To head up "his" inquiry commission ("his" because he was the only one gunning for it), he found a prestigious judge who agreed to the mandate and the six-month deadline, no questions asked [...]. The inquiry will focus solely on judicial appointments. What will Mr. Bastarache have to say about the Liberal organizer who had a little chat with a minister and, soon after, celebrated his son's appointment to the bench? Will he read the selection committee's report and find—surprise, surprise—that the lawyer in question had the requisite skills? Of course he will! This is familiar ground for Mr. Bastarache, whose own Supreme Court appointment, some said, was partisan because of his professional and political connections to Prime Minister Jean Chrétien. Yet he was an excellent judge, wasn't he?

Émilie and Jean-François, my years at the Supreme Court of Canada left me with an aversion to that kind of media commentary. That opinion piece in Le Devoir surprised me. I had a clear mandate from the government. I had the authority and independence to lead an inquiry commission on the process for appointing judges, not a commission to protect Jean Charest. Not a political tool or a diversionary tactic. Let me remind you that this was a legal and administrative commission, and when I accepted the mandate, I made sure I was not getting involved in a commission on the construction industry and political party fundraising, issues the Charbonneau Commission would deal with a few years later. I was well aware it would

> Émilie and Jean-François, my years at the Supreme Court of Canada left me with an aversion to that kind of media commentary.

cover a lot of ground, take a long time, and involve hundreds of witnesses. I had no experience with commissions, so I would not have agreed to get involved in something fiendishly complicated. The nature of this commission was strictly legal, very much in my wheelhouse, which made it much less of a stretch.

Before we got to work, disconcerting media reports surfaced. For example, I had not heard that the son of a person of interest had secured an appointment. When the former minister responsible for the Outaouais, Norm MacMillan, told the commission that he had pushed for an aspiring judge to be considered, that really worried me. Had I known there was so much political conflict around judicial appointments, I can say with absolute certainty that I would never have accepted the Government of Quebec's mandate.

I fully expected a reaction from the media and politicians because a lot of people wanted the government to create something essentially like the Charbonneau Commission. That made my commission look like a poor excuse to focus on something else. Still, I thought I was entitled to fair, honest treatment.

"It is ironic, to say the least, that the Chair of the inquiry into the judicial appointments process is a man whose 1997 appointment to the highest court in the land stirred up controversy because of his connection to Jean Chrétien and the Liberal Party of Canada," wrote *Le Devoir* columnist Michel David. "Mr. Bastarache may be competent, he may be a man of integrity, but he will certainly have a hard time convincing the public that he's not a party to a blatant diversionary tactic. One might even wonder whether he really understood what he was getting himself into."

I figured efforts to attack Charest by discrediting my commission would simmer down within a few weeks and leave me to do my work in peace, but they never let up. What is truly "ironic," as David put it, is that eighty percent of the recommendations in my report were adopted by Liberals and the PQ alike.

⁂

The commission had a two-part mandate: to inquire into Bellemare's allegations and to examine the judicial appointment process. I addressed each individually from the start. I began with Mr. Bellemare. When that was done, my team would tackle the second part with three or four outside experts.

I was facing two major challenges. I had never headed an inquiry commission, and I did not know any city of Québec lawyers. I immediately reached out to judges I knew in the provincial capital to ask for references. I had to find a very good lawyer to serve as chief prosecutor, a key position in this kind of commission. The chief prosecutor's job was to handle questioning based on evidence gathered throughout the inquiry. Three or four of the judges I talked to suggested Pierre Cimon. The first time I called him, I had no idea who he was, just that the judges had recommended him. I met him a few days later to find out more about him. I wanted to know if he had previous involvement in inquiry commissions and if he was politically involved. I wanted my team to be as neutral as possible, starting with my chief prosecutor. I asked him to give me a sense of how he would organize and supervise the work. From the get-go, I ran background checks to rule out any conflict of interest. This process is consistent with the Quebec Bar's rules: identify the individual and identify people who know them and can attest to their identity and reputation. I also checked to make sure they had their licence and insurance and found out if they had ever been sued. That kind of thing.

During our meeting, Cimon disclosed that he had donated to the Quebec Liberal Party. Not huge sums of money, just cheques for three hundred, four hundred, two hundred and fifty, and five hundred dollars every year or so. Out of personal conviction, he said. He had never been a political attaché or strategist, not even an adviser. That was fine by me. It was all above board, no real or perceived conflict of interest. Every single one of us has the right to donate to a political party. Never did I think it could have caused a problem. Had he been a PQ supporter, that would have been fine by me. Over the years, I have met plenty of people in sensitive positions of a legal or political nature who had been party members. Nobody ever questioned that.

A few days later, though, Cimon's political past sparked a media frenzy, and the opposition parties took full advantage. "Let's keep in mind the fact that his job is to question witnesses about allegations that top Liberal Party fundraisers influenced the judicial appointment process [...]. That taints things right off the bat [...]. In justice as in ethics, appearances are just as important as the facts of the matter," said the Parti Québécois's justice critic, Véronique Hivon. Québec solidaire MNA Amir Khadir added, "Quebec Liberal Party fundraising is the reason this province is in a state of political uproar. The Minister of Justice should, at the very least, have given Mr. Bastarache clear instructions to avoid this kind of appearance of conflict of interest in selecting the commission's prosecutors."

Even the President of the Quebec Bar, Pierre Chagnon, called the impartiality of my commission into question in full view of TVA cameras at the National Assembly. I could not believe it. We encourage law students to join political parties, yet a qualified, competent man of integrity was being punished precisely because he did so. What kind of message does that send? To this day, I do not see the sense in it.

★★★

The government gave me full control over whom I hired, their job descriptions and my own role in relation to them. There was just one exception: the administrative services manager. I contacted the woman who had been in charge of that aspect of Pierre Marc Johnson's inquiry into an overpass collapse, but the executive committee was not in favour, instead suggesting Daniel Legault, a top-notch administrator I really enjoyed working with.

While developing the commission's overall approach, I consulted several people who had ample experience with inquiry commissions. No, I did not call John Gomery, the famous head of the Commission of Inquiry into the Sponsorship Program. I was mindful of a Federal Court judge's findings of bias in his case. I focused on establishing a process and assembling an elite, professional team.

The first person I talked to as I was setting up my commission was Denise E. Bellamy. I was acquainted with Judge Bellamy, who had led an inquiry into inappropriate spending by the City of Toronto, and she gave me some advice. I also talked to a judge I knew at the Court of Appeal of Quebec and a former deputy minister from Quebec who specialized in inquiry commissions.

I also called Justice Jeffrey Oliphant, who was wrapping up his inquiry commission into the relationship between Karlheinz Schreiber and former Canadian Prime Minister Brian Mulroney following the Airbus affair. Mr. Oliphant, the Associate Chief Justice of the Manitoba Court of Queen's Bench, carried out a very rigorous inquiry. I asked him if he had any good lawyers to recommend. He immediately suggested Giuseppe Battista, so I hired him as deputy chief prosecutor and moved him into the chief prosecutor role when Cimon left. Battista had been a lawyer with the Poitras Commission and specialized in criminal and disciplinary law.

Next to join the team was Éric Downs, a high-profile Quebec lawyer who was a perfect fit as deputy chief prosecutor. I knew him a little because he had made a good impression representing Quebec's financial regulator in the trial of Vincent Lacroix, who had defrauded a lot of Norbourg investors. Downs was appointed to the Superior Court of Québec in 2016.

Children, I was not given a lot of time, but I felt I had put together a strong team of principled people who would get to the bottom of what happened. I wanted to dig deep. Of course there was criticism. For one thing, none of the prosecutors were female. There were women on my team;

in fact, I wrote the report with Professor Martine Valois. Still, we would have been better off with a woman on the core team. I actually wanted two male and two female lawyers. I extended the offer to four women, all of whom promptly and categorically refused it. I asked them for names of other qualified women, and they all replied that any first-rate lawyer with one of the big firms would never work for the Government of Quebec's hourly rate.

★★★

I refused to let my opinion be informed by what I read in the papers because I no longer trusted reporters. My approach was that of a judge. Judges do not make up their mind based on commentary. Hearing both sides of the story before coming to a conclusion has always been my MO. In Bellemare's case, I wanted to wait and see what he had to say in his defence. I did not know what had happened between Bellemare and Charest. I did think it was pretty stupid for a justice minister to make comments like that in public seven years after the alleged incidents, but it is a long way from that to figuring out if those allegations were true. I was determined to probe deeply and find out what really happened. And we did find out. Unfortunately, Bellemare had a politician's mindset, and he made me his target of choice. Journalists, politicians, and some members of the public wanted a commission on Quebec Liberal Party fundraising, but that is not what I was going to deliver. What I delivered was evidence that he had lied.

One morning in May 2010, I spotted a headline in *Le Devoir*: "Bellemare fears facing clique." In the article, Bellemare said my commission was rigged because we were not sufficiently independent from the government. What was that accusation based on? According to Bellemare, "The government appointed Mr. Bastarache, an associate at a legal firm that's very closely connected to the government, specifically through Pierre Marc Johnson."

Where do I even start with this? I wanted to give everyone the benefit of the doubt. I wanted the commission to be a forum for genuine debate so we could learn about how judges were appointed. Was there real political pressure? Hearings were not even underway yet, but there was Bellemare, viciously attacking me. I thought it was cheap, not the best defence. How was suggesting there were ties between my office and the government going to help him prove he was forced to make improper appointments? Then, right in the middle of summer, with hearings yet to begin, Bellemare asked the Superior Court of Québec to shut down my commission and cancel my appointment. That was way out of line. In an interview with *Le Devoir*, Bellemare alleged that the commission was an "abuse of power" by Premier Charest, who acted "illegally." Bellemare said the Premier was using my commission to further his defamation lawsuit. Bellemare also claimed the facts pointed to "complicity" and an "incestuous" relationship between the executive branch of government and me. Then he went on and on about my personal relationships with Minister Jacques Dupuis and the Premier himself, whom I knew "very well," to hear him tell it. Well, as I said earlier, that is all completely false.

We were all targets of Bellemare's smear campaign. He was the reason the commission was created, yet he subjected us all to daily mudslinging. Plainly stated, that was irresponsible of him and his lawyer, Jean-François Bertrand. TV gave everyone in Quebec and even across Canada the opportunity to see how boiling mad I sometimes got at them. Children, I am especially grateful to Infoman for using my red face as his show opener for several weeks. Had my job description allowed me to speak to the media, I would happily have explained to Jean-René Dufort that my scarlet countenance had nothing to do with Bertrand's behaviour but was due entirely to a skin condition called rosacea. When I get hot, I turn red. Ever since childhood, I have looked so sunburned that people regularly ask me if I just got back from Florida. My father had the same condition, which is not actually harmful. During the inquiry, the lighting and the pressure made me hot, so I turned red. That said, rosacea or not, Bellemare's lawyer really pushed my buttons.

Yolande would tell you that I was so mad, she thought I would "throw them in jail." People had warned me Bertrand would do that on purpose and told me he had a reputation for being arrogant and insulting. That was his MO, if you will. He wanted me to lose my cool. During the cross-examination of Liberal fundraiser Charles Rondeau, Bertrand relentlessly questioned him about QLP fundraising practices and the mechanics of government appointments. He must have thought I would say something to undermine the commission, but all I did was focus on him. If I had to do it over again, I would manage Bertrand differently. I should not have walked into his trap and lost patience. I can see why some individuals and the public as a whole would think I could not have cared less about what he was saying. That is not true. His questions were not relevant. Our topic was the appointment of judges, not government representatives abroad. Let us just say that Bellemare did not help his case. His and his lawyer's behaviour and tactics did not convince me that the facts he alleged were true.

His version of events, as presented to me at the hearing, is as follows: Bellemare claimed he met with Premier Jean Charest on September 2, 2003, and said he wanted to talk about Franco Fava and Charles Rondeau's insistence on appointing certain candidates to the bench. After listening to the Justice Minister's complaints about Marc Bisson and Michel Simard, the Premier allegedly said to Bellemare, "Franco is a personal friend and an influential party fundraiser. We need these guys, so listen to them. He's a pro fundraiser. If he says to appoint Bisson and Simard, do it."

Jean Charest said he was never told Bellemare was under any pressure to appoint Justice Bisson or promote Justice Simard. He said he did not remember a call from Bellemare on August 24, 2003, or a meeting on August 27, 2003, to set up a meeting for September 2. On that day, according to his agenda, his last meeting ended at 7:30 p.m. Although he could, by his own admission, have had later meetings that were not recorded in the agenda, he confirmed that he had not.

Apparently there had also been a meeting on January 8 at which Bellemare discussed Line Gosselin-Després's appointment. Charest said that was not true and her name had never been mentioned.

Who was telling the truth? It was a monumental task for one simple reason: we had to figure out what really happened without influencing the civil suits against Charest and Bellemare in the Superior Court of Québec. In response to Bellemare's allegations, Jean Charest sued him for defamation. The former justice minister felt the Premier's claim was unjustified, so he filed a counterclaim.

It was all very complex, but I wanted to unpack all the details. Gilbert Lavoie wrote in *Le Soleil* that I had not done a thorough job, but I most certainly did. I just could not publish all the evidence I had gathered because that could have influenced the court hearing the two civil suits. Now, though, children, let me tell you what we discovered.

> It was a monumental task for one simple reason: we had to figure out what really happened without influencing the civil suits against Charest and Bellemare in the Superior Court of Québec.

***

Every day, I scheduled meetings with the commission's lawyers. Our two leads were criminal lawyers. One day, I sat down with the two of them to share a concern I had. In essence, I said they knew more about it than I did, so I wanted their advice. I did not want any conflict between the two civil suits and my report. I did not want to be accused of imposing a solution on a criminal or civil court. There were several relevant Supreme Court precedents, and I was determined to avoid entering into conflict. Together, we decided the prosecutors would not ask any questions similar to those that would be asked during the trial and that I would try to prevent the witnesses from talking about anything that was not specific to my mandate.

For example, when Bellemare said he went to Charest's office on the evening of September 2, 2003, and there was nobody there to have him sign the guest book, we questioned his driver. Bellemare said he had a government driver take him there, but he refused to tell us the driver's name, so I sent an investigator to question every Government of Quebec driver, and we found the one who had picked Bellemare up that night. For one thing, the driver picked him up at a time that was not at all consistent with Bellemare's claim, and for another, he never went to Charest's office. He went somewhere else instead.

Then I had my people question two other individuals who were at that other place, and they confirmed having seen Bellemare there at that exact time. There was no truth to the claim that he went to Charest's office that night, but I did not put that in the report because Charest's defence hung on that detail. Charest said he was not at his office that night and that Bellemare never went to see him. Had I included that in my report, every last Quebecker would have thought I was helping Charest with his lawsuit, and I definitely did not want to go there. I decided the Premier could figure it out on his own. All he had to do was find witnesses who would tell him the same thing they told my investigators.

***

Ferocious opposition party attacks became an almost daily occurrence. They usually took aim at the Premier, but I was not immune to their criticism for the simple fact that it pertained to the subject of the commission I was leading. Early on, I decided we would set up a ten-year sample. That is a typical approach when you are trying to evaluate whether a system is working and identify points of comparison. In other words, our plan was to examine how things were done from 2000 to 2010, which included the time PQ Premiers Lucien Bouchard and Bernard Landry were in office.

Some people said my decision was influenced by my political allegiance. Can you believe it? Politics did not play into any of my decisions about what to do or not do during my inquiry. To suggest otherwise is absurd. I wanted the whole undertaking to be above board and highly professional. I wanted no accusations of political bias. That is why I decided not to react to all the newspaper reports.

Bernard Landry even went so far as to say, in public, that he had some concerns about what motivated my decision. "Why try to expand the inquiry to a party that has not been accused of anything and is no longer in power? No former Supreme Court justice would ever be sympathetic to separatists. Quite the contrary," he said. In fact, as I said earlier, I was not unsympathetic toward credible sovereignists like René Lévesque, Claude Morin, Camille Laurin, and Louise Beaudoin, but I was not keen on Bernard Landry and his ilk.

Then PQ MNA Véronique Hivon started taking up more and more space during the commission. Hivon was the official opposition's justice critic, and she was particularly hard on me. I did not know her then, but when she started making political hay at my commission's expense by saying the most ridiculous things imaginable, any respect I might have had for her evaporated. You see, I never gave the official opposition intervener status in the inquiry because I did not think it had anything to contribute. It had no direct interest in the inquiry and no important information to provide. Moreover, I thought giving them intervener status would further politicize the debate.

Hivon disagreed and was deeply offended. At a press briefing, she said, "We wanted to have our say, play our role, but it's clear the commission is completely one-sided. We now have every reason to wonder about its true objective. At this point, I think it's just as hard for us as it is for the general public to trust this commission and not wonder what good the millions being spent on this will do other than maybe help Jean Charest save face."

That comment was politically motivated, period. It had nothing to do with the commission's mandate. I was not working for Jean Charest. I was there to carry out a specific, defined mandate, and that is what I was doing. I was not working for the QLP or Charest personally. They tried to make it political. It was ridiculous, but the media ate it up. It was a media feeding frenzy.

Commentary by Radio-Canada's lead political analyst, Michel C. Auger, struck me as particularly surreal. In a June 2010 blog post, he kindly wrote, "Structurally, the commission is above reproach. Justice Bastarache's reputation is impeccable." But then he added, "Regardless of what one might think of the legal firm he is attached to." He was referring to some of my colleagues at Heenan Blaikie, who, unfortunately for us all, had spent time in politics. "The commission put together a good team, and its early work was carried out with the professionalism one would expect under the circumstances," he wrote.

A few lines later, he dropped this bomb: "In terms of appearances, one other element weighs heavily against the commission: the fact that the Premier himself selected the judge [...]. According to an age-old legal precept, justice must satisfy the appearance of justice. That's turning into a serious problem for the Bastarache Commission." Well, thank goodness for my impeccable reputation!

Auger frequently showed up on the evening news program, Le Téléjournal 22 h, during my commission's hearings, and once saw fit to say quite blatantly, "This commission isn't running smoothly," and "it's not altogether clear where the commission is going with this." He said we were communicating poorly. Fortunately, this renowned expert on legal matters informed us, "It's not a lost cause, but it needs a major course correction." Unbelievable! You would think my commission was a hockey game.

In contrast, when the Charbonneau Commission got up and running, Auger deemed them all top experts and gave them his blessing.

Compared to the Commission of Inquiry on the Awarding and Management of Public Contracts in the Construction Industry, my commission may not have been quite as exciting, but nearly all my recommendations were adopted by the Liberals and the PQ. Hivon herself was in government at the time. Most importantly, we discovered that Bellemare was a liar.

★★★

Children, let me tell you a story about Post-it® notes. Every inquiry commission has its share of surprises: Jean Chrétien's golf balls in the Gomery Commission, "Mr. 3%" in the Charbonneau Commission. In my case, two things stand out as particularly fascinating. The Post-it® notes shared by two witnesses and the diskette provided by Bellemare's wife that contained his agenda and ultimately proved he was lying. Let us talk about the Post-it® notes.

Georges Lalande, who served as associate deputy minister in Quebec's justice ministry under Bellemare, corroborated the former minister's allegations that party bagman Franco Fava pressured the office to appoint certain people. Lalande kept all his agendas from that time and wrote fairly detailed notes about the events. Interestingly, he mentioned Fava's impatience with Minister Bellemare, who did not seem to understand that he was supposed to hand judicial appointments to the party faithful. "Franco again with more talk of appointments," he wrote in his agenda in the summer of 2003.

We had gathered quite a lot of evidence relating to Bellemare's claims, and everything led us to conclude that he lied. By backing up the former minister, Lalande exposed himself. He clearly was not telling the whole truth. When he was shown some of the evidence, his response to the commission was, "Oh, well, let me look at my agenda." When the agenda confirmed what we said, he quickly added, "Oh, wait, there's a little note here." It was a Post-it®, one of those little sticky notes. I had a hunch he was lying, but I wanted to be sure. In August, I asked him to turn over his agendas and his notes, which we kept until the commission wrapped up. We sent everything off to a handwriting expert. It turned out that the ink on any given page in the agenda never matched its corresponding Post-it®. I knew that kind of thing could happen; he could certainly have used a different pen each time. My commission colleagues said, "Really? He used a different pen every day?" We were no further ahead. There was still some doubt. I ended up telling my team to ask our expert if the kind of ink that was used existed five, six, seven, ten years ago. I asked because it occurred to me that companies could change their ink formulations. It turned out that the ink used for those entries did not exist at the time they were supposedly written. The agenda entries and the Post-it® notes were not written at anywhere near the same time. He was lying.

The second Post-it® incident occurred on September 27, 2010, a pretty busy day for the commission. One of Charest's staffers, Chantal Landry, who was responsible for appointments, testified that, if she knew a judicial candidate's political allegiance, she would let the Premier know. And just how did she do that? She put a little Post-it® on their folder. As she was telling me this, I thought it was a pretty strange way of doing things. Landry was not a high-profile witness; she did not have a stake in the appointments. She had nothing to hide. All she had to do was explain how things happened and describe a system.

Anyway, it turns out Post-it® notes are pretty useful in Quebec.

★★★

The commission was without a doubt one of the most trying ordeals of my professional life. I did not get death threats like I did in the early 1980s when I chaired the official languages commission in New Brunswick, but the media coverage really took a toll on me. Everything we did was scrutinized, often by mean-spirited journalists with axes to grind.

For example, the media seized on the fact that one of the two Government of Quebec prosecutors, Patrick Girard, once clerked for me at the Supreme Court of Canada. *Le Devoir* journalist Robert Dutrisac saw fit to make a big deal of it just over a week before I submitted my report. In his article, he said our prior relationship had not been disclosed at the start of the commission. Naturally, Bellemare's lawyers leaped at the chance to discredit my commission. "It's appalling. Pardon me for laughing, but I'm laughing in disgust," said one of them, Rénald Beaudry. What disgusted me was the fact that a lawyer, a member of the Bar, saw that as a conflict. To this day, I do not see how there could have been a conflict of interest with a law clerk who had worked for me twelve years earlier. I certainly did not need to make it known to anyone that he was my former clerk. You cannot go around creating controversy where none exists. Name one lawyer in all Canadian history who ended up in a conflict of interest because of their clerkship. In court clerks are support staff, interns essentially. They do not represent anyone or anything other than justice. Clearly, some people failed to grasp that notion during the commission.

With all the political and media pressure, I thought about resigning a couple of times. From the moment I was appointed to the moment I submitted my report, all the comments were political. It was way too much. I often wondered if it was still possible in our society to do one's job and deal with an issue professionally without everything being discredited because of the political context. The most intense part was when Franco Fava and Charles Rondeau testified. They were being taken to task for acting as Quebec Liberal Party fundraisers. I had to tell my lawyers not to question them about that because it was not part of our mandate. That was for a future commission to address. I gave the prosecutors strict instructions to ask only the following questions: Did you interact with Bellemare? Did you communicate with Bellemare or his employees in order to influence judicial appointments? And so on. Those were the questions they asked, and I had to prevent Bellemare's lawyer from asking them about their contributions to the QLP because it was not a commission of inquiry into the QLP. Naturally, I was accused of protecting the Liberal Party.

Some editorialists and columnists claimed that I myself was biased because of my supposed illegitimate Supreme Court appointment. I thought that was pretty low. If that was what people thought, I had half a mind to tell them to take the job and shove it. I was this close to packing it in, but I did not because I talked to my commission colleagues and decided it would be wrong not to follow through on my commitment. If I stepped down, how would the Government of Quebec get its inquiry done?

As much as I wanted to resign, I do not regret my involvement in the commission. I would have regretted it if things had ended badly and the report had been rejected. We managed to produce a three-hundred-page report, and nearly all our recommendations were accepted by the government at the time and its successor. In the report, I made the following recommendations: create a secretariat for judicial selection and appointment that reports to the National Assembly; create a standing selection committee made up of thirty paid, trained individuals, twelve of them members of the public; have the National Assembly decide, by way of statute or regulation, whether the minister of justice may consult the premier during the judicial appointment process; expressly list nepotism, cronyism, and political allegiance as factors irrelevant to a judicial appointment; prohibit ministers and members of the National Assembly from taking any steps to promote a candidate; require the minister of justice to provide reasons for their choice of appointee by providing Cabinet with certain documents; announce each judicial appointee publicly along with reasons the candidate was chosen.

I think we did a very good job, and I believe the Government of Quebec now has the best judicial appointment system in Canada. It is possible to make good appointments despite a bad system if you have good people making the decisions. But if the system allows or even facilitates bad decisions, you have to change it because we cannot take for granted that we will always have decision makers who make good choices and do not give some individuals preferential treatment. I think the system needs institutional protection. Discretion will always be a factor, of course. That is the very nature of governance, and it is a good thing. Politicians have to appoint judges, but the process has to be properly regulated and we need institutional barriers to partisan appointments. We looked at how all the other provinces and the federal government handle this, and I think there is room for improvement across the board, especially within the federal government's appointment process—the very process that made me a judge at the Court of Appeal of New Brunswick and the Supreme Court of Canada.

One Last Fascinating Chapter

CHILDREN, in the early 2010s, I was in charge of a team of young legal practitioners at Heenan Blaikie. Nothing big was happening. The Quebec Commission was running its course, and I was taking on a few cases here and there. Over in New Brunswick though, something big was happening. I saw on the news that Father Charles Picot of the Diocese of Bathurst had been accused of sexually assaulting young children as far back as the 1970s. This was Father Picot's second encounter with the justice system; he had been sentenced to seven months in jail in the 1990s. I did not know it then, but on January 22, 2010, Father Lévi Noël, also of the Diocese of Bathurst, was sentenced to eight years in prison after pleading guilty to twenty-two charges of gross indecency and indecent assault. The incidents occurred between 1958 and 1981, and the victims were all boys between the ages of eight and sixteen. It was an unprecedented time. Internationally the Catholic Church was embroiled in a scandal involving child sex abuse by priests, a scandal with no end in sight. Some very powerful bishops had been blamed for repeatedly covering up the crimes.

Then I got an extraordinary phone call. The caller, Mark Frederick, a Toronto lawyer I did not know, was representing Monsignor Valéry Vienneau, the Bishop of Bathurst. Msgr. Vienneau was dealing with a difficult situation: two priests facing criminal charges and constant media attention. He had met with some of Father Picot's victims and was shaken by their accounts of what happened. He agreed to compensate the victims for the harms they endured. During our phone call, Frederick explained that the bishop wanted help not with defending the diocese but with establishing a victim compensation process. Off I went to Bathurst to meet with the bishop, his assistant, and Frederick.

They told me that, even though only a few victims had come forward during the criminal trial, apparently there were more. There were also Father Lévi Noël's ten or so victims. In 1999, when I was a judge, our ruling in *Bazley* established that a third party that controls the conduct of an assailant has a civil liability toward the victim.

Msgr. Vienneau and his assistant were concerned that a large number of victims might sue the diocese and said the diocese's insurer had rejected their claim. The bishop and his assistant said they did not have the financial resources to pay.

The bishop also felt that it would not be fair if only individuals who were psychologically capable of coming forward and participating in a trial received financial compensation. Msgr. Vienneau said to me, "If we compensate only those who come to see us, that's not really fair. Those who want to remain anonymous won't have an opportunity to claim compensation, and they might actually be the hardest-hit victims."

I agreed with him on that, of course. Just because ten victims came forward did not mean there were not others keeping quiet. He wanted to set up a process that would enable all victims to obtain fair compensation while remaining anonymous. Frederick thought I could help them by serving as a sort of judge who would make fair decisions about financial compensation for each victim who came forward. In his view, it was crucial that the victims trust me. They felt I was the best person for the job because I was from New Brunswick and had been a Supreme Court justice.

I had no interest in representing the diocese. The Church acknowledged its responsibility. Great, but I would not be representing it or helping with its defence. I was firmly on the victims' side. During the meeting with Msgr. Vienneau, I clearly stated, "I don't want to be the diocese's lawyer because that would conflict with every one of my values. I think what the priests did is appalling. And don't forget, Msgr. Vienneau, I'm not even a believer!"

"Mr. Bastarache," responded Msgr. Vienneau, "you will be completely independent. You decide the criteria, the categories, the amounts, how you want to proceed. I will go along with whatever you say. Once you've figured it out, tell me exactly how much money you need, and I'll give it to you. If I don't have it, I'll get it somehow." With that, we had an agreement.

★★★

I felt like a conflict arbitrator, but unlike in conventional arbitration—the diocese on one side; victims on the other—my role was to develop a process that involved investigating and making decisions about compensation. I was completely independent. I developed a process to identify victims of sexual abuse and assess the severity of the acts perpetrated against them as well as the long-term consequences.

I set to work. First, I created a detailed application form for each victim to fill out. I developed a rubric that took all the factors into account and used the information from the victims' forms to analyze the severity of the abuse in each case. There were five categories plus the amount of compensation for each category, as well as a timeline and the conditions under which I would meet with each victim. In designing the rubric, I consulted some two hundred sexual assault rulings to identify the criteria the courts employed and amounts of compensation typically awarded. I determined that a victim could receive between five thousand and two hundred and fifty thousand dollars. The criteria were very precise because I wanted to be very consistent in my analysis of each case. For example, compensation for unwanted touching was five thousand dollars. If a priest invited a boy to his office and sexually assaulted him in some way, that was twenty-five thousand dollars. If a priest treated the child like a sexual object and assaulted him on a regular basis for months or years, that was dangerously close to the two hundred and fifty thousand dollars cap. I also had to take long-term effects into account in determining the final amounts. I just want to point out that the Court of Queen's Bench agreed that my rubric was perfectly acceptable. I do not think two hundred and fifty thousand dollars could ever repair the damage done, but I did not have a choice. I had to award an amount equivalent to what a New Brunswick court would deem acceptable. The amounts were based on precedent.

Things have changed a bit since then. Recently, there have been cases with one-million-dollar awards. While I was on the job, there were lawyers who said that the victims did not get enough money. They claimed that if those victims became clients of theirs, they could win a lot more money. Those were lies. "A $10,000 offer bothers me because it's peanuts," said Robert Talach, a lawyer, in a 2016 Radio-Canada interview. "I can't think of a single sexual assault case in which such a pittance was offered, even in the least serious ones. In our system, $10,000 is what you get for a bad haircut." He was referring to the amounts offered to victims of Father Camille Léger in the Diocese of Moncton. With that statement, Talach showed the whole world that he clearly had no understanding of the matter. He thought he could get hundreds of thousands of dollars based on court cases that awarded victims one million dollars. That was just not true. Million-dollar cases in Canada had been settled out of court and had nothing to do with the Catholic Church. They were cases involving father-daughter incest over long periods of time. I am still at peace with the amounts I established, which were higher than what was offered to victims of Indigenous residential schools, for example. In Bathurst, the average compensation amount was around fifty-seven thousand dollars and about twenty percent of the cases were awarded the maximum amount, if I remember correctly.

As I was developing my rubric, I felt there was something missing. Obviously, what happened was an important factor, but the long-term effects were even more important. I did not know what criteria to go by. There was very little information in the jurisprudence about that, so I called a psychiatrist I knew well. Céline Finn was the daughter of my former boss at Assumption Life and the Université de Moncton, Gilbert Finn. Céline was a child psychiatrist, and my job involved people who had been victims in childhood. Céline had just wrapped up some work with Canadian soldiers suffering from post-traumatic stress disorder. I thought she was exactly the person whose help I needed. We met several times, and I showed her my list, which she analyzed and amended as needed. Céline was there for me throughout the process. I requested the victims' medical reports, and she helped me decode them. She assisted with some of the victim interviews, when they gave permission for her to be there, of course. I told them, "I'm trying to understand the impact of these assaults. Lots of things happen to people throughout their lives, right? You were molested at the age of ten, but fifty years later, it's not clear that that's what caused all your problems. We need to establish causality." Some of the victims complained, with reason, but I told them, "You might not like me asking you that question, but if you had to testify in court, what would you do?" Céline was a huge help.

Preparations complete, I was ready to receive the victims' forms. I put the word out in newspapers and online, asking victims to contact me. As the weeks went by, the forms piled up. And up. I realized the diocese was gravely mistaken in thinking there were probably twenty or thirty victims. I received dozens and dozens of applications. I even extended the deadline. In the end, I received 117 applications. I was astounded. Then I started looking at the forms. The list of priests involved got longer and longer. We weren't just talking about two individuals. Other names I'd never heard before were mentioned. I went to the bishop's office and told him he had a serious problem. His two priests were not isolated cases. In all, over one hundred victims named some ten priests. Msgr. Vienneau was livid. He could not believe it. These priests had never been charged. I turned to the bishop's assistant and told him he would have to look into the priests' files. Had there been complaints? Did they know anything? I gathered all the information and met with trustworthy victims who were eager to talk. I learned that the diocese was aware of some of the goings-on and that the priests who were named had been transferred from parish to parish for all kinds of made-up reasons. On average, priests remained in a parish for about seven years. Known pedophiles were moved much more frequently. It also looked like two of the priests whose names came up during the conciliation process may have been wrongly accused.

★★★

Émilie and Jean-François, your mother and I always enjoy watching good movies. During our time in Nice, we gained an appreciation for the acting skills and screenplays that were hallmarks of great films. At home in 2016, we watched the movie everyone was talking about: *Spotlight*, a Tom McCarthy film about child sex abuse by priests in Boston and the investigation by *Boston Globe* reporters. Just twenty minutes into the film, I was stupefied. I could not believe my eyes. "That's exactly what they told me!" I exclaimed the first time the reporters met with a victim. It was identical. I could have played that role.

Every one of the victims in the film was like someone I saw in Bathurst and then in Moncton when the diocese asked me to do the same thing again a few years later. I met a victim just like the one in the film. He was from an underprivileged background, and he confided that it really meant something when the parish priest paid attention to him. He was honoured when the priest asked him to do chores at the church or the rectory. Just like in the film, victims told me it felt as though the Good Lord Himself had asked them to help. The priest was a leader in the community, an almost godlike authority figure. If a priest cracked a slightly off-colour joke, that meant a lot because it was like he trusted the boy to keep a shared secret.

The priest's next move might be to offer the boy a massage, and the boy would agree. Things escalated from there. Eventually, the priest would ask the boy to masturbate or fellate him, and the boy would obey. I heard all those things. The priests bewitched the children and convinced them that sex with them was okay and acceptable.

Soon after I started meeting with victims in Bathurst, I realized the priests had a pattern, an MO. Charles Picot always said the same thing to his victims, something like, "This is just how people learn about sex, it's fine, everyone does this." Children could not say no. Abuse is physical, but it is psychological and spiritual too.

The victims I interviewed ran the gamut. Some used drugs or alcohol to calm down because they were so nervous about coming to see me, they had not slept in three days. I could tell right away. These people were stressed and anxious. Others were well dressed and very elegant even though they claimed to be unemployed and penniless. They trusted me and said they did not have a problem telling me what happened. I was surprised for sure. As one meeting led to the next, I asked them if they found the acts they had experienced humiliating. Were they afraid they might be seen? Afraid someone would find out? One thing many victims told me helped me understand how serious the situation was. "I was afraid people would think I was gay." That sentence broke them all. Nearly all of them were terrified people would think they were homosexual. The New Brunswick Acadian community was clearly very conservative in many ways, at least back then. The people I interviewed were worried that, if people knew they had been victims of pedophile priests, their wives would leave them, their children would stop talking to them, and they would for sure lose their jobs. Whether they came in cool and collected or visibly agitated, nearly all of them panicked at that thought.

People experience these situations very differently. I interviewed two or three men who were subjected to horrendous abuse for months but overcame it. They started their own companies and were successful businessmen. Others who had been exposed to objectively less serious abuse were more profoundly affected. They became alcoholics or drug addicts and had never been able to work. I had to evaluate these people's resilience, which is an important factor, as well as the support they got from loved ones. Some people got help from family and friends. Others were not so lucky. Some were kicked out at fifteen because they had the nerve to tell their parents what happened.

★★★

One man I interviewed was a little younger than the others. He was tall and slim, and he carried himself with pride. Children, this man was not like the others. Most of the victims had very little education and were not very articulate. He was the opposite. He did not shed a single tear during our meeting. As he took his seat, he said, "Listen, Mr. Bastarache, I'm going to tell you what happened to me. I want you to know I've never talked to anyone about this. I've never told a single human being because it's humiliating and I blame myself." He told me his story, frequently insisting on the fact that he still wonders why he did not have the courage to run away when the priest wanted to satisfy his sexual impulses with him. His was one of the most serious cases I examined. At the end of the interview, I told him that long-term effects are typically significant. This man, however, had not become an alcoholic or a drug addict. He told me he had a very hard time holding down a job. Still, he was not prone to depression, had never been hospitalized, like so many of the other victims. He completed his account and calmly stated, "Mr. Bastarache, I've rationalized this whole thing. I know how it affected my life. I just want to know when I'll get the money."

I was taken aback at that and asked him right away if he had come to see me just because he wanted money. Straightaway, he said yes. I told him that surprised me. I would never have expected him to say something like that. Then he explained: "I know exactly what I need. I need that money to send my two nephews to university. They're from a very poor family, you see. They have nothing. I'm going to give them the money, and then I'm going to kill myself."

I was speechless. He went on to say that he did not have any immediate family and no reason to live, certainly not if it meant he would have to keep reliving those memories. He had constant nightmares. He was done. He could not carry on. "I'm going to kill myself," he said. Calmly, I offered to help him by setting up an appointment with a psychiatrist so he could talk about what happened. I explained that there are ways to treat people who have gone through the kind of terrible trauma he experienced. He listened, but did not say a word. His mind seemed made up. I told him to give me a week, which was how long it would take for the cheque to get to him. I tried to find psychiatrists to help him. Five or six days later, I called him and asked if he had received the money. Not yet. Then I said I was calling because he had said he wanted to commit suicide and I wanted to convince him not to. He said, "Of course. I understand. I remember what you said to me." I talked to him, but he did not say anything. Not a word. He said,

"Yes, yes, I understand," one more time. Then I asked if he had changed his mind. He said, "Let it go, Mr. Bastarache. You've accomplished your mission." And he hung up. The following week, I opened up the paper and saw that he had killed himself.

Children, I really blame myself for what happened. Over the next two years, I often thought about what I should have done. What an idiot! I should have been able to persuade him not to do it. I should have forced him to go see a doctor with me. I should have done something. I talked to a few friends about it, and they said they would not have believed it. After all, lots of people contemplate suicide but never go through with it. I asked myself why I sent him that cheque. Why did I not try harder to get him to see a psychiatrist? I often wonder if I should have done more. How do you force a fifty-year-old man of sound mind not to do it? How do you force him to go to the hospital? It was not as if he was obviously depressed. I could not have had him committed.

I know I was the only person who tried to change his mind. I was also the only person who knew his story. I could not talk him out of it. I failed.

> Children, I really blame myself for what happened. Over the next two years, I often thought about what I should have done. What an idiot! I should have been able to persuade him not to do it. I should have forced him to go see a doctor with me. I should have done something.

⁂

No lawyers were allowed to be present during my private meetings with claimants in Moncton. I did have a couple of assistants from Heenan Blaikie who took notes so the victims could not come back and say I promised something I did not deliver. I had to do due diligence to ensure the alleged victims were telling the truth and were not trying to trick me. I sympathized with their situation, but I did not want anyone to deceive me and use me for financial gain. The minute I set eyes on a claimant, I had a sense of whether he was really a victim. It was quite obvious when they were lying. By looking them in the eye as I started describing what was written on their form, I would see if they were detached or emotional. Some started crying. When a sixty-year-old man starts crying, sometimes inconsolably, it is hard to believe he is making it up. Only an Oscar-winning actor could make me think otherwise. That is how the vast majority of them reacted.

Some were almost cheerful as they told me their story. That raised some doubts. I had a list of questions to catch them out. Before meeting with the first claimants, I carefully studied what the priests did at the time, so I knew their patterns. I would ask the victims what the priest said at the time of the incidents. One of the priests always took the boys into his car. A black Buick station wagon. I would ask the victims what colour the car was. "Black." "Black." "Black." "Blue four-door Chevy." That is when I knew there was a pretty good chance it was not true.

After I wrapped things up in Bathurst, I did the same thing for the Diocese of Moncton. At Cap-Pelé, where Father Camille Léger preyed on boys for decades, I got calls from people who tried to take advantage of the system. One day, a man called me and said, arrogantly, "Hey, you gave my neighbour three hundred and fifty thousand dollars, and he was there at the same time as me, and the same thing happened to both of us. It's not fair. I want the same compensation he got." I calmly replied that it simply was not true. He shot back, "How dare you say that to me; that's outrageous!" Remaining calm, I explained that I could easily tell he was lying because I had written no cheques for that amount. I suggested he bring me a photocopy of his neighbour's cheque. He hung up.

One day I ran into two men who had just come out of the Cap-Pelé bar (which is close to the church). What they told me really worried me: "We just left the bar. At the table next to us, four guys were talking, and one or more of them had just gotten money from you. The others were taking notes about what they told you to get them money, and they said they were going to tell you the same thing." I do not know if it was true. I asked if they knew the men's names, but they could not help me with that. There was not much I could do under the circumstances, but it shows that some people could very well have lied. I fully expected some dishonest people to try to work the system. I did what I could to shore up weaknesses in the system, and most of the time it worked, but I am sure some people succeeded where others failed. To put that into perspective, three to four percent of guilty people are found innocent by the courts. There is no perfect system. There are always some people who get away with it, but if the overall good outweighs the harm, it remains worthwhile. I had 117 applications in Bathurst, and I caught about five or six people whom I felt were lying. There were slightly more in Moncton.

★★★

When it was over, more than two thirds of the Bathurst victims accepted the compensation I offered them. That percentage was higher in Moncton. As a result of my work, the two dioceses each had to pay the victims about four million dollars. The system was voluntary, of course, and any participant who refused my offer was free to take the diocese to court. The only thing they could not do was ask me to be a witness or refer to anything I said to them during the interview. In some cases, I actually suggested that the victims lay criminal charges. I told them that if confidentiality and being subjected to questioning were not major impediments, criminal charges could be an effective way to obtain reparation. I encouraged them to find other people who had been molested and pursue the matter together. Two of the victims did so.

I believe the process was a huge success because the number of individual lawsuits and potential associated costs were dramatically reduced. In addition, each victim could be compensated without being identified. Very few cases ended up in court because Frederick was able to negotiate agreements with most of those who opted not to participate in the process or refused my offer. These people realized that individual lawsuits would take a long time and that legal bills would take a huge chunk out of their compensation. I still believe that most of them would have ended up with less money than what I offered them.

Of course it helped the diocese, which could never have borne the cost of fifty lawsuits, and, of course many people opposed the process. "Parallel" justice to save the diocese from bankruptcy may seem odd at first blush, but mediation and arbitration are parallel procedures too. Personally, I think there is no better way to resolve such matters. How could the diocese possibly have dealt with 50, 100, or 117 lawsuits? Bankruptcy? Yes, businesses go bankrupt when they get taken to court, and some see that as justice served, but given the type of offences in this case, most of the victims would never file lawsuits because they would not want to disclose their identity. That is why I got involved. I still feel it would have been totally unfair if compensation had gone only to those comfortable speaking openly about what happened, with others getting nothing at all.

I think this kind of process goes some way toward redressing the harm of sexual assault. I interviewed people who were poor and ended up with tens of thousands of dollars. Some of them turned around and gave it all back to the Church or other charities. It is hard to prove assault, but it can be done, especially when there are so many people.

★★★

I thought all that was behind me, but one day, my friend Robert Décarie, a former Federal Court judge, invited me to one of his election-night parties. Every time there was an election in Quebec, Canada, or the United States, he hosted a pizza party in his basement and we all watched the results together. I have been a number of times.

In 2012 or 2014, I do not remember exactly, I was there chatting with an acquaintance, another Federal Court judge, when I was introduced to another judge's wife, Liliana Longo, who joined our conversation. She was a lawyer and senior general counsel for the Royal Canadian Mounted Police (RCMP). She asked me what I was up to, and I told her about the process that had been set up for the two New Brunswick dioceses. She was intrigued and said she had never heard of anything like it. We had a short conversation about it, then I turned to the TV to watch the election results. I heard nothing more about her for about two years. Then, when I heard about the class-action lawsuit for sexual harassment of women within the RCMP as far back as 1974, I had a chat with my Heenan Blaikie colleague, Simon Ruel. "We should call the RCMP and suggest they do something like what was done in New Brunswick rather than be destroyed in court." Simon made the suggestion to another acquaintance, and the idea eventually made its way to the commissioner.

If I remember correctly, Longo may even have discussed my suggestion with RCMP higher-ups, but they decided against it and tried to shut down the class action.

Later on, I got a call from Longo, who told me the RCMP had spent two years negotiating with the two groups of plaintiffs but had failed to reach a settlement. She asked me if I would help the team that was working out a settlement with the lawyers representing the two groups of women. I agreed right away and attended the negotiations. In my opinion, what was on the table at the time was unlikely to lead to a settlement. I suggested they let me draw up a new settlement proposal based on what was done in New Brunswick. The RCMP team agreed to my proposal and asked me to present it to the lawyers for the other two parties. Talks eventually led to an agreement. Really, the main sticking point was how much the lawyers would get paid.

Along the way, the parties agreed that I would shift from participating as a member of the RCMP delegation to acting as a lawyer for all the parties. Representatives for the victims and the RCMP seemed to appreciate my contribution, and I think that is why they asked me to implement the agreement. The process was similar to what I set up in New Brunswick. First, the RCMP and the federal government came up with one hundred million dollars for the settlement fund. At first, I was quite reluctant to participate because I knew quite well the process would be time-consuming and difficult, but I agreed when the parties told me there would be between eight hundred and one thousand claims and I would not have to interview all the claimants, just those who experienced the most serious injuries. I also wanted to conduct the process myself, which really irritated one of the lawyers, who wanted to hand it over to a big accounting firm.

In October 2016, Commissioner Bob Paulson made an emotional announcement about the settlement that was reached with the two groups of women and my appointment as commissioner. I do not know Paulson; I met with him only once, at his request. That is when he told me, "You know, Mr. Bastarache, I was not keen to approve this agreement, if only because of the lawyers' fees. They don't do any work for it. But there was no way to convince my lawyers to negotiate something else, so I had no choice but to approve it."

He was dead right about that. Only two legal firms were involved in the class action, which ended up costing the government about one hundred and thirty-seven million dollars, and when all was said and done, the lawyers pocketed twenty-five percent of that. I would like to see stricter, tougher rules for lawyers' fees. I think they should be taking a huge risk or doing a whole lot of work to earn that much money. In this case, they charged clients eighteen percent for completing their claim forms.

★★★

Once I was appointed, I started by setting up an actual office. Unlike in New Brunswick, I was able to hire employees to help me, but as an independent assessor, I alone would decide how much compensation each claimant would receive based on the criteria the parties adopted. Halfway through the process, the Federal Court agreed to bring two retired judges on board to do interviews for me. Neither my decisions nor theirs were subject to judicial review or appeal. I hired an executive director and a lead counsel, as well as some part-time assistants to analyze files and handle financial administration. I was responsible for two budgets, one for operations and the other for victim compensation. The office was up and running fairly quickly, but we had to wait several months for the order from the Federal Court.

Once the action was certified, we had to wait for a period of time during which the women of the RCMP could opt out of the process. I spent the time working with my staff to develop a very detailed claims process, set up a website, and develop an online claim form. Collaboration on the part of RCMP lawyers was excellent every step of the way; collaboration on the part of the other lawyers less so. The legal firms refused to use the electronic claim form for their clients, which was disappointing. It meant we had to hire additional administrative staff to input the claims, many of them handwritten, into our system, which was essential to generating the information we needed to produce the final report.

We received some one thousand three hundred claims during the first six months of the claims period, including about three hundred filed by lawyers, who also asked the court to grant an extension for women who had expressed an intention to participate before the end of the first claims period. During the extension, the lawyers filed about four hundred claims. When all was said and done, we had received just under three thousand three hundred claims.

We were set up to handle about a thousand claims. One of the lawyers, who had fewer than a hundred clients, complained that we were moving too slowly. He did not seem to care that we were not equipped to handle over three thousand claims, nor did he explain why the lawyers withheld hundreds of claims, only to file them all at once. The most uncooperative lawyer also complained about the fact that twenty percent of the claims were denied during the first few months. That number was high, and many of those claimants had been harassed, which caused resentment. The problem was that, in nearly every case, it was not sexual harassment, which was all my mandate covered. Regardless, the unhappy lawyers wanted me to justify my decision in every case. One of them also asked for a copy of my budget and the name of the assistant who had prepared the file for each claimant. He also wanted me to ask the court to hire more assessors, whom he insisted should have the same management powers as me. Three months later, I asked the parties to approve the appointment of two retired female judges to speed things up. That same lawyer objected to my request, delaying the process for months. In the end, the two judges conducted interviews on my behalf in the Western provinces. About fifty percent of the claims were from British Columbia and Alberta. The process established six categories of claimants, but only those assessed at level 3 or higher were interviewed, which was about twenty-five percent of the total claims. The interviews were a challenge, not only because there were so many of them, but also because we had to travel to various Canadian cities to speak to the claimants. Most of the claimants were interviewed in Vancouver and Calgary. They told me about how they were victims of gender-based discrimination, sexual harassment and, in many cases, sexual assault.

I had to accept claims if the perpetrator was an employee of the RCMP and the incidents were related to the workplace. It was absolutely clear to me that the RCMP was very ill-prepared to integrate women into its ranks from day one and that the administration was incapable of properly handling problems that arose. According to the claimants, discrimination and harassment existed across Canada at every level of the hierarchy.

Despite the administrative difficulties I encountered, I have to say it was gratifying to be able to help the women who experienced long-lasting harm due to the behaviour

> It was absolutely clear to me that the RCMP was very ill-prepared to integrate women into its ranks from day one and that the administration was incapable of properly handling problems that arose.

of people who did not want them in the police force. Many of them cried as they told me how the stress led to depression, alcohol or drug addiction, job loss, and the loss or reduction of their pension. In some cases, what happened to these women resulted in personal and family crisis, divorce, and the inability to maintain good relationships with their children. Some confided that they had attempted to take their own lives.

Émilie and Jean-François, it is hard to hear these things, but the mission is important. I have to try to help these women not only financially, but also psychologically. I have to find a way to make recommendations that will change things. I have to find a way to make myself heard and achieve meaningful results. That is my challenge. I will succeed.

Conclusion

IT WAS SO HOT. Over 30 °C for sure. The air was heavy and sticky. Alberta was in the middle of a heat wave, and I could have driven. I love cars, and I can drive for hours, no problem. I do not know how many times I covered the one thousand two hundred kilometres from the national capital to Moncton. The distance never bothered me; in fact, I think driving had a calming effect on me. Long distances also gave me a chance to discover little surprises all across our great country.

It was the late 1980s, and I was in Alberta to meet with a group of parents from Peace River who wanted to meet with me to assess the feasibility of a French school in the northern part of the province, some five hundred kilometres from Edmonton.

I could have driven there, rolled the windows down and left the city behind. I could have taken Highway 16, then turned right to head north on Highway 43 past wheat fields so vast they defy description. Four or five hours on the road is nothing to Albertans, especially not those in the northwest, where communities are seemingly endless fields apart. I could have shared the road with pickup trucks speeding with impunity, no law enforcement for miles around. It is a two-lane road much of the way, with vehicles passing at breakneck speed. Off in the distance, massive flare stacks rise out of the ground, torch-like, spouting constant flame. This is black-gold country. It is peaceful. The landscape is so linear, so flat, so calming. Far away, the pumpjacks nod up and down, their flares burning. The clouds are so low you can almost touch them. The Alberta sky is no match for the firmament in neighbouring Saskatchewan, whose grandiose celestial display is truly worthy of its "Land of Living Skies" licence plate slogan. In Alberta, the evening sky in late summer in particular is leaden and dark, a dead sky.

Driving the 43 would have done me some good. Jean-François, you had left us a short time before, and a little time on the road would have immersed me in the kind of silence I yearned for, I have to admit. But I did not drive. For that trip, the Association canadienne-française de l'Alberta had chartered a little plane to facilitate travel. Honestly, I do not think I had ever been in such a small plane. It was so small that only two people could fit in the cockpit. I had never been afraid of flying, so I boarded the craft without so much as a second thought.

Inside, it was unbearably hot. Thank goodness the flight was only an hour. The engine made an infernal racket in the tiny plane's belly. I did not ask any questions. My fate was in my private pilot's hands; I trusted him implicitly. An uneventful takeoff from the capital, and we ascended into a blue sky. Way off to the west were the Rocky Mountains of Jasper National Park, miniature from our perspective. Below us, fields as far as the eye could see.

I was hot. We had been in the air for thirty, maybe forty-five minutes when the engine started going "puttaputta-putta." Then it shut down altogether and we were gliding. I turned to the pilot and, not wanting to seem panicky, asked him, "Um, excuse me, what's going on?" He turned to me as though nothing had happened, and said, "That happens sometimes when it's hot. Don't worry. It'll restart."

He tried to restart the motor. He tried again. I was sweating bullets. The pilot tried five or six times. Every time, the cockpit filled with smoke. We could hardly breathe. We choked on gas fumes. We could not open the windows. We were suffocating, but somehow, I was not afraid. Isn't that odd? I was not really worried because the pilot was cool as a cucumber. Still, I wanted to know what was happening.

"OK, what's going on?" I asked.

"Well, it looks like I won't be able to restart the engine, so we're going to have to land," he replied.

"I didn't notice an airport around here!" I joked.

Judging from the pilot's big smile, I suppose he appreciated my attempt at humour, but what I was really asking was, would we be able to land in a field?

"Not a chance!" he exclaimed. "It's way too soft. The second the wheels hit the ground, we'd flip and be done for. No, we have to land on the road."

Without an engine, we had to land on the road and cross our fingers we would not get hit by a tractor, a truck, or a car.

The engine had been out for at least ten minutes, and we were approaching our final destination. We were so far from the capital there was not much traffic below us. Telephone wires would not be a problem because the wingspan was so small. Again the pilot said, "Don't worry, we'll be fine." I was not worried. My mind was blank. I was motionless, frozen, just waiting for something to happen.

Suddenly, we began to lose altitude. Fast. Without an engine, we had no brakes.

Ever calm, the pilot said, "It'll probably bounce pretty hard on the road, but I'll keep it good and straight, and we'll be fine." It was very risky. I realized that if the plane hit the ground at an angle, we could roll. Our chances of survival would be slim. The cockpit was utterly silent. I looked out the window and watched the road rise up to meet us. Fast. It all happened so fast.

★★★

Jean-François, I came very close to joining you that day. But I am still alive. Sometimes I feel like I should not be. Your passing and Émilie's a few years later left a gaping hole in my life. The older I get, the more your absence hurts, children. My parents are dead. My brothers and sisters are far away. Loneliness is creeping in.

At the start of my career, I very much wanted to accomplish something of value to society. Today, I am not so sure what I achieved. I will obviously never be able to say mission accomplished. As the writer Philippe Forest said, "[...] it all ends in confusion, indecision and world-weariness, my own story a mere blip in history [...]."

Despite all the career opportunities that have come my way, the only life I ever truly desired could never be mine. All I ever wanted since coming of age was a full, busy family life. I wanted several children. I wanted to teach them everything, show them everything. I wanted to be surrounded by their activity, their noise, their liveliness. Perhaps, unconsciously, that was my way of escaping my loneliness? I wanted a real home, a safe, loving haven for my whole family. Children, your death was the greatest failure of my life.

All my love,
Papa

Biography and Memoirs

As its name implies, the focus of this collection is to feature the life and work of prominent anglophone and francophone Canadians whose distinctive contributions have marked our collective society and history. In chronicling the lives of these leading figures, each title explores their life's work and the era in which they were active.

Combining scholarship with an accessible voice, the Biography and Memoirs collection is contributing to building an archive of Canadian achievements in culture, science, and beyond.

Previous Titles in the Biography and Memoirs Collection:
Stéphane Desjardins, *La famille Fermanian : l'histoire du cinéma Pine de Sainte-Adèle*, 2022.
Constance Backhouse, *Deux grandes dames : Bertha Wilson et Claire L'Heureux-Dubé à la Cour suprême du Canada*, translated from the English by Karine Lavoie, 2021.
Michel Bastarache and Antoine Trépanier, *Ce que je voudrais dire à mes enfants*, 2019.
Monique Frize, *A Woman in Engineering: Memoirs of a Trailblazer*, 2019.
David M. Culver, with Alan Freeman, *Saisir sa chance : mémoires de David M. Culver*, translated from the English by Christine Gonthier, 2018.
Ruey J. Yu, with Kate Jaimet, *Journey of a Thousand Miles: An Extraordinary Life*, 2017.
Michel Bock, *A Nation Beyond Borders: Lionel Groulx on French-Canadian Minorities*, translated from the French by Ferdinanda Van Gennip, 2014.
Jacqueline Cardinal and Laurent Lapierre, *Taking Aviation to New Heights: A Biography of Pierre Jeanniot*, translated from the French by Donald Winkler, 2013.
Ralph Heintzman, *Tom Symons: A Canadian Life*, 2011.

Other Titles Related to this Collection:
Andrew Donskov (ed.), *Sofia Tolstaya, the Author: Her Literary Works in English Translation*, Translated from Russian by John Woodsworth and Arkadi Klioutchanski, 2022.
Andrew Donskov (ed.), John Woodsworth, Arkadi Klioutchanski and Liudmila Gladkova (trans.), *Tolstoy and Tolstaya: A Portrait of a Life in Letters*, 2017.
Andrew Donskov (ed.) and John Woodsworth (trans.), *My Life: Sofia Andreevna Tolstaya*, 2011.
Hartmut Lutz (ed. and trans.), *The Diary of Abraham Ulrikab: Text and Context*, 2011.
Ernest Adolphe Côté, *Réminiscences et souvenances*, 2006.

For a complete list of titles published by the University of Ottawa Press, please visit:
www.press.uOttawa.ca